CINEPHILIA AND THE ADVENTURE
FOR EXISTENTIAL HEALTH

SUPERIMPOSITIONS
PHILOSOPHY AND THE MOVING IMAGE
Series editor Brian Price

Superimpositions: Philosophy and the Moving Image takes philosophy and visual media as related practices. Books in this series do not simply apply philosophy as a method for reading art or redundantly representing its extant ideas. Following the visual logic of superimposed imagery, we see what philosophy and art share and what remains distinct, and distinctly generative. Superimposition, moreover, resembles thinking itself: an encounter with an object summons the idea of something like it and yet not the same. Twentieth-century philosophers turned increasingly to literature to replace generalized axioms with thick descriptions of the world and our psyches. *Superimpositions* takes the moving image, in all its limitations and possibilities, as central to the task of twenty-first-century philosophy and its refusal to foreclose either thought or difference.

SERIES EDITOR
Brian Price

Cinephilia and the Adventure for Existential Health

RECOMPOSING SUBJECTIVITY
AT THE CINEMA

Adam Szymanski

NORTHWESTERN UNIVERSITY PRESS
EVANSTON, ILLINOIS

Northwestern University Press
www.nupress.northwestern.edu

Copyright © 2025 by Northwestern University. Published 2025 by
Northwestern University Press. All rights reserved.

Printed in the United States of America

10 9 8 7 6 5 4 3 2 1

Library of Congress Cataloging-in-Publication Data

Names: Szymanski, Adam (Film scholar), author.
Title: Cinephilia and the adventure for existential health :
   recomposing subjectivity at the cinema / Adam Szymanski.
Other titles: Superimpositions.
Description: Evanston, Illinois : Northwestern University Press,
   2025. | Series: Superimpositions | Includes bibliographical
   references and index.
Identifiers: LCCN 2025016563 | ISBN 9780810149144 (paperback) |
   ISBN 9780810149151 (cloth) | ISBN 9780810149168 (ebook)
Subjects: LCSH: Assayas, Olivier—Criticism and interpretation. |
   Motion pictures—Philosophy. | Motion pictures—Health aspects.
Classification: LCC PN1998.3.A7645 S99 2025 | DDC
   791.430233092—dc23
LC record available at https://lccn.loc.gov/2025016563

Contents

    Introduction: The Cinema, an Ally of the Sick *1*

1   Really Existing Instrumentalizations *17*

2   A Machine for Transversality *37*

3   A Cinephilia of Existential Adventure *59*

4   Seeing Intrusive Images *79*

    Conclusion: Existential Health contra Public Health *99*

Acknowledgments 113
Notes 115
Filmography 147
Bibliography 149
Index 163

[INTRODUCTION]

The Cinema, an Ally of the Sick

Cinema and literature have often been compared with one another, especially during those moments in the twentieth century when cinephiles felt compelled to defend the art which profoundly moved them as being, indisputably, art. Alexandre Astruc conceptualized the film camera as a pen, and François Truffaut believed that literary scenes once thought to be un-filmable could find their cinematic equivalents in the hands of an exceptionally adept filmmaker who warranted the designation of "auteur." The auteur was a creative genius, and auteurist methods were generally grounded in a director's biography and personal intentionality. A few decades later, Gilles Deleuze's cinema books introduced a new way of thinking about the auteur. They put forth an experimental taxonomy of cinematographic concepts in which auteurs function as "signifiers for singular modes of creative production."[1] The name of the auteur came to designate an event of pure semiotic assemblage rather than an individual person.

Viewed in this light, the cinema auteur, literary author, and philosopher are all remarkably similar for reasons other than their art forms being equally valuable. Each of these figures uses their chosen material to create living concepts, and in doing so, they each become symptomatologists of civilization by composing with significations drawn from genealogically divergent regimes to produce novel signs which bear their proper names. It is amidst this conceptual landscape that the author becomes "a path," literature becomes "a health," and the work is "a voyage, a journey."[2] Deleuze specifically wrote these words about literature in *Essays Critical and Clinical*. This book, subtitled *Recomposing Subjectivity at the Cinema*, takes as its starting point the idea that these words apply equally to cinema. If cinema too, is a health, then perhaps it is no coincidence that Gilles Deleuze and André Bazin both approached it with the fragility of illness and found in it an intercessor for belief in a world of inexhaustible potential. The cinema is an ally of the sick.

The following study explores the cinema's therapeutic value, and it does so through the invocation of a contemporary auteur whose oeuvre has little to do with mental illness or therapy, but whose film style and artistic ethos encapsulate the spirit of openness towards the world and the penchant for surprise and wonder that so attracted Bazin to the cinema. The name of the auteur is Olivier Assayas. Over the course of this book, three films directed by Assayas will act as intercessors for thinking through conceptual impasses in the film theory of spectatorship. Whereas film spectatorship has historically been theorized through the prisms of identification, fetishism, and voyeurism, Assayas's oeuvre offers up images that chart a more generous path through the film-spectator relationship, one where a primordial cinephilic desire catalyzes a transversal adventure in seeing.

The organizational logic at work in the chapters that follow is admittedly unconventional for a study that builds on the legacy of auteurism. Although the book is auteurist in its intellectual orientation for the reasons outlined above, it does not provide the kind of overview that is normally found in books devoted to a single director. An example of that format can be found in the book *Olivier Assayas* edited by Kent Jones, for instance, where an essay of film criticism is dedicated to each film in Assayas's filmography up to the date of publication. Alternatively, the scenes and films discussed at length in this book are like nodes of exceptional intensity that pop out of Assayas's oeuvre when it is approached with the question of spectatorship and cinema's therapeutic value in mind. Their inclusion in this study arises from their conceptual allure and should not be mistaken for a value judgment, for the act of putting an auteur in play as an intercessor for thought is not a practice of pantheon-building, but of philosophy. In this regard, cinephilia functions as both the topic and the method.

Ultimately, Assayas acts as an intercessor for thinking through what it means for cinema to indeed be considered "a health." As the title of this book suggests, its working hypothesis is that if the cinema is truly "a health," that is because the cinema harbors the potential to recompose spectatorial subjectivity. Guiding this line of thought is Félix Guattari, whose work offers a vision of subjectivity beyond the human and irreducible to the individual. Guattari proposes that subjectivity is a dynamic relational process of machinic composition among heterogeneous material, the social and semiotic components of subjectification.[3] His life's work at La Borde clinic consisted of experiments in the recomposition of the collective subjectivity of the clinic, and his writings on art and cinema gesture towards their potential to do the same. In an essay on cinema where he refers to it as "The Poor Person's Couch," Guattari writes:

> One doesn't go the cinema with one's ego, one's childhood memories, the way one goes to a psychoanalyst. One accepts in advance that it robs us of our identity, our past and our future. This is due to the fact that cinema intervenes directly in our relations with the external world.... In the worst commercial circumstances, good films can still be produced, films that modify the arrangements of desire, that "change life."[4]

This book takes seriously the idea that cinema can change life. That is why the "health" that this book attributes to the seventh art, much like the health that Deleuze explicitly attributes to literature, is a uniquely "existential health." The concept of existential health ascribes a fundamentally eventful character to health, and suggests that the freedom to make meaningful contributions to how the ecologies in which subjectivity has a lived stake are composed is paramount to its valorization. Existential health thus avoids the psychologizing and personalizing tendencies encapsulated by the notion of "mental health" wherein individuals are assigned diagnoses that betray the relational complexity of symptoms. Most importantly, the concept of existential health presents itself as a foil to the authoritarian spirit that guides the recently emboldened institution of "public health."

If the cinema can recompose subjectivity in the valorization of existential health, it is due to the spirit of adventure at the core of the cinephilic disposition, and the fact that the cinema is an aesthetic zone of encounter. It is for this reason that the title of this book speaks specifically of recomposing subjectivity "at" the cinema despite it being increasingly rare to write about the cinema in such terms, given how the vast majority of film screenings have taken place outside of physical cinemas for some time now. Regardless of where a film is viewed and whether or not the viewing situation meets the ideal technical specifications of the classical apparatus, the cinephilic disposition approaches cinema with a certain measure of reverence so as to demarcate film screenings from the banal flow of screen-based information which makes up much of daily life. It is an approach that recognizes the cinema as a site of encounter, even in an era when the space of the theater has been decentered, miniaturized, and expanded. The cinema's alliance with the sick is struck amidst this ecology of auteurism, cinephilia, and the adventure for existential health.

The following introduction stages how it is possible for an alliance to exist between the cinema and the sick, particularly those whose style of suffering is liable to be diagnostically categorized as a mental illness.

Nevertheless, it deliberately avoids the invocations "mental health" or "mental illness" without an appropriate qualification which would situate these terms within the institutions of medical power that attribute meaning to them and render them operational. For as Herbert Marcuse writes, "The insistence on operational and behavioral concepts turns against the efforts to free thought and behavior from the given reality and for the suppressed alternatives. Theoretical and practical Reason, academic and social behaviorism meet on common ground: that of an advanced society which makes scientific and technical progress into an instrument of domination."[5] To take the significations of "mental illness" or "mental health" as fait accompli and amenable to revision only through the professional avenues offered by the medical-industrial complex would be to corroborate these signifiers' official denotations and obscure the polyphonic field of existential questions generated by any and every instance of sustained distress. In their most intellectually fertile expressions, the overlapping disciplines of psychiatry and psychology have historically found the means to ask such questions, usually through theories of the subject sprung from the well of psychoanalytic theory. The dominant mental health discourses of today are the result of the "evidence-based" revisionism that has followed from the blotting-out of psychoanalytically informed concepts from the *DSM-III* in 1980. A rigid commitment to statistical evidence in the medically objective treatment of organic disease now masks—though only very thinly—an aura of anti-intellectualism and strict adherence to protocol at the expense of lay analytic experiments in subjectivity production. *Cinephilia and the Adventure for Existential Health* sidesteps the hegemonic idea of "mental health" by alternatively opting to think through a paradigm of existential health. When the terms "mental health" or "mental illness" are used in this text, it should be noted that they carry a deliberate existential inflection: an awareness that neither the existential coordinates of neurosis, psychosis, nor perversion can be adequately modeled by the biological reductionism which grounds medical treatments of psychiatric conditions, popular discussions of mental illness, and policy positions on public health. Conversely, an existential approach to health offers a line of flight from the mental health-industrial complex and the recognizable, yet sclerotic essentialisms which lend influential credence to its (commonly iatrogenic) practices. To break away from the medical image of thought which couches mental illness in a scientism that leaves the lay multitude of nonprofessionals in a compulsory state of passivity, and in the worst of cases, learned helplessness, requires a renewed attention to how modes of existence are opened, foreclosed, and delineated by the relations which engender subjective life. The pages of this study are devoted to expounding the virtual relationality of the cinema and the novel existential territories that it generates. The relation that is forged across the sick and the cinema can be thought of as a therapeutic alliance whose stakes are nothing less than the wager of existence itself. Thinking the cinema and its therapeutic potential through the optique of existential health breathes a politics, an ethics, and an erotics into the administered domain of mental health services.

"Therapeutic alliance" is a technical term that refers to the unique working relationship between a psychotherapist with professional qualifications and a patient who seeks treatment for a mental illness.[6] The last decade has witnessed a concerted interest in the therapeutic alliance, and a plethora of research now unequivocally indicates that the quality of this alliance is one of the main predictors of treatment outcome. The work of the psychologist John Norcross and his collaborators has found that the two most important indicators of treatment success are the person in therapy's will to change and how positively that person views the relationship they have with their therapist.[7] "Second only to the client's individual efforts, the therapeutic relationship accounts for most of the success of what we do," says Norcross.[8] These results may seem benign or even self-evident to the lay population, but they border on being outright scandalous in a climate of psychiatric orthodoxy that is increasingly committed to "manualized treatment"—that is, the treatment of psychiatric disorders through therapies such as cognitive behavior therapy (CBT), which have a large evidence base of statistical data supporting their efficacy and whose techniques have been standardized by treatment manuals that are upheld as gold standards of medical practice. The rationale behind the "manualization" of therapy is that the set of dialogical protocols meticulously detailed in the therapy manual, if administered correctly, should be able to treat a given disorder with predictable efficiency. Manualized therapy's purpose is to maintain the integrity of an evidence-based medical technique as it is transposed to treat the same mental illness in different people and across different clinical settings.

Even in the context of manualized therapies which have a reputation for encouraging strict adherence to their written protocols, Norcross's findings about the importance of the therapeutic alliance hold true.[9] One of the conclusions that can be drawn from his studies is that different types of therapists and therapies work for different types of people.[10] Research such as his effectively subdues claims for the universal applicability of manualized therapy by emphasizing that the therapeutic techniques embedded in manuals require relational activation through an alliance which is conditioned by external factors.[11]

The renewed emphasis that researchers have placed on the quality of the therapeutic alliance as an indicator for treatment outcome serves as a strong counterpoint to the increased push for manualized therapies which are expected to be transposed into different clinical contexts with little variation, and with slight regard for the particularities of the therapist and the client who are to be affected by the manual's therapeutic techniques.

In presenting large samples of statistical data which suggest that a therapeutic technique's effectiveness is highly dependent on the strength of the therapeutic alliance, as it is perceived by the person in therapy, Norcross's research consequently implies that the concerted wave of institutionally sanctioned efforts to disseminate manualized therapy through computer programs is predestined to fail should it do away with the interpersonal therapeutic alliance altogether. The scientific literature articulates the therapeutic alliance in the language of an interpersonal relationship, and the aptitude of an effective therapist is described through recourse to a uniquely human set of skills and virtues. According a meta-analysis of more than "over 200 research reports based on 190 independent data sources, covering more than 14,000 patients,"[12] the esteemed qualities of a therapist who creates a positive working alliance include the classical Rogerian core conditions of congruence (authenticity), unconditional positive regard, and empathy, along with the habit of collecting client feedback, repairing alliance ruptures, and managing counter-transference.[13] The successful therapeutic alliance is thus conceived as a relationship which maximizes virtuous human qualities to create the interpersonal conditions for the procedural deployment of therapeutic techniques. With traditional interpersonal psychotherapy up against the threat of being eroded by the joint forces of managed care, manualization, and computer-based therapy, research which correlates a positive therapeutic alliance with successful treatment outcome constitutes a defense of person-centered approaches.

The contradiction between psychology's veneration of the therapeutic alliance as interpersonal relationship on one hand, and the push towards technologically disseminated psychotherapy on the other, has led to a serious reappraisal of the therapist-client relationship. It is not uncommon for psychotherapy sessions between a human therapist and a client to be conducted over videoconference technology, and recent years bear witness to a growing automation of psychotherapy, as evidenced by the upsurge of therapy smartphone apps and desktop computer programs, as well as chatbots and smart speakers powered by artificial intelligence.[14] The definition of the therapeutic alliance is beginning to change in tandem with the implementation of computerized therapy in treatment programs, and research is now being conducted so as to corroborate the clinical utility of computerized psychotherapy and encourage its systematic implementation via public health programs.[15] As a result, a slate of new studies and tools is seriously seeking to gauge the therapeutic alliance between patients and digital technology.

How is it possible to measure the strength of a therapeutic alliance between a computerized therapy program and a person in therapy? Current attempts suggest that little attention is being paid to the qualitative differences of the relationship which distinguish it from its in-person counterparts. The California Psychotherapy Alliance Scale[16] is a respected tool for measuring the traditional interpersonal alliance between client and therapist. It asks clients to respond on a seven-point scale to questions such as "Did you feel accepted and respected by your therapist for who you are?" and "When important things came to mind, how often did you find yourself keeping them to yourself rather than sharing them with your therapist?" A similar measurement tool, the Working Alliance Inventory (WAI), now has an adapted version for technology-based interventions called the WAI-Tech.[17] The WAI and WAI-Tech ask very similar sorts of questions, with the questionnaire for technology-based interventions instructing participants to replace the name of their human therapist with the name of their computer program. Participants are asked to rank their response to statements such as "I am confident in the CBT4CBT program's ability to help me." In situations where it would be nonsensical to replace the name of the therapist with the name of a computer program, the wording is slightly changed. "I believe the therapist is genuinely concerned with my welfare" is rephrased as "I believe CBT4CBT is genuinely relevant to my well-being."[18]

The WAI-Tech's logic of substitutionality mirrors current attempts by mental health policy-makers to implement computer-based interventions which replicate the presence of a human therapist as much as technologically possible. One of the reasons why computerized therapy takes its cues from the interpersonal therapeutic relationship is that programs which include an animated computer character or videotaped narrator who simulates face-to-face conversation using "social-emotional behaviors" tend to score better on working alliance measurement tests.[19] These human or anthropomorphized characters are referred to in the scientific literature as "relational agents" for their ability to retain user interest in the computer program and give the fictitious impression that the patient is in a therapeutic relationship with another who can empathize with emotions and relate to difficulties.[20] Even though therapy administered through a computer program aims to reduce actual face-to-face therapist hours in the name of economic efficiency and wider public access, it invokes the audiovisual specter of the expunged therapist as a relational agent who improves the therapeutic alliance between the computer program and its users. Since the most widely accessible computer programs have been relatively rudimentary, to the extent that an attentive user would never catch herself believing that she is in dialogue with another human capable of mentalization and symbolization, the image of the therapist in the computer program is an attempted diversion from this deficiency of therapeutic resources.

The dawn of artificial intelligence in the sphere of psychotherapy promises to erase this deficit between human therapists and computer programs altogether, and signs even point to the creation of an inverse deficit wherein human therapists are at a disadvantage compared to AI bots with vastly better memory, rapid access to clinical data, facial recognition skills, and emotional intelligence. The implications for the delivery of psychotherapy could be immense.

One of the guiding premises of this study into the recomposition of subjectivity, at the cinema, is that the fault lines of a productive therapeutic alliance bisect the stratification dividing humans from cinema and media technologies. Even if the current implementation of computerized therapy is a symptom of the brazen neoliberalization of mental health treatment, it would be a mistake to reduce technological therapeutic alliances to the logic of neoliberalism, just as returning to the recognizable safety of the interpersonal therapeutic relationship would offer a false sense of oppositional politics, especially given how psychiatric power has never had any trouble operating through the interpersonal dyad of classical analysis to reinforce overlapping operations of sovereign and disciplinary power.[21] This book shares an affinity with the mental health researchers and practitioners who value the therapeutic alliance, while at the same time it takes a line of flight from the clinical scene into the sensuous landscape of art to discover the workings of a therapeutic alliance between the cinema and the sick which is machinic rather than interpersonal. What it desires to actualize is nothing more than an existential territory for therapeutic experimentation in the recomposition of subjectivity via the resources of moving image art, as a singular contribution to a polyphonic play of efforts—both clinical and critical—to prompt becomings that transform inhibiting symptoms into opportunities for lived, creative elaboration. The promise of a machinic therapeutic alliance immanent to the cinephilic encounter with cinema is thus most productively engaged with as a speculative proposition. The hope guiding the writing of this book is that this proposition will be discovered as ripe for relay to new linkages, and that it will survive on a different plane of intelligibility than that of the reigning medical imagination, which is cluttered with protocols that systematically reify mental disorders as diseases and thus silence the cry of existential grievances which beckon from the relational fabric of every psychic affliction.

AN UNNATURAL ALLIANCE

The cinema's therapeutic proposition percolates amidst this field of therapeutic practices, alliances, and logics, differentiating itself from them on multiple fronts. It is telling that the therapeutic alliance proposed by the cinema would not register in an alliance measurement tool like the WAI-Tech, and that an attempt to enact such a measurement would be an exercise in absurdity. Clearly the cinema as a whole or the title of a particular film could not seriously be inserted for the name of a therapist or computer program in an alliance measurement tool. From the point of view of film philosophy, this sort of instrumentalizing gesture would grossly undervalue the cinema's artistry, history of political relevance, and subjectifying powers. The discipline of psychology would find the move equally unsatisfying, since the cinema could not be expected to follow an evidence-based treatment manual, or replace a therapist in the same way as a computer program with built-in response functions. The therapeutic alliance between the cinema and the sick is of a different order than clinical psychotherapy altogether; an order that is imperceptible to the psychological research tools used to quantify the quality of alliance.

Whereas the therapeutic alliance in clinical psychotherapy is a means to an end, the therapeutic alliance offered by the cinema is an end in its own right. The explicit purpose of the alliance in clinical psychotherapy is to facilitate the procedural application of therapeutic techniques designed to relieve the person in therapy of aggravating symptoms. Therapies which are undertaken in the context of a weak alliance are less likely to have a positive outcome, and the psychoanalytic origins of modern talk therapy bear this out: the hermeneutics of dream interpretation or free association would lack the credibility of their empirical link to the material of the case study if transference and counter-transference were not active in the clinical scene.[22] With regard to CBT and its goal-oriented pragmatism, it would be hard to imagine that the therapist's probing invitation for the person in therapy to rethink his strongly held views of the world, and seriously question their veracity, would be successful if the therapist herself was not held in high esteem. In clinical psychotherapy, a positive working alliance lends therapeutic technique its rightful statistical chance at fulfilling a positive prognosis.

Clinical psychology's structural instrumentalization of the alliance to the ends of a technique's procedural application mirrors the social contractualism of extensive alliances. In *The Elementary Structures of Kinship*, Claude Lévi-Strauss identifies the incest taboo as the transitional point from nature to culture and extrapolates the social structures of alliance-making from the universality of this prohibition. After considering various hypotheses as to the origins of the taboo against incest, Lévi-Strauss settles on an explanation which reverses the interdiction to not have sexual relations with immediate family members into the positive command that these members be exchanged. He writes: "The prohibition of incest is less a rule prohibiting marriage with the mother, sister or daughter, than a rule obligating the mother, sister or daughter to be given to others. It is the supreme rule of the gift."[23] The sociogenesis of alliance-making through the exchange of women imbues alliances with an extensive character that is capable of indexing transactions. In the imaginary of structural anthropology, gifts are given neither freely nor indiscriminately. They are accounted for in a historically accurate balance sheet of social transactions that recognize the parties involved as global persons organized under the family name of a filial tree. The instauration of social alliances through the extensive exchange of women is structured subserviently to filiation.

Ordered kinship, however, is but one actualization of extensive alliance-making. Exchange between global persons also rules the domain of psychotherapy, where the therapeutic relationship is delineated according to contracted mutual responsibilities grounded in the economic privileges and ethical standards of chartered professionalism. The paradox of the therapeutic alliance which expresses itself as a contract of economic exchange is that it creates an extensive pairing which reifies both signatory parties who are responsible to one another and allied out of mutual interest. The therapeutic alliance, for as long as it is professional, is prohibited from recomposing the subjectivity of the clinical encounter across predetermined thresholds. The insights brought about by the work of therapy may prompt a cascade of changes to be lived outside of the therapist's office, and yet the terms of the extensive alliance's exchange remain remarkably consistent. The therapeutic alliance, as articulated by clinical theory and practice, is a properly extensive alliance. Intensive components of the alliance such as transference and counter-transference are overcoded by the defined terms of contractualized extensivity and guaranteed in the exchange of time for money.

At the conclusion of *The Elementary Structures of Kinship*, after delineating the primordial cultural practice of alliance-making through the exchange of women whereby women are made to function culturally as signs of their exchangeability, Lévi-Strauss nevertheless affirms the non-instrumentalizability of value and maintains a view of sexual relations irreducible to the elementary social structures formed by such exchanges. Lévi-Strauss writes: "In contrast to words, which have become wholly signs, woman has remained at once a sign and a value. This explains why the relations between sexes have preserved that affective richness, ardour and mystery which doubtless originally permeated the entire universe of human communications."[24] Even when extensive structures of marriage alliances appropriate women as signs of possible exchange, the reduction is incomplete: women and the relations of sexual difference they engender retain an irreducible richness of individuation *in potentia*.[25] This pre-individual potential transversal to sexual relations is an incipient value.[26] Exchangist transactions may capture such value in the creation of extensive alliances based on credit, yet such accounts are exercises in the quantification of quality, in the structural extensification of polymorphous intensity. What remains, irreducibly, is the value of quality.[27]

Alliances of intensity wherein the order of signs is not yet determined by laws of exchange bubble up through the cracks in the extensive logic of the clinical. It is in such intensive ruptures that the cinema's therapeutic alliance with the sick is made palpable. If the alliance offered by the cinema overruns attempts at instrumentalization and enjoys the fact of being an end in its own right, it is because the cinema, as an occurrent art, exists as ripe to be encountered, and the indeterminacy of the encounter holds value.[28] Like the figure of the woman in structuralist anthropology, the cinema is both sign and value, and its therapeutic value is engendered by the intensive quality of its alliance with the sick. On the plane of molar existence, there certainly is an extensive contractualism to the practice of cinema spectatorship, most overtly codified in the space of the theater. The spectator pays the price of admission in exchange for an aesthetic experience that is expected to meet minimum criteria which are culturally defined and genre-specific.[29] From the perspective of this molar plane of individuated people and objects, the cinema's therapeutic value is minimal. According to a clinical logic where the therapeutic alliance is necessarily an extensive alliance, the cinema can at most serve as a tool to improve the interpersonal alliance between client and therapist, as well as aid in the application of institutionally backed therapeutic techniques. Whereas in the molecular universe of values, "the cinema" and "the spectator" exist in nascent states, composing a relational bloc of sensation where subject and film object are yet to be wholly differentiated.[30] The cinema's indeterminate quality as an art of occurrency with therapeutic value comes to the fore on this molecular plane of subjective mutation. At the most primary level, the bloc of sensation knows no difference between subject and object: discrete human spectators and film objects appear only after the de-subjectifying and re-subjectifying experiential primacy offered by the cinematic arts.[31] The intensive therapeutic alliance found here is not one between cinema and persons identified as mentally ill, but a quality of relation which recomposes how the contingency of their encounter may lead them to become other than what they are already identified to be.

How is it that an alliance can take shape on this molecular plane of pre-personal becomings, where the terms of an exchange have not yet been individuated? The challenge is to imagine a non-exchangist conception of alliance. In *Anti-Oedipus*'s rereading of *The Elementary Structures of Kinship*, alliance and exchange are respectively paired as foils to filiation and production, and their role in the production of sociality is brought under scrutiny.

> The criticism of all "exchangist conceptions" expressed by *Anti-Oedipus* is grounded on a counter-theory of Oedipus in which filiation and production, rather than alliance and exchange, are primary. In this and other senses, *Anti-Oedipus* is an anti-structuralist book. . . . Against the theme of exchange as the socio-institutive synthesis of opposing (contradictory) interests, *Anti-Oedipus* puts forth the postulate that the social machine works paramountly to code the flows of desire. Social production is desiring production in a coded state.[32]

Eight years later in *A Thousand Plateaus*, Deleuze and Guattari return to Lévi-Strauss's anthropological material to excavate a pattern of non-exchangist alliances as disjunctive syntheses. On the tenth plateau, "1730: Becoming-Intense, Becoming-Animal, Becoming-Imperceptible . . . ," alliance takes on a "dangerous and contagious power" and comes to describe the relations of anomalous, trans-species intensities that are provocative of qualitative change.[33] The intensive alliances of becoming-other in *A Thousand Plateaus* are minor recompositions of the extensive alliances recorded on social balance sheets found in *Anti-Oedipus*. This shift in the conceptual performance of alliance across the two books leads the anthropologist of the Amazon Eduardo Viveiros de Castro to assert: "Every becoming is an alliance, which does not mean that every alliance is a becoming. There is extensive alliance, which is cultural and socio-political, and intensive alliance, which is unnatural and cosmopolitical. . . . When a shaman activates a becoming-jaguar, he does not 'produce' a jaguar, he does not 'affiliate' himself to the descent of jaguars either; he makes an alliance."[34]

In order to see the cinematic experience and the indeterminate quality of its molecular stratum as offering a therapeutic alliance, it helps to situate the becomings of intensive alliances found in *A Thousand Plateaus* in light of Deleuze and Guattari's critique of psychoanalysis. Of the two *Capitalism and Schizophrenia* volumes, *Anti-Oedipus* contains the more sustained references to psychoanalytic tenets and the book concludes by way of an introduction, opening onto a speculative field of therapeutic praxis with the final chapter being titled "Introduction to Schizoanalysis." Concepts take on an ethological and ecological dynamic in *A Thousand Plateaus* which can, if read in isolation, obfuscate the broader reasons for Guattari's involvement in the project. It is important to remember that *A Thousand Plateaus* is an intellectual expression of Guattari's lifelong therapeutic activism. The concepts which populate the plateaus were partly invented to enrich the experimental clinical practice at La Borde and move past the reigning impasses of psychoanalytic theory, particularly around the organization of part-objects, desire as lack, and the triangulated unconscious. While much has been written about becoming as a minor *détournement* of Being and the importance of this concept's appearance in the history of twentieth-century philosophy, its implications for clinical practice are easily overlooked.[35]

A becoming is a becoming-other.[36] At first glance, it may seem as if becoming-other is the strategy of psychotherapy par excellence, but in fact, the philosophical underpinnings of psychiatry suggest the very opposite: most mental illnesses are conceived of as organic diseases in need of pharmaceutical intervention so that the person who is posited as existing independent of the disease is restored to health. Even in the case of personality disorders whose relational qualities are sometimes emphasized in lieu of organic hypotheses, psychotherapeutic interventions attempt to consolidate a restoration of the personality.[37] The molecular becomings of intensive alliances found in *A Thousand Plateaus* made the Oedipal master narrative of psychoanalysis stutter, and they remain anomalous to the commanding trends in today's psychotherapeutic landscape, namely positivity, rationality, and mindfulness—all approaches which reify and responsibilize the individual as agent of health. Guattari's clinical approach stands as an ethico-aesthetic paradigm of becoming-other through encounters with alterity, of inventing new subjectivities and experimenting with collective situations. For Guattari, experimentation with subjectivity was an end in its own right and he went so far as to claim: "The only acceptable finality of human activity is the production of a subjectivity that is auto-enriching its relation to the world in a continuous fashion."[38] This adventure of experimentally recomposing subjectivity through the forging of transindividual alliances is the practice of a schizoanalytic psychoanalysis freed from libidinal economies of exchange. It is a process of unnatural alliance-making at the cusp of the clinical becoming creatively critical, of the Apollonian becoming Dionysian.

The customary nomenclature of an alliance "between" terms is an unfortunate misnomer, and is appropriate solely in instances of an exclusively extensive alliance. There is no intensive therapeutic alliance between the cinema and the sick; an intensive alliance is constructed with the cinema and the sick by putting into indeterminate relation alterious tendencies, yet to be individuated as discrete terms, whose novel relation is productive of qualitative change—an evental aesthetic bloc of becoming-other. The cinema's therapeutic alliance conceived here is not between a "film object" and a "spectator," but emerges in the withness of difference, disjunctively synthesizing singularities in becoming.[39] Relation is not what links discrete terms as in the concepts of "intersubjectivity" or "interactivity," but is a differential force cutting tangentially across their molar existence. Recomposing subjectivity, at the cinema, is a creative entering into the eventfulness of the bloc's auto-poesis, an entering whose effects are non-causal, and whose artful indeterminacy in a "world-integrated" medical-industrial complex is a potency.[40] The art of cinema is an art of staging indeterminate, intense encounters. The potential of this encounter to upset existence in a recomposition of subjectivity is its therapeutic value.

The cinema's therapeutic alliance with the sick accomplishes machinically what the most well-meaning therapist could only fantasize of undertaking on her own. In response to a stubborn analytic case which posed many difficulties, Sándor Ferenczi and his analysand Elizabeth Severn developed the technique known as mutual analysis whereby the analysand analyzes the unconscious of the analyst. Ferenczi kept word of this radical inversion of psychoanalytic power secret during his lifetime. He only made note of it in his personal diary and never mentioned it in any public-facing publications.[41] The invention of mutual analysis was instigated by Severn's deep mistrust of Ferenczi. She convinced him that her own analysis would not progress until she was able to reverse their roles and analyze him instead. Ferenczi agreed to go along with this unlikely proposition for mutual analysis even though it risked his credibility among Freud's other disciples who, like Freud, had come to abandon the seduction theory. Ferenczi was acutely aware that the power imbalance of incest is re-created in the power dynamics of the analytical scene and posited that an experiment in mutual analysis could assist in the psychoanalytic treatment of trauma related to childhood sexual abuse.[42]

Jeffrey Masson, former director of the Sigmund Freud Archives, goes on to describe what came of this experiment in mutual analysis and how it challenged the extensive alliance of exchange upon which the psychoanalytic edifice was built. Masson relays the following anecdotes from personal correspondence with Anna Freud:

> Ferenczi said that many patients told him they felt that love coming from the therapist could cure them, that if Ferenczi could simply be there, more or less silent, without any attempt to interpret, this would help them. Ferenczi found this was true, and wondered if this love acted as a salve for the wounds left by early traumas. But he also recognized that the feeling the patient had of being helped did not always last beyond the end of the session. He asked whether this is not because "our imagination endows us with more love than we in fact possess." After all, he pointed out, when the analytic hour is over, the therapist simply sends the patient away and ushers in the next. . . . Anna Freud and Ferenczi once discussed this very topic, and Ferenczi said to her that one hour of treatment was a very artificial time barrier, and that he preferred to give his patients however much time they wanted. Anna Freud said she raised the obvious objections: What if the patient wanted all afternoon; what did one say to other patients who were waiting? Ferenczi thought for a while and then said to her: "Maybe one should have only one patient." Anna Freud told me she was very impressed by this remark.[43]

To have only one patient: Ferenczi and Anna Freud's therapeutic fantasy could be mistaken as a desire for friendship or coupling, but what their conversation hints at more than anything is their shared technical aspiration for releasing the productive forces of the therapeutic alliance from the terms of exchange which extensivize the relation. Their fantasy entertains the possibility of a therapeutic relationship free to expand and contract in accordance with the appetite immanent to its unfolding—the possibility of a pure alliance.[44] They dare to imagine the therapeutic alliance as a generalized mode of existence, predisposed for activation.

The cinema imparts a giving disposition that Ferenczi and Anna Freud could only dream of offering their analysands. In contradistinction to the therapist who has a finite number of hours to share, and who would be limited to only one patient should he want to fulfill the fantasy of being ever-present, a multiplication of existential engagements with the cinema does not diminish its aesthetic resources in the slightest. Each additional interlocution brings a new existential situation to the cinema for potential recomposition on the wager that a cinematic sign may index the pathway to a hitherto unforeseen composition of existence—a future health. The cinema is not causative of mental health, but it gives existential health a chance.

[CHAPTER ONE]

Really Existing Instrumentalizations

Epidemic rates of mental illness pose a unique challenge to theories of political aesthetics, which despite their indebtedness to the psychoanalytic tradition, have from their very beginnings absconded from any therapeutic endeavors. Given the continuing global crisis in mental health, must a contemporary political aesthetics of cinema double as a therapeutic aesthetics?[1] Following Félix Guattari, whose lifelong work combined a fascination with the cinema's subjectifying powers with political activism and psychotherapeutic experimentation, this question can be answered in the affirmative.

Contemporary thinkers who carry forth Guattari's intellectual ethos have continued to insist on the productivity of the conjunction between art, therapy, and politics. The autonomist Franco "Bifo" Berardi explicitly argues that "political action must happen according to modalities analogous to therapeutic intervention."[2] Invoking Guattari directly, Erin Manning writes: "All of Guattari's theory and practice emerges from the necessity to bring out the collective resonance of the event, to see illness not as a personal problem to be analyzed outside of the field of relation, but as an event, an ecology. . . . Conditions of well-being cannot be abstracted from the social field."[3] Josep Rafanell i Orra, in turn, concludes his fascinating book on neoliberalism's integration of therapeutic institutions with the words, "Before wanting to ask, 'How can I heal?' therapy presupposes a prior question: 'Which world must be actualized?'"[4] In connecting the question of how to create conditions of well-being with the question of what world must be actualized, rather than which medical technique from a psychiatric manual to deploy, these thinkers each formulate political aesthetics in a therapeutic key. Their allied approaches also call forth a politicized mode of institutional participation which echoes Guattari's assertion that "people who work in therapeutic systems, or in the universities, who consider themselves to be mere depositories or channels for the transmission of scientific knowledge, have already made a reactionary choice."⁵

If a political aesthetics of film may create the material conditions for a recomposition of subjectivity that has therapeutic effects, then film theory first requires knowledge of and engagement with the psychological practices which currently put the cinema to medical use. An analysis of the mental health institutions, discourses, and practices which render cinema medically useful is offered here as a way to contextualize the subsequent chapters which excavate modern film theory's attachment to the concepts of identification, fetishism, and voyeurism so as to explore cinephilia's therapeutic dimension.⁶

Despite the institutional use of cinema in medical settings, knowledge which is relevant to the mental health field that has been produced by the humanities has little purchase amidst an institutional landscape where the question of what constitutes a life worth living is increasingly left up to the scientific disciplines which have hegemonically claimed mental health as their rightful domain. In ancient Greece, before philosophy became an isolated discipline, what is today called "mental health" belonged to the tradition of *epimeleia heautou* (care of the self)—a tradition that was equally philosophical, medical, theological, and ethico-aesthetic. Martha Nussbaum has shown that for the learned ancients, philosophy, like medicine, was a "rigorous science aimed both at understanding and at producing the flourishing of human life."⁷ It is worth keeping this genealogical lineage of the mental health sciences in mind, as well as remaining cognizant of their mutable nature, when asking how the cinema can play the politically therapeutic role of cultivating subjectivities that enable sustainable modes of collective existence worthy of the name "health." For, as the following pages demonstrate, if the therapeutic value of cinema is left to be decided by the institutions which are publicly vested with responsibility for the management of mental health, then the cinema is liable to witness a yoking of its powers of subjectification to the protocols embedded in mainstream mental health services and their historic complicity in reifying the reigning reality principle.

The medical practices presented in this chapter are exactly that—practices—and building on the thinking of Tobie Nathan, they are approached as such. Nathan fruitfully underscores the importance of studying institutional practices by asserting his belief that, above all, "the only legitimate scientific object of psychopathology should be the most detailed description possible of therapists and therapeutic techniques—never the sick."⁸ To emphasize the historically contingent and processually dynamic character of medical-scientific cultures, this chapter will pair observations on how film is used in various psychotherapeutic and psychiatric contexts with an analysis of the assumptions that these practices—often unconsciously—harbor about the cinema, subjectivity, and power. This line of analysis aims to foster knowledge of well-being, mental health, and therapy on the humanities' own epistemological terms, knowing that the humanities have a different, yet equally valid claim on truth as do the medical sciences.

The notion that humanistic inquiry has a crucial role to play in re-existentializing the mental health fields, and that this role is grounded in its own unique claims to validity, finds support from disparate corners of the humanities: in the affect theory of Brian Massumi and the Christian theology of Joseph Ratzinger. Each in their own way, Massumi and Ratzinger affirm the possibility of encountering truth through nonscientific methods, without falling into a postmodern abyss of endlessly slipping arbitrary signifiers.

Drawing on William James's philosophy of radical empiricism to valorize nonscientific modes of knowledge-production, Massumi suggests

> that philosophy, art, and even cultural studies are empirical enterprises in effective connection with the same reality science operates upon, generating results with their own claim to validity. The astonishingly workable results that science regularly generates gives it a well-earned claim to realism and validity. But it does not give it a monopoly on them.... Philosophical speculation has just as much a claim to empirical truth as science does. It just has a different claim on it.[9]

In a parallel move found in a book from the same era, Ratzinger defends theological truths which cannot be proven through scientific methods but which can be arrived at through religious experience. He writes: "When science becomes the dominant element in a view of the world, this absolute value becomes exclusive.... It moves within the limits of certain categories, within which it is strictly valid; but to maintain that it is only within these categories that man can know anything at all is an unfounded presupposition, which in any case is found by experience to be untrue."[10]

Remarkably, but perhaps not surprisingly, given the theological references of William James, John Dewey, and Alfred North Whitehead, the fields of speculative pragmatism[11] and Christian theology find communion here, in their mutual embrace of the radically empirical tenet that experience—particularly experience outside of the laboratory—is grounds for knowledge production. These radically empirical orientations buttress challenges to the hegemonic imperative that all therapeutic endeavors be "evidence-based."

Recent years have witnessed a series of debates and shifts in power colloquially known as the "therapy wars," where cognitive behavioral therapies have sought, and largely achieved, institutional dominance and wide public acceptance due to the sheer quantity of studies which show evidence of their effectiveness in reducing the symptoms of common mental illnesses such as anxiety and depression.[12] As the clinical psychologist Jonathan Shedler has pointed out, therapeutic approaches whose effectiveness has been either understudied or misrepresented by selective readings of the scientific literature have found themselves denigrated by influential figures in the mental health industry.[13] According to the logic of some mental health policy-makers, the pursuit of psychodynamic psychotherapies, for example, could at best be assessed as ineffective, and at worst categorized as blatantly dangerous, because according to an "evidence-based" logic they could be framed as preventing someone from obtaining a more effective treatment.[14] Even a brief glance at a discussion with David Clark, the Oxford psychologist responsible for establishing the Improving Access to Psychological Therapies (IAPT) program with Richard Layard after Tony Blair's 2005 electoral victory, helps to paint a picture of the rhetoric in favor of evidence-based treatments. Over the span of a short interview, he uses the word "evidence" no less than sixteen times, and summarily states, "There's clear evidence that certain ways of doing therapy work better than others."[15] By 'certain ways of doing therapy,' what he in fact means is CBT, or some variant of it, access to which was significantly expanded in 2008 through the IAPT program and is provided through public health insurance in the United Kingdom.[16]

Armed with a broad evidence base, cognitive behavioral therapy—a "common-sense" and "manualized" treatment for neuroses and personality disorders—has now long supplanted psychoanalysis as the zeitgeist therapeutic modality and has cast a shadow of doubt on therapies still trafficking in psychodynamic principles. CBT is fast (usually less than sixteen sessions), effective at symptom relief (with a massive evidence base to prove it), and cost-effective (CBT claims to "pay for itself" by relieving the economic burden of lost productivity). Its rise in popularity can be attributed to all of these factors, and also to how well it lends itself to neoliberal management techniques such as performance evaluation, with the IAPT priding itself on the "transparency" of its results.[17] The psychoanalyst and art critic Darian Leader has lamented this attribute of CBT: "In today's outcome-obsessed society," he writes, "people must become countable, quantifiable, transparent. And this leads to a grotesque new misunderstanding of psychotherapy."[18] Leader's denunciation of CBT has as much to do with its relatively simplistic modelization of the psyche as with its political ascension as a tool for governing a labor force whose cognitive and behavioral deviations—if left to their own devices—could put the economic base of late capitalism in serious jeopardy through a wave of massive withdrawal from the economic scene: a refusal of work on behalf of the sick, the exhausted, and the stressed.

In contrast to the narrow confines of CBT and its quantitative fixation, the psychoanalytic tradition does not eschew the complex intricacies of the unconscious and desire. Rather, it embraces them as foundational ideas used to conceptualize the meaning of health, and even its very possibility. Film theory's historical imbrication with the psychoanalytic tradition puts it in a unique position to work with these concepts and stage an intervention into the medicalized film and media ecologies where existential grievances are expressed—an intervention which disrupts the way that manualized therapies gloss over the discontents of civilization.

The cinema is implicated in medical efforts to determine the therapeutic climate to come. The pressing question is not whether film will play a role in future psychotherapeutic initiatives, but whether the critical ethos and conceptual resources of film philosophy will have a hand in shaping—and if necessary, shaking—this development. If the humanities have a truth claim on empirical reality that is as equally valid as science, then it seems entirely appropriate that when the art form which has most thoroughly capitalized on the activation of unconscious psychic processes is put to psychotherapeutic uses, the thinkers who know the intricacies of that art most intimately should be present. Otherwise, the cinema's subjection to powers that the history of film studies has sought to contest may become increasingly reified by the cloak of scientism.

The following sections present four different contexts in which cinema is put to therapeutic use by professionals in the mental health fields: art therapy, outpatient psychotherapy, psychiatric inpatient care, and positive psychology. In application, these approaches overlap with one another, but their distinctiveness is worth holding onto since they each operate on different assumptions about the nature of mental illness and what the role of film should be in achieving mental health outcomes. The purpose of walking through them is to become acquainted with how the cinema is instrumentalized by medical methodologies wherein films are used as tools, and thus to establish a backdrop against which this book's exploration of the recomposition of subjectivity at the cinema can be contrasted.

ART THERAPY

Once could reasonably hypothesize that art therapists would use films in therapy sessions much more than orthodox psychologists. However, interviews with art therapists reveal this not to be the case. Exact figures on the topic do not exist, probably in large part because such statistics would be generated by art therapist associations, and they have much fewer resources at their disposal than their psychological and psychiatric counterparts. The best assessment of the situation comes from the introduction to the only anthology devoted to filmmaking as psychotherapy, and it readily admits that "the number of clinicians practicing film and video as therapeutic tools has been relatively small."[19] Surprisingly, statistics on the use of film in non-art psychotherapy are available and suggest the complete opposite. In a survey of 827 practicing psychologists licensed with the American Psychological Association, "67% reported the use of motion pictures to promote therapy gains, and most of these practitioners (88%) considered the use of motion pictures as effective in promoting treatment outcome."[20] The fact that two-thirds of psychologists reported using cinema as a therapeutic strategy is remarkable in its own right, and testifies to both the ubiquity of this practice and the need to understand it better.

Why do most art therapists not use film in their practices, and why do most psychologists use film in theirs? The answer has to do with the split between the production of art and the consumption of art, with art therapists' work falling into the former category and the psychologists' work falling into the latter. Creative arts therapies, as they are often called, are focused almost exclusively on art production: painting, mask-making, drawing, dance, theater, performance, and on occasion, filmmaking. With the exception of filmmaking, all of these modalities are conducive to amateur art-making and the format constraints of the art therapy session. Even though cellphone cameras and simple-to-use digital editing suites are now ubiquitous, filmmaking is generally still too laborious for standard art therapy sessions, particularly since art therapists work mostly with non-artists who produce art as amateurs for therapeutic purposes. In a media ecology where anxiety, addiction, and self-esteem issues have been linked to social media usage, it also makes sense that art therapists would prefer their clients to engage in artmaking practices which do not pass through their daily-use devices. Another practical reason why there is relatively little filmmaking in the field of art therapy could be due to the fact that art therapy disproportionately works with children, compared with other psychological approaches. There are also special legal and privacy considerations around filmic representation (especially of children) that must be considered when incorporating filmmaking into an art therapy session, and which do not affect other modalities of art-making to the same degree.

On a more theoretical level, one could reason that art therapists generally tend not to make films with clients because of the likelihood that their art therapy techniques are designed to work with the expressive therapies continuum (ETC). The expressive therapies continuum is based on the idea that the way people make art mirrors their way of living, and it promotes using diverse types of artistic materials to prompt different ways of making art, with the goal of stimulating different, healthier, life patterns. According to the ETC, the psychologically mature and healthy individual is one who can move between different materials and styles, avoiding neurotic obsessions and structures. These layers of style and material are thought to help build and strengthen different facets of the personality. An illustrative example would be an art therapist who encourages a client obsessed with drawing rigid lines and boundaries with pen to try using watercolor painting as a way of relinquishing control. Given the prominence of this theory, art therapy practitioners tend to offer their clients a diverse slate of art-making materials to choose from: pencil, crayon, marker, paint, fabric, and so on. Even though film could express these different facets of materiality through changes to the mise-en-scène (lighting, costume, makeup) and cinematographic techniques (altering lenses, filters, and shooting styles), it is less straightforward than using different art materials for illustrating or painting, to achieve a fuller range of stylistic expression. Nevertheless, some examples of art therapy through filmmaking do exist, and they are catalogued in an anthology entitled *Video and Filmmaking as Psychotherapy: Research and Practice*. The book is edited by Joshua Cohen and Lauren Johnson, both of whom are psychologists and filmmakers.

Depending on the jurisdiction, art therapy may or may not qualify as a registered psychological practice, and this distinction has tangible consequences for the range of freedom offered to practitioners. Art therapists are themselves divided on whether or not art therapy should be officially recognized and licensed by governmental bodies as a form of psychotherapy. Those in favor make the argument that art therapy techniques, much like other psychotherapies, can be effective in relieving symptoms of mental illness, whereas other art therapy professionals prefer to eschew the licensing framework altogether and consider art therapy to be more analogous to personal development or coaching. Whether or not art therapy is a registered field in a given jurisdiction can have drastic ramifications on a practitioner's income level and ability to find employment, since public health insurance generally does not cover art therapy sessions in outpatient settings and private insurance plans usually only cover "evidence-based" psychotherapies administered by licensed psychotherapists.

As important as it is that art therapists be adequately compensated for the work they do, the fact that art therapy is often not officially recognized as a psychotherapy can actually give it a creative advantage. For example, in many jurisdictions, art therapy is an unchartered practice, meaning that art therapists cannot legally provide psychotherapy or treat mental illnesses. This has the negative repercussion of limiting the reach of art therapy, but the silver lining is that as a result, art therapy can advance a sense of health that need not reduce the suffering of personal existential impasses to the disease model of mental illness, which evidence-based psychotherapies assume as the basis of their intervention. It is in contexts such as these—where art therapy, working on the margins of the psychotherapy establishment, does not seek to treat specific mental illnesses that are strictly defined according to a disease model—that a re-existentialization of mental illness may be witnessed. By insisting that psychic pain is irreducible to a disease, that it is expressive of a unique constellation of existence, a singular manner of becoming constituted as a subject in a relational field shaped by desire and power, art therapy presents itself as an ally of the belief that a political aesthetics should double as a therapeutic aesthetics.

Filmmaking may not be the most viable way of practicing art therapy due to the technical limitations alluded to above. For this reason the use of film in art therapy, compared to other psychological and psychiatric fields, is infrequent. Nevertheless, even if art therapy chooses to foreground the therapeutic value of non-cinematic artistic production, it can be seen as an ally in theorizing the therapeutic value of film spectatorship, precisely because it grants an existential dimension to psychic disturbances and sidesteps the reductionism at the core of the most institutionally dominant etiologies and therapies.

CINEMATHERAPY

A shift in focus from art therapy to the use of film directly in outpatient psychotherapy settings introduces the practice of "cinematherapy." Cinematherapy arose out of the long-standing practice of bibliotherapy in the 1980s as home movies became widely accessible in the form of VHS tape technology.[21] According to Cathy Malchiodi, "cinematherapy is generally defined as an intervention used by a variety of helping professionals that directs clients to watch specific movies for psychotherapeutic reasons and/or to report their impressions to their therapist for further discussion."[22] There are a variety of ways for this to be accomplished, and it is possible for this strategy to be based on diverging conceptual models of psychological health. Most often it takes place in a one-on-one client-therapist setting. Some examples will be outlined to give a better sense of the general attitudes undergirding this psychotherapeutic usage of cinema, and the extent to which it sidesteps the crucial questions about the cinema's subjectifying powers which are posed by film theory.

Cinematherapy initiatives have given rise to a body of psychology literature explaining, rationalizing, and "manualizing" the practice. Of the representative books on the topic which will be touched upon, Birgit Wolz's *E-Motion Picture Magic* is the most sophisticated. Wolz is one of cinematherapy's main advocates, a psychotherapist with a private practice who offers continuing education courses in cinematherapy for therapists and nurses. Her practice is oriented in the tradition of depth psychology and uses "the impact of movies to help clients change negative beliefs, manage destructive emotions, develop self-esteem, discover forgotten strengths and grow in the face of a loss or disappointment."[23] *E-Motion Picture Magic* is filled with short self-help exercises and plot previews of films about dealing with such challenges, and Wolz's practice seriously considers how mindfulness exercises, or "conscious attention" can be applied to watching a film.

Mindfulness techniques have become commonplace in psychological discourses and practices, particularly since Marsha Lineham developed "dialectical behavioral therapy" for people with borderline personality disorder (BPD) in the late 1980s. The techniques are primarily based on a secularization of ancient Buddhist meditations, wherein the mindfulness practitioner observes his or her thoughts without judgment and in a disposition of non-attachment. "Though these [mindfulness] practices were and are helpful, I became excited when I noticed that it seemed easier to practice conscious awareness while watching a movie than it did in everyday life situations," writes Wolz.[24] "The experience of watching movies can be seen as a metaphor for [a] trance or illusory state. Becoming consciously aware in the moment helps to wake us up."[25] In cinematherapy, the film viewing is posited as an opportunity to practice mindfulness free from the distractions that can accompany other more abbreviated forms of media consumption.

On a related note, Gary Solomon has published on cinematherapy from within the twelve-step tradition inaugurated by Alcoholics Anonymous. The principle therapeutic benefit that he ascribes to the cinema is its ability to undo denial: "Movies help break through the walls of denial in a very special way. They help us to see and hear things that we were unwilling or unable to acknowledge on our own. . . . Suspension of disbelief is coming out of denial."[26] The first step of the twelve-step program—admission of one's powerlessness over addiction and that life has become unmanageable—is aimed precisely at overcoming denial and the admitting of a problem whose severity had gone previously unacknowledged by the person with an addiction.

Jan and Jon Hesley use films in a similar fashion to prompt difficult discussions with their reticent clients. According to the two therapists, "VideoWork is a therapeutic process in which clients and therapists discuss themes and characters in popular films that relate to the core issues of ongoing therapy. . . . In VideoWork, we use films to facilitate self-understanding, to introduce options for action plans, and to seed future therapeutic interventions."[27] The Hesleys offer a number of reasons why they think therapists should introduce films into their psychotherapeutic practices. The first reason they provide is compliance, meaning that clients are likely to give the therapy a chance. Films are accessible and require less concentrated attention than reading, and this can be conducive for clients who are anxious or depressed. They are also easily available and familiar; popular films are already a part of the client's vernacular and require no specialized knowledge or language. Additionally, the authors argue that using cinema in psychotherapy improves the rapport between client and therapist by giving them an experience in common. The Hesleys also emphasize how films can be used to build rapport and reframe life problems so that self-defeating thinking and behavior patterns can be sorted out with sharper reasoning.

As a whole, this genre of cinematherapy writing encompasses both self-help literature for commercial audiences and cinematherapy training manuals for psychotherapists.[28] Its texts move from offering motivational quotes to then providing instructions on how to bring popular film into the therapist's office. They also draw upon a variety of psychological models, with Wolz drawing from Jungian depth psychology and Buddhist spirituality, Solomon emphasizing how cinema can help a client to accomplish the first of the twelve steps by breaking out of denial, and the Hesleys opting for a "homework-based approach for therapists working from an outcomes perspective with a brief therapy orientation."[29] The decisive factor common to all these cinematherapy practices is that film is instrumentalized and made useful in the service of an extraneous therapeutic system or technique.

INPATIENT ENCOUNTERS

In the outpatient settings of cinematherapy, film functions as a tool to assist in a talk therapy process aimed at treating the symptoms of neurosis. Conversely, psychiatrists working in inpatient settings such as hospitals make use of film to socialize, discipline, and diagnose psychosis. A study by Turkish psychiatrists, "Use of Movies for Group Therapy of Psychiatric Inpatients: Theory and Practice," details the operations and objectives of the Watching Cinema Group Therapy program at a psychiatric clinic in Kocaeli. The authors based the study on the premise that using cinema in group therapy could help to address symptoms particular to impatient populations, "such as refusal of treatment, lack of cooperativeness, lack of social responsiveness or interest in others, serious communicative impairments, failure to develop normal relationships or friendships, and other cognitive disabilities caused by illness."[30] According to the group's organizers, these psychiatric inpatient populations "need therapeutic treatment in addition to medication . . . group psychotherapy may support medicines as a complementary approach."[31] Watching and discussing films in a group setting led by a psychiatrist qualifies as one of these group psychotherapies, which they recommend for use as a complement to psychotropic medication. The program included a mix of Hollywood and popular Turkish films for accessibility purposes, though the psychiatrists found that patients (much like the general public) did not like to watch subtitled films.

The study's authors readily admit that their sample size is small and that the same sort of conclusions cannot be drawn from their report as would be from a meta-level study. Yet the psychiatrists responsible for the program point to the positive outcomes of their working group as reason for optimism about the use of cinema in psychiatric institutions. They even go to the length of identifying sixteen benefits from the program, most of which can be boiled down to assisting social integration, improving communication between patient and psychiatrist, and facilitating behavioral education.[32] Going to see a film in a common room in the hospital became a way of integrating the patients socially because they were able to successfully perform a normative activity which made them feel connected to people outside of the hospital who also spend their time watching films and television. At the first screening, patients showed up in their normal clothes, but at subsequent meetings doctors noticed that the patients began to place special emphasis on their appearance, choosing to wear their best clothes or put on makeup, as if for an important social outing. The screenings also improved communication between psychiatrists and patients, since many of the patients had a hard time speaking about their case history and sharing confidential details of their lives with unfamiliar persons. In the group discussions held after each film screening, patients often spoke with ease about matters of personal importance which gave the doctors insights into their mental health conditions. These conversations carried over from the group sessions into individual medical appointments, facilitating doctor-patient communication and helping to smooth the hospital operations.

The film screenings were also seen by the psychiatrists running the pilot group as assisting in behavioral education. There are certain social norms that are implicitly expected to be adhered to when watching a film, and the doctors encouraged these behaviors, such as being quiet during the movie, and waiting for one's turn to speak during the discussion afterwards. The patients were observed during the movies for indicators pertaining to their clinical status, and as a way to gauge how the patients might fare in the outside world. When patients behaved poorly at a film screening or subsequent discussion, a reward-punishment system barred them from returning until they showed that they could modify their behavior in ways deemed socially acceptable for the screening.

Compliance, docility, and discipline are also at the core of the therapeutic strategy of psychiatrists at the Quincy Mental Health Center, Massachusetts Department of Mental Health. Two of them, Michael Fleming and Ericka Bohnel, authored the paper "Use of Feature Film as Part of Psychological Assessment" published in the journal *Professional Psychology: Research and Practice*.[33] The article recounts their experience in using film as a tool to aid in conducting diagnostic interviews in an emergency ward, particularly when dealing with patients whose acute distress makes them uncooperative with medical personnel. In the words of Bohnel and Fleming, "The introduction of feature films may make the patient more positive and ready to engage with the interviewer, as well as more motivated to speak about his or her mental illness."[34]

The authors give an example worth citing at length because of how boldly it illustrates the efficacy of film in diffusing turbulent situations on the psychiatric ward.

> A 68-year-old man was hospitalized after engaging in a successful auto-castration that resulted in his nearly bleeding to death. After a week of hospitalization on a medical surgical unit, he was transferred involuntarily to the psychiatric inpatient unit. On admission, he refused to meet with Michael Fleming or any of the clinical team members (medical doctor, licensed social worker, registered nurse, and occupational therapist) for assessment purposes. He appeared to be steadfast in his resistance and noncompliance. When asked what film he would suggest, he stated *2001: A Space Odyssey* (Stanley Kubrick, 1968). . . . Slowly, the patient seemed to become more engaged in the discussion of the opening scene. He appeared more animated as he spoke about his remembrance of what he emphasized was the "historical" importance of the film. The initial discussion of the film lasted almost an hour. An attitudinal shift seemed to

have taken place in the patient that created a point of engagement with the assessor. The next day, the patient was willing to engage in a more formal MSE (Mental Status Exam).

This excerpt points to a couple of key differences from the way that film is used in outpatient cinematherapy. The first is that these clinicians encourage patients to choose their own films for viewing. This seemingly "democratic" or patient-centered strategy differentiates itself from the other cinematherapy approaches that have been presented thus far, in which the therapist or psychiatrist chooses the films for the clients to watch. (The title of Solomon's book *The Motion Picture Prescription* encapsulates this attitude, in which the doctor prescribes an appropriate film to a client whose knowledge of film history is presumed to be inferior to the therapist's.) However, Fleming and Bohnel's decision to grant patients their choice of film isn't motivated by an orientation towards auto-directed therapy or the belief that patients possess the cultural awareness to select films that will help them to exteriorize their psychological problems.

Instead, these psychiatrists make use of film in response to urgent medical scenarios in psychiatric inpatient environments, particularly when patient behavior challenges compliance. When patients who exhibit such behaviors are given the option to select their own film, psychiatrists leverage the cinema's capability to pacify agitated individuals. This tactic effectively fosters compliance with the overarching psychiatric authority and its corresponding regimes of subjectification—these being prerequisites for carrying out the standard diagnostic procedures integral to the admission protocol in psychiatric hospitals.

POSITIVE PSYCHOLOGY

Building on the utilization of film in both outpatient and inpatient clinical settings, it is relevant to consider another context where film is rendered useful: the sphere of positive psychology. Positive psychology isn't entirely separate from ordinary psychology or cinematherapy, since therapists of many orientations have incorporated the main ideas of positive psychology into their practices, and the cinematherapists mentioned above all traffic in some of positive psychology's key preoccupations, such as improving self-esteem and cultivating character strengths. That said, positive psychology has emerged as a stand-alone branch of psychology that has developed a unique approach to using cinema for the promotion of mental health, one which differs from the examples presented thus far.

Danny Wedding and Ryan M. Niemiec are the coauthors of *Positive Psychology at the Movies* and prominent proponents of using cinema to advance the aims of positive psychology. However, their journey began with a different focus—they originally used films as a tool to aid in psychiatric diagnosis, similar to the approach of Bohnel and Fleming. In their earlier work, Wedding and Niemiec led a project resulting in the creation of a handbook titled *Movies and Mental Illness*. This publication, modeled after the *DSM* (*Diagnostic and Statistical Manual of Mental Disorders*), serves as a training manual for student psychiatrists and enables students to practice their diagnostic skills by analyzing the symptoms of characters in commercial films. The book categorizes hundreds of popular films based on the specific mental health conditions they portrayed and this method of categorization was carried over to *Positive Psychology at the Movies*, but with a significant change reflecting the difference between traditional psychology and positive psychology. Instead of categorizing films based on *DSM*-recognized mental illnesses, *Positive Psychology at the Movies* groups films according to the virtues of positive psychology that their narratives encapsulate.

Positive psychology distinguishes itself from standard clinical approaches because it chooses not to focus on clinically diagnosable mental illnesses and their correlate symptoms. Most psychotherapeutic approaches begin with a clinical diagnosis of what is conceived of as an underlying mental illness, and then seek to diminish the presenting symptoms associated with that illness. Martin Seligman, a depression researcher, former president of the American Psychological Association, and progenitor of the positive psychology movement, has argued that psychiatry's fundamental flaw and "dirty little secret" is that it has settled on symptom relief and has abandoned any and all pursuit of cure.[35] Touted as a corrective to entrenched methods of treating mental illness, positive psychology proposes to begin with people's character strengths and to improve on them so as to promote human flourishing rather than mere symptom relief.[36] Positive psychology is also predicated on the idea that human suffering is not merely caused by an underlying illness but by difficulties which are unavoidable facts of life. It supposes that the ability to express one's strengths and live according to one's highest values are key factors in determining whether or not a client can overcome these challenges without succumbing to behavioral and cognitive patterns which will exacerbate life's problems and deteriorate one's mental health. Positive psychology came about after Seligman searched through all major religions and cultures across recorded history to deduce the virtues and character traits they all supposedly hold in common. He settled on precisely six virtues and twenty-four character traits, which he assembled in the *Character Strengths and Virtues Handbook*.

The diagram in figure 1.1 is taken from *Positive Psychology at the Movies*, which is closely modeled after the *Character Strengths and Virtues Handbook*—positive psychology's systematized response to the *DSM*. It visually reflects the field's organizing ideas and situates the role that the authors believe film can play in positive psychology practice by adding film titles to the outermost ring of the chart. For positive psychology, there are five fundamental aspects to well-being: positive emotions, engagement, relationships, meaning, and achievement. These are found listed in the center of the chart. According to the positive psychology system, character strengths and virtues are what allow people to flourish, and the field is focused on developing character so as to facilitate flourishing.

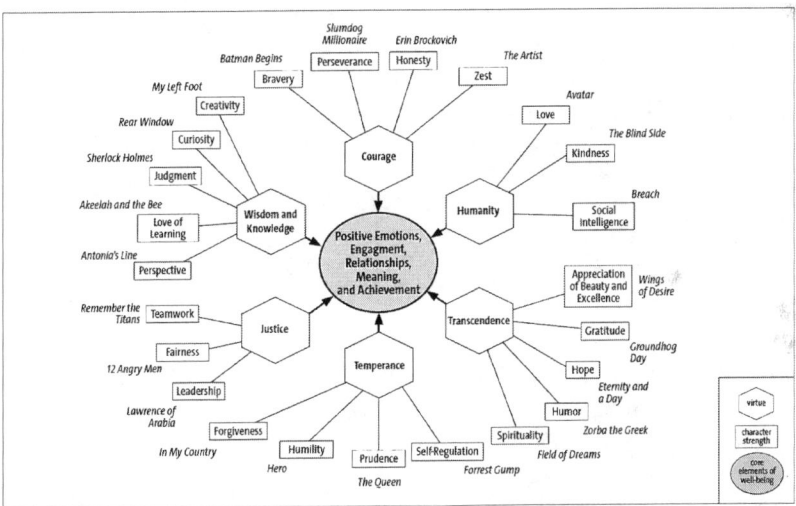

FIGURE 1.1. The VIA classification of character strengths and virtues. As it appears in Ryan M. Niemiec and Danny Wedding, *Positive Psychology at the Movies: Using Films to Build Character Strengths and Well-Being*, second edition (Boston: Hogrefe, 2014). Adapted from Christopher Peterson and Martin E. P. Seligman, *Character Strengths and Virtues: A Handbook and Classification* (New York City, Oxford University Press, 2004).

The therapeutic strategy expressed in Wedding and Niemiec's *Positive Psychology at the Movies* manual is very similar to that found in the cinematherapy books, in that it is based on the principles of "observational learning"—the idea that people can take solace and find inspiration in what they see on screen, with the goal of changing unhelpful patterns of thought and behavior. *Positive Psychology at the Movies* posits four criteria of a positive psychology film: the portrayal of a character with the character strengths; the depiction of obstacles and adversity; the overcoming of obstacles; and lastly, an uplifting tone.[37] The diagram lays out the role of cinema in this therapeutic system quite clearly. If the aim is to arrive at "the core elements of well-being" positioned at the center, then the positive psychology client is tasked to arrive there by developing their "signature" character strengths which are reflective of a universal virtue. Depending on what facet of themselves a client seeks to work on, a particular film is recommended. For example, *Slumdog Millionaire* (Danny Boyle, 2008) is prescribed for people who seek to develop perseverance, which is an expression of the virtue of courage, and could lead to meaningful achievements in the client's life. The *Positive Psychology at the Movies* manual offers a comprehensive list of recommended films in the index, organized according to the field's standard classification of character strengths and virtues, so that a positive psychologist can find a film which represents the strengths and virtues that they wish to cultivate in a client.

CRITICAL FRIENDSHIP

Having reviewed the various ways that cinema is used in psychological and psychiatric practices, this final section of the chapter offers a critique in the spirit of cultivating the type of "critical friendship" between the medical sciences and the humanities advocated by Nikolas Rose.[38] A politically committed humanities scholarship is liable to take exception to two characteristics of the aforementioned clinical uses of cinema. The first has to do with their implicit defense of professionalization, which has the effect of abnegating the therapeutic potential immanent to the cinematic encounter by situating the therapist's office as the default site of therapy.

Cinematherapy's defense of the profession of psychology is understandable given that its practitioners are educated and licensed in the discipline and make their living off of its monopolization of psychotherapeutic services. However, these practitioners have not identified anything intrinsic to the cinematic experience which has therapeutic value. Despite their books being filled with claims regarding the "healing qualities" of the "movies," they primarily view the cinema as a tool for assisting in whatever talk therapy method they already espouse. In these really existing instrumentalizations of cinema, it is not the cinematic experience which holds therapeutic promise, it is the traditional client-therapist relationship and its gamut of psychological counseling methods. Nowhere is this summarized more clearly than in the preface to an edited anthology on cinematherapy where Florence W. Kaslow writes: "Films can be rich adjuncts to therapy and provide excellent stimulus for in-session discussions."[39] Much can certainly be accomplished in the therapist's office, but it does mean that the name "cinematherapy," for all its catchiness, is more than a bit misleading, since the cinema is rendered a mere tool in a manualized psychotherapeutic process. In cinematherapy, the cinema is instrumentalized and made useful.

As a consequence of not giving due consideration to the therapeutic potential of the cinematic experience in its own right, these writers and practitioners are able to completely sidestep the long-standing film-theoretical problem of how the cinema produces subjectivity. The cinematherapists effectively reduce the cinematic experience to a talking point, and elide the question of the apparatus altogether, to say nothing of visual pleasure, primary identification, fetishism, or voyeurism. Despite its best intentions, by skirting how the cinema produces subjectivity, cinematherapy offers a model of mental health which borders on false consciousness.

The two examples of psychiatrists who use film in institutional settings also warrant critical engagement. The first initiative of employing cinema within a group therapy context undeniably demonstrates greater ambition and complexity among the two applications, as it cultivates a degree of social interaction that is often challenging to foster within the confines of a psychiatric ward. However, the program is guided by a normative current in which the psychiatrists' main preoccupation is to use the cinema to prompt socially acceptable behavior in the patients. In this context, the cinema is effectively turned into a disciplinary apparatus.

The second inpatient iteration is intentionally drained of the productive ambivalence that the first example conveyed in its openness towards the indeterminacy of cinema-initiated patient sociality. Instead, it focuses on rendering psychotic patients docile, primed for diagnosis, and prepared to be interned. The scene of psychiatric diagnosis condenses the three disciplinary techniques which figure in Foucault's definition of a disciplinary society: hierarchical observation, normalizing judgment, and examination: the doctor must be in a position of hierarchical authority, expressed physically and spatially; must subject the patient's symptoms to a normalizing judgment, represented by the *DSM*, the diagnostic document which conveys the consensus of the psychiatric discipline with regard to nosology; and lastly, an examination interprets the patient's symptoms through the lens of medical perception to reach a diagnosis.[40] Based on this configuration of power in the diagnostic scene, it is easy to see why, in his lectures on psychiatric power, Foucault claimed that medical authority "functions as power well before it functions as knowledge."[41] Regardless of whether such power is posited as repression or aide, it clearly amounts to a reduction of whatever therapeutic potential may be found in the encounter with the cinema. The role that the cinema plays in these psychiatric operations is one of persuading compliance with a larger psychopharmacological treatment regime through the offer of visual pleasure.

As for positive psychology, a critical appraisal of its use of cinema reveals an entrenched American-centrism and unconditional allegiance to the U.S. military during its invasion of Iraq. It must be pointed out that never does positive psychology ask whose interests are served by positive thinking, or whether or not the mission of a given institution warrants positive reinforcement. The U.S. military is a perfect example because the positive psychology founder Martin Seligman designed a military "global assessment test" "to measure the psychosocial well-being of soldiers of all ranks in four domains: emotional fitness, social fitness, family fitness, and spiritual fitness," with the aim of improving the success of American military missions.[42] He provides the following rationale for designing the test: "Unfortunately, all the wars that we have fought recently are human wars and we are zero for seven in these."[43] The "we" in "wars we have fought" is the United States, reflective of positive psychology's lack of critical reflexivity towards what people supposedly ought to think positively about.[44]

The American-centrism of positive psychology extends beyond the militaristic orientation of its main progenitors to include the claim that its scientific findings can "transcend particular cultures and politics and approach universality."[45] This logic replicates that of orthodox psychiatry, with its reliance on the disease model of mental illness, and its embedded assumption that cultural and subjective differences are masks which must be stripped away to uncover a discrete, underlying disease which is coherent and consistent across historical and cultural contexts.[46] The work of ethnopsychiatrists and anthropologists, such as Tobie Nathan's accounts of West African therapeutic modalities and Robert Lemelson's investigation of the unique cultural underpinnings of mental illness in Indonesia documented in the ethnographic film series *Afflictions*,[47] lays out the therapeutic inefficacy of applying universal models of pathology to singular assemblages of subjectivity that arise in different cultures.

These observations and critiques of the really existing instrumentalizations of cinema by medical practices reveal two noteworthy tendencies. The first is that film studies has historically advanced a plethora of ideas about the cinema's powers of subjectivization which are absent from the medical literature on the therapeutic uses of cinema. And secondly, whatever therapeutic value the cinema may harbor is systematically foreclosed by these medical discourses and practices, which ask merely how the cinema can be used to serve preexisting clinical methods. The following chapters affirm film theory's long-standing engagement with the psychoanalytic tradition in order to explore the therapeutic potential of the nonclinical and nonprofessional mode of creative activity that is engaged, cinephilic spectatorship. For if the therapeutic value of cinema is reduced to the ways in which film is made useful in clinical settings, then those who could stand to benefit most from an ethos of lay therapeutic experimentation will be abandoned to the medical-industrial complex's naturalization of the reality principle, surplus repression, and an ensuing erosion of existential health.[48]

[CHAPTER TWO]

A Machine for Transversality

In the middle of the film *Paris s'éveille*, or *Paris Awakens* (Olivier Assayas, 1991), Louise (Judith Godrèche) and Adrien (Thomas Langmann) meet around a blazing trashcan fire. They have gathered with friends to party but they also have things to discuss. After all, they are in a relationship with one another, but life's pressures are ripping them apart. Adrien is wanted by the police and is plotting an escape to South America with a forged passport. Louise has reached her limit living with him in an abandoned Parisian squat after having discovered his black-market activities. She is in love but has a taste for the high life, and their current living situation does not match her ambitions.

The scene which stages their predicament is composed of alternating medium close-up shots of Adrien and Louise moving around opposite sides of the fire in unison, shot through a clockwise swivel pan. What is remarkable is the way the scene condenses the film's extenuating formal pattern of oscillating back and forth between the two characters' pursuits: *Paris Awakens* opens with a shot of Adrien roaming the city and it ends with Louise having achieved her career goal of working as a television personality. In between these beginning and ending points the film articulates their respective movement profiles which begin apart, conjunct, and eventually lead on in separate directions according to their singular appetites, having changed them both irreversibly.

The way that *Paris Awakens* ends on the note of the couple's dissolution contributes to a motif of loss and rupture found across the early Assayas oeuvre.[1] His films exhibit a sustained interest in group dynamics and repeatedly conclude with the breakup of relationships and friendships, along with an overwhelming sense of the loss of youth and innocence. In the films of Assayas, the reality of social dynamics and their imperfect negotiation of the contradiction between the pleasure and reality principles take precedence over narrative closure.

38 · CHAPTER TWO

FIGURE 2.1. Adrien at the opening of *Paris Awakens* (Olivier Assayas, 1991).

FIGURE 2.2. Louise at the closing of *Paris Awakens* (Olivier Assayas, 1991).

Paris Awakens, like other works from Assayas, offers multiple avenues for analysis. The developmental path chosen here adopts the film as an intercessor for rethinking the problematic of the production of subjectivity beyond the logic of identification which structures modern film theory, particularly its discourse on the cinematographic apparatus. *Paris Awakens* makes itself amenable to the task by virtue of its restaging of the fundamental concern of modern film theory: the problem of identification. Modern film theory probes how psychic processes of identification with an impression of reality determine the position of the spectatorial subject. Inasmuch as modern film theory understands identification as an unconscious psychic process, its mechanisms are explained with

FIGURES 2.3 AND 2.4. Louise and Adrien meet around the blazing trashcan fire in *Paris Awakens* (Olivier Assayas, 1991).

recourse to the Oedipus complex, which, true to the psychoanalytic foundations of modern film theory, is held responsible for the psychic emergence of subjectivity. In 1973, upon leaving the screening of an F. W. Murnau film, Roland Barthes posed the question, "Doesn't every narrative lead back to Oedipus?"[2] The quotation would guide modern film theory's orientation and provide weight to the idea that the production of the cinema's spectatorial subject through identification could be elaborated through the analysis of Oedipalized desire.[3]

At first glance, *Paris Awakens* may give the impression that it too can be read as the story of Oedipus, since its coming-of-age narrative contains elements of Oedipal teleology. Adrien meets Louise towards the beginning of the film when he returns home to live with his father Clément (Jean-Pierre Léaud). It turns out that Louise is Clément's new live-in girlfriend. Louise and Adrien then develop their relationship clandestinely behind the father's back; and in spite of her provocative warning to him—"Be careful what you do, I'm your stepmother"—they eventually decide to leave the father's apartment together after he attempts to clamp down on Louise's heroin use. Given that the film traffics in the son's aggression toward the father and his desire for the (step)mother, it could certainly lend itself to the type of structural film analysis practiced by Raymond Bellour—and inspired by Roland Barthes—that takes all instances of narrative cinema as variations on the foundational myth of Oedipus. Up until a certain point—the scene around the blazing fire—and up to a certain degree—the degree of narrativity—the film does lend itself to interpretation through the stages of male psychosexual development culminating in mature object choice and genital love.

Nevertheless, the film's aesthetic construction thwarts subsumption to the Oedipal master narrative. In the aforementioned scene, Adrien and Louise face off in a shot-reverse-shot schema which condenses how the film is split between allegiances towards their divergent escapades. The formal structure of the scene foregrounds the problem of identification in its equally patterned oscillation between the characters. By evenly distributing scopic agency, this scene avoids dividing the pair into the subject and object of the gaze, and resists positioning Adrien as the sole protagonist and narrative point of identification. The film's scopic development is as committed to Louise as it is to Adrien. The film is *découpé* through the relationality of their relationship, not through either one of them individually. *Paris Awakens* and its affinity with the pre-personal force of relational dynamics offers a jumping-off point for thinking about the cinema's production of subjectivity as emergent to its encounter with singular existential constellations that overrun the lines of identification drawn by the triangular striations of Oedipus. In aesthetically composing relationality in such a way that troubles the habituations of spectatorial identification with on-screen characters (secondary identification), *Paris Awakens* acts as a lure for thinking through the elements of the spectator-image relation which are irreducible to identification with the apparatus (primary identification) as well.

The following pages are designed to erode the striated directionality from inside the discourse of apparatus theory and supplement its lacuna around transference. As Paul Willemen aptly notes, transference is gapingly absent from apparatus theory's conceptualization of the spectatorial subject in spite of transference being a companion concept to identification in psychoanalytic theory.[4] If one were to deduce the reason for this omission, it could legitimately be posited that the concept of transference simply carried too much baggage for a theoretical enterprise whose vision of emancipatory politics required breaking with social institutions which retained vestiges of the reigning reality principle. For all of the radical developments around Lacan in France and psychoanalysts such as Fromm and Marcuse who came out of the Frankfurt school, psychoanalysis as a whole, not to mention the "helping professions" more generally, certainly retained such vestiges and often explicitly acted on the side of surplus repression—as they still so often do.[5] Reintroducing the neglected concept of transference into the theorization of the cinema's production of subjectivity raises the question of the cinema's therapeutic valence in a manner that better reflects apparatus theory's indebtedness to the psychoanalytic tradition, and in turn, the psychoanalytic tradition's imbrication in the history of the healing arts.[6]

An image of thought has structured film theory of the spectatorial subject: the unidirectionality of the cinematographic apparatus's productive, "impressive" forces, reinforced and coordinated by unconscious identifications with a parental imago. This chapter takes a conceptual line of flight from the aforementioned image of thought through an alternative attunement to the vicissitudes of nonclinical transferences at the cinema that allows for a more contingent theory of subjectivity production rooted in the machinic assemblage of anoedipal transversality. The wager of this encounter with film theory is made with the aspiration of rendering palpable the cinema as a machine for transversality, and thus facilitating an analysis of the production of subjectivity sensitive to how the cinema relationally conjuncts singular existential constellations to therapeutic effect.

AN APPARATUS OF IDENTIFICATION

The scene of Adrien and Louise circling the fire, looking at one another, ostensibly raises the question of how to identify, and with whom to identify. In the terminology of apparatus theory, the scene stages the interlinked problems of primary and secondary identification. Apparatus theory defines secondary cinematic identification as the identification between the spectatorial subject and a character on screen. It posits primary cinematic identification as the condition for the cinema's existence. The two types of identification depend on each other, with the interpersonal, character-centered quality of secondary identification being made possible by the transcendental subject position offered by primary identification with the apparatus itself—a primary identification with what stages the cinema. On this differentiation between primary and secondary identification, Jean-Louis Baudry writes:

> One can distinguish two levels of identification. The first, attached to the image itself, derives from the character portrayed as a center of secondary identifications, carrying an identity which constantly must be seized and reestablished. The second level permits the appearance of the first and places it "in action"—this is the transcendental subject whose place is taken by the camera which constitutes and rules the objects in this "world." Thus the spectator identifies less with what is represented, the spectacle itself, than with what stages the spectacle, makes it seen, obliging him to see what it sees, this is exactly the function taken over by the camera as a sort of relay.[7]

Christian Metz builds on Baudry's schema of primary identification to posit a spectator who "*identifies with himself*, with himself as a pure act of perception (as wakefulness, alertness): as condition of possibility of the perceived and hence as a kind of transcendental subject, anterior to every *there is*."[8]

According to Baudry and Metz, secondary identification is grafted onto primary identification. The spectator's secondary identifications with a character on-screen are activated by primary identification with the basic cinematographic apparatus itself. In this schema, primary identification delineates the imaginary relationship between the apparatus and the spectator for whom the apparatus has prepared an empty place. Through primary identification with the apparatus and its designated place, the spectator becomes subject. Apparatus theory posits that once subject to the basic cinematographic apparatus, spectatorial identifications with on-screen characters (at least in the classical formulation of cinema) are mobilized in the service of voyeuristic pleasure and fantasies of bourgeois ideology structured around the binary of sexual difference. The discourse of political modernism which sought to delineate the (gendered) ideological operations of the classical text was founded on the a priori fact of the spectator's primary identification with a transcendental subject position.[9]

The previous passages from Metz and Baudry imbue the apparatus with a sense of unidirectionality and technological determinism. Unidirectionality is manifest in the way the apparatus is theorized as producing the subject without being mutable in return (which would admit of a bidirectionality to the encounter). Technological determinism also undergirds Baudry and Metz's conceptualizations of the apparatus as unerringly effective in its production of a standardized subject.[10]

Baudry's term of choice when describing the subjectifying effects of the apparatus is "impression of reality." The word "impression" has two meanings which come through both in English and in the original

French. The first implies the material effect caused by an act of impressing, such as is accomplished by a stamp in wax. The second meaning of "impression" denotes an indistinct or imprecise mental configuration, such as an idea, memory, or mental image. Apparatus theory intentionally plays on the dual meaning of the word "impression" in the phrase "impression of reality" to polysemically signify that the cinematographic apparatus impresses reality onto the psyche of the spectator, and that the reality which is impressed is only an impression of reality in the second sense of the word, an illusion and not reality itself. [11]

The impression of reality appears in apparatus theory as unidirectional since it is the apparatus which impresses onto the psyche of the spectator, producing the spectatorial subject. The apparatus wields the power to impress reality; the spectator is impressed, like wax. There is no consideration in Baudry or Metz's configuration of apparatus theory of the spectator in turn affecting the cinema.[12] Consider these lines from Baudry's essay "The Apparatus" where he draws his well-known analogy between Plato's cave and the cinematographic apparatus: "If this apparatus really produces images, it first of all produces an effect of specific subjects—to the extent that a subject is intrinsically part of the apparatus; once cinema has been technically perfected it produces this same effect by the words 'impression of reality.'"[13] The subject is here an effect of a unidirectional impression. The subject is also technologically overdetermined since, as Baudry says, the apparatus has been "perfected." Mary Ann Doane cues into this technological determinism of the spectatorial subject and astutely laments it when she writes: "The problem with the theory of the cinematic apparatus is that the apparatus always works. It never breaks down, is never subject to failure."[14]

Ultimately, according to apparatus theory, spectatorial subjectivity is unidirectionally impressed and technologically overdetermined via the apparatus's activation of primary identification. Through identification, the subject becomes "intrinsically part of the apparatus," leading to a "denial of difference," to evoke the phrase of Anne Friedberg, between cinema and spectator.[15] In this schema, the relation that the apparatus has is unproblematically, seamlessly—and at the end of the screening, still—only with itself. It is endowed with the power to produce subjectivity, but only in its own image.[16]

The philosophical underpinnings of the psychoanalytic term "identification" belie the unidirectional determinism which effaces the singular existential constellation that accompanies each spectator to the cinema and the myriad ways that subjectivity can find itself recomposed in the encounter. In *The Language of Psychoanalysis*, Laplanche and Pontalis define identification as the psychological process whereby the subject assimilates an aspect, property, or attribute of the other and is transformed, wholly or partially, after the model the other provides. It is by means of a series of identifications that the personality is constituted and specified.... In Freud's work the concept of identification comes little by little to have the central importance which makes it, not simply one psychical mechanism among others, but the operation itself whereby the human subject is constituted.[17]

The Freudian roots of identification are more flexible than the totalizing impulse canonized in apparatus theory, even if identification performs a constitutive role in both formulations of the subject. In Freud's teleology of infant development, the subject assimilates an aspect or attribute of the other, and may be partially transformed by the model the other provides. Conversely, in Baudry's conceptualization, the spectator's primary identification with the place made for it by the apparatus produces a coherent transcendental subject. There is no sense that primary identification may be incomplete or that its effect may only be partial. The obligatory identification with the impression of reality constitutes a transcendental subject of identity; a subject identical with that very impression; a subject of similitude subsumed to the imaginary mechanisms of the apparatus.

Joan Copjec helps to picture how the ontology embedded in the apparatus theory of primary identification constructs a unified subject which betrays the elementary teachings of Lacan (despite the fact of his work being foundational to apparatus theory). Her words follow:

When Metz refers to the "already constituted ego" of the film spectator, when he says that "cinema demands that the psychical apparatus of its participants be fully constituted,"[18] he forgets, if only momentarily, what the spectator also forgets, that the psychical apparatus is never fully constituted in the sense of its ever being complete, a product, as we have said, of an infinitely iterable process. Identification is not an encounter of one fully present subject with another—fully present.[19]

In Lacanian thought, the ego is not constituted "once and for all" by a primary identification, but by "'a real patchwork of disparate images' which leads Lacan to call the ego a 'hodge-podge of Identifications.'"[20] It is also important to remember that identification for Lacan is indeed the mechanism by which the ego is constituted, but these productive identifications take place solely in the realm of the Imaginary which is but one ring in the Borromean knot which Lacan uses to diagram subjectivity. Apparatus theory's formulation of the spectatorial subject based on primary identification gave rise to a plethora of metaphors about the cinema as dream and the cinema as mirror, further demonstrating that its theory of spectatorial subjectivity is based on the restricted purview of the Imaginary ego and a more totalizing view of subjectivity production through identification than exists in the primary texts of Freud and Lacan.[21]

Given the primacy that identification assumes in modern film theory's attempts to theorize spectatorial subjectivity through the tools provided by psychoanalysis, theories of political aesthetics responded with recourse to Brecht to advance a counter-cinema capable of shattering the impression of reality's illusionism by foregrounding the semiotic labor of the film-work and hence breaking the imaginary identifications which artificially regressed the spectator to the mirror stage.[22] This political strategy which catalyzed much of 1970s film theory was foreshadowed and germinated by the work of Metz himself, who prescribed a killing off of the "love object"—the cinephilic "attachment"—in order to reapproach the cinema from a purportedly more mature and objective position. To accomplish this, Metz transposes the structure of the relationship between the analyst and analysand in the clinical scene onto the ideal relationship between the film theorist-as-spectator and the cinema. Metz then endows the film theorist before the cinema with a task analogous to that of the psychoanalyst before the analysand: that of winning the imaginary identifications of the ego for the symbolic. He writes: "Reduced to its most fundamental procedures, any psychoanalytic reflection on the cinema might be defined in Lacanian terms as an attempt to disengage the cinema-object from the imaginary and to win it for the symbolic, in the hope of extending the latter by a new providence."[23]

The Metzian paradigm figures the cinema as an apparatus of imaginary identification, only to pathologize the operations of this apparatus and the subject it produces, and prescribe psychoanalytic symbolization as a type of corrective analogous to the cure—after which the cinema may be loved again, albeit differently.

The following lines articulate how Metz repudiated the imaginary pleasures of his cinephilia with the aim of economically converting the relationship into symbolic epistemophilia.[24]

> To be a theoretician of the cinema, one should ideally no longer love the cinema and yet still love it: have loved it a lot and only have detached oneself from it by taking it up again from the other end, taking it as the target for the very same scopic drive which had made one love it. Have broken with it, as certain relationships are broken, not in order to move on to something else, but to return to it at the next bend of the spiral. . . . I have loved the cinema, I no longer love it, I still love it.[25]

The love for cinema that appears "at the next bend of the spiral" is a distanciated love that holds the object (of study) in place through a logic of secondarization that prevents the theoretician from being carried away by the primary processes of imaginary identification. Only by first dispelling the image's seductive lure[26] for identification, and detaching from the cinephilic love that he once uncritically indulged in, can the psychoanalytic theoretician then study the apparatus's subjectifying power and secondarize the primary processes involved in cinephilic desire.[27] In the words of Nico Baumbach, what Metz proposes with this maneuver is "a double consciousness that acknowledges that while cinephilia may resist theoretical knowledge, it was at the same time a precondition for theory. For Metz, theories of cinema shouldn't be beholden to the affective attachments of cinephilia, yet at the same time, they are futile if they do not grasp the 'specific kind of love' that cinema inspired in its devotees."[28]

This self-conversion process by which Metz transforms from a cinephile who passionately loves the cinema, to an analyst of the cinema who loves it from the position of symbolic detachment, parallels the therapeutic teleology of Lacanian psychoanalysis which, based on Lacan's 1953 lecture "The Function and Field of Speech and Language in Psychoanalysis," finds its end point in the subject's capacity for the "advent of a true speech."[29]

At this "other end of the spiral," where the egoic illusionism of identification has been sublimated into a symbolic discourse on desire which aims at truth, identification returns. It returns as identification with the (desire of the) analyst.[30] Apparatus theory, for all its denunciation of the cinema's idealism and integration into the realm of the imaginary, and for all its self-repudiation of its having taken pleasure in the identifications which the cinema offers, nevertheless, in the last instance, identifies with the analyst as ideal ego. The cinematographic apparatus, like the theoretical writing about it, is an apparatus of identification.

IMAGOS OF TRANSFERENCE

Apparatus theory's Lacanian account of subjectivity production concludes by way of an identification with the analyst. Lacan was clear, however, that identification with the analyst does not mark the end of an analysis. As John Müller writes, Lacan

> criticizes this "terminal identification" of the patient's ego with the analyst's ego because it leads to a "reinforced alienation" . . . In this paradigm of analysis, the identification of the patient's ego with that of the analyst

is a repetition of the original mirror-phase transference onto an idealized image taken as oneself, and is always a narcissistic and aggressive attempt to shore up a faltering sense of coherence and mastery. Clearly it will occur, but just as clearly it cannot be a goal of treatment.[31]

It is remarkable how the content of this passage parallels the language of apparatus theory. Just as with the men in chains in Plato's allegory of the cave, or the film spectators in the darkened cinema, the analysand forms an imaginary identification which lends a false sense of coherence and mastery (i.e., a transcendental subject position) that is indicative of regression to the mirror stage. What Müller adds here to apparatus theory's account of identification is the vector of transference that identification makes repeat.

Despite the focus on identification across the corpus of apparatus theory, the conjoined concept of transference which is fundamental to psychoanalytic theory and clinical technique is glaringly absent.[32] As a result, what gets lost in apparatus theory's idea of cinema, despite the theorist's identification with the analyst in the last instance, is the therapeutic aim of psychoanalysis.[33] To reintroduce the question of the therapeutic value of cinephilia requires destabilizing the underlying paternalism of the theory of identification and finding a basis for articulating the relationship between spectator and cinema that is productive of subjectivity beyond the technological determinism and unidirectionality implied by the apparatus of identification. It requires winning the imaginary—not for the symbolic, but for the image—in the real machinic materiality of the relational encounter with it. The remainder of this chapter asks how transference is active in the spectatorial situation, how identification's yoking to the primal imagos of the Oedipal complex attempts to girdle transference, and how in the last instance, the materiality of the transference exceeds the triangulated lines of identification in tending towards an intensive constellation of anoedipal transferences that one could call transversality—the basis of a purely machinic therapeutic alliance immanent to the encounter with the cinema.

It must be established: there is no psychoanalysis without transference.[34] In the clinical scene, the presence of alterity in the form of an other (the analyst) is the precondition for the unconscious production of analytic material. Whether it is viewed as resistance or progress, transference is the material basis of the therapeutic alliance without which the analytic endeavor would be sterile. There is, however, transference without psychoanalysis. As regards the specificity of transference to the psychoanalytic scene, Laplanche and Pontalis ask: "Does not the analytic situation, given the strictness and constancy of its conditions, merely offer an especially favorable ground for the emergence and the observation of phenomena that are actually present elsewhere?"³⁵

The spectatorial encounter with cinema is one of these "elsewheres." The acknowledgment of transference in the spectatorial situation defies the two problematic tendencies of apparatus theory's account of subjectivity production couched in the operations of identification: the unidirectionality of the "impression of reality," and its unceasing overdetermination. Unlike apparatus theory's schema of identification which results in the production of a standardized subject, admitting of transference in the encounter with cinema implies a singularity of the relational composition shaped as much by the unique mix of semiotics particular to each film, as by the unconscious elements brought to the material encounter with cinema's signs and signals by the spectator. Transference indexes relationality in the stead of unidirectional determinism, and contingency in the stead of standardization. An analysis of transference in the cinematic encounter could thus pose as an alternative to the totalizing tendency of apparatus theory, if only the chaosmic spasm of its relationality and contingency were not triangularly striated by Oedipal identifications. If only the cinema's images (its transference material) could stand up as images, and resist being transduced into imagos.³⁶

The imago is a familialist image. Most often in psychoanalytic discourse, it is a parental image, and even more specifically, a paternal image. Freud "pointed out that, although various types of transference can be identified (maternal, fraternal, etc.), 'the real relations of the subject to his doctor' mean that 'the 'father-imago' . . . is the decisive factor.'"³⁷

Why is the transference, which psychoanalysis itself readily admits can appear elsewhere than its analytic situation, identified with a parental imago? This was a pivotal point of contention between Freud and Jung which led to the cessation of their collaboration. Deleuze and Guattari relay the schism in the pages of *Anti-Oedipus*:

> When the break between Freud and Jung is discussed, the modest and practical point of disagreement that marked the beginning of their differences is too often forgotten: Jung remarked that in the process of transference the psychoanalyst frequently appeared in the guise of a devil, a god, or a sorcerer, and that the roles he assumed in the patient's eyes went far beyond any sort of parental images. They eventually came to a total parting of ways, yet Jung's initial reservation was a telling one.³⁸

The reason why Freud rejected Jung's insistence on non-familial transference is that he considered transference a repetition of infantile desires which are unconsciously displaced onto the person of the analyst, thus re-creating pre-Oedipal and Oedipal family dynamics under the artificially favorable conditions of the analytic relationship.[39] Freud viewed transferences as "new editions or facsimiles of the impulses and phantasies which are aroused and made conscious during the progress of the analysis; but they have this peculiarity, which is characteristic for their species, that they replace some earlier person by the person of the physician."[40] Transference thus became for Freud a transference neurosis, an artificial illness which displaces parental imagos from the analysand's past onto the analyst. Through the vehicle of transference, the analyst came to be systematically and unerringly identified with an unconscious familial imago. Returning to a familiar refrain, the analyst was then tasked with the transferential imago's methodical analysis—with once again winning the imaginary identification for the symbolic.[41]

Paris Awakens proposes to conceive of an encounter with the cinema as catalyzing a transferential process that deviates from identification with a parental imago. On the level of the film's molar representation, there are three possible points of secondary identification, three imagos for transference which together make up the Oedipal triad: child, mother, and father. Except that this staging of a would-be Oedipal drama undergoes a slippage of positionality, and ultimately a molecular rupture of its signifying coordinates. The slippage begins from the second scene in the film when Adrien meets his father Clément in a café. Clément plays the archetypal father figure, reprimanding his son for his delinquency and laying down the rules Adrien must obey if he is to be welcomed back into the home. While the acting is completely sincere and without a hint of irony, the identification of Clément with a father imago deliberately falters because of the history of the actor who plays him. Jean-Pierre Léaud's most famous on-screen performance is as Antoine in François Truffaut's 1959 film *The 400 Blows*.[42] In that film he incarnates the youthful, rebellious spirit of the French New Wave. The film famously follows his brushes with authority at school, in the family home, and in juvenile detention, and concludes with one of the most famous scenes in the history of cinema in which Léaud runs along the beach in a final stab at freedom.[43] It is difficult to envisage Léaud in *Paris Awakens* as activating a paternal transference, given that the iconicity of his persona is intimately associated with a spirit of defiance. The early filmography of Judith Godrèche is equally as destabilizing of her role of stepmother. Her previous three starring roles in *The Disenchanted* (Benoît Jacquot, 1990), *Stormy Summer* (Charlotte Brandstrom, 1989), and *The 15 Year Old Girl* (Jacques Doillon, 1989) all emphasize her pre-maternal youth.

FIGURES 2.5 AND 2.6. Jean-Pierre Léaud as a child in *The 400 Blows* (François Truffaut, 1959).

FIGURE 2.7. Jean-Pierre Léaud as the father, speaking sternly to Adrien in *Paris Awakens* (Olivier Assayas, 1991).

The polysemic slippage of these iconic signs is reinforced by the exchange of roles and dissolution of identities that the plot hinges on. Clément begins the film as the father, but his position is quickly challenged and displaced. After an argument at a nightclub, Louise speeds off on a motorcycle with her drug dealer, leaving Clément behind, as well as her role as mother-in-law to Adrien. Clément's son Adrien then defies the law of his father and becomes romantically involved with Louise, flouting his designated role as child. Once Adrien and Louise live together in their squat apartment, Adrien begins to take on the characteristics of his imperious father, jealously asking Louise about her daily whereabouts. Eventually she leaves him as well. Adrien then flees to Argentina to evade the police, never to be seen again. *Paris Awakens* is constructed around this taking of turns laying down the law and then transgressing it. None of the characters can be pinned to the familial role that they occupy in relation to one another. They all seek ways out of these roles, and they find them. Not only does the iconicity of their faces slip, and the positionality of their familial roles exchange, but in the turbulent movements of the group desire, the law of the father which holds the signifying series in place and secures the extensive logic of exchange breaks apart from the inside—composing images of difference in lieu of imagos of identification.

Admittedly, the relational aberrancies of the film's characters could be read through Oedipal triangulations as a barometer of normativity: the father "regresses" to an infantile state after the trauma of object loss; the child fails to develop out of the pre-Oedipal phase by retaining a taboo maternal object-choice; the mother hystericizes her resistance through acting out, and so on. The pathologized readings could continue. From such a perspective, secondary identifications with any of these three characters could prompt transferences with an imaginary familial imago consolidated during the mirror stage.

However, what if the aberrancy of desire honored by the film's découpage, an aberrancy which dissolves identities, asymmetrically intensifies filiation, and ultimately schizophrenizes the Oedipal family, was itself the lure for the transferential relation? In *Paris Awakens*, the transference discovers a molecular autonomy from the triangulating repetitions of identification anchored in the typical familial imagos.[44] Immanent to this relational juncture where an emergent spectatorial subjectivity percolates in tandem with the desiring commotion of a film, the apparatus loses the bearings of its identificatory mechanisms, the transcendental distinction between primary and secondary transference erodes, and the cinema takes on the chaosmic productivity of a machine for transversality. To think of "technology as dependent on machines, not the inverse,"[45] offers a way out of apparatus theory's unidirectional technological determinism, and towards the singular contingency of the machinic production of subjectivity.[46]

A MACHINE FOR TRANSVERSALITY

Transversality liberates transference from the Oedipalism of identification. Guattari invented the concept of transversality to map out the group dynamics of La Borde, an experimental inpatient clinic mainly for people with psychoses.[47] Based on his immersion in the daily *ritournelles* of the clinic, Guattari was acutely aware that the multitude of polydirectional transferences across the collectivity exceeded the classical analytic scene of transference. He also speculated that an emancipatory politics of desire-in-the-making required unfixing the fixity of transference:

> A fixed transference, a rigid mechanism, like the relationship of nurses and patients with the doctor, an obligatory, predetermined, "territorialized" transference onto a particular role or stereotype, is worse than a resistance to analysis: it is a way of interiorizing bourgeois repression by the repetitive, archaic and artificial re-emergence of the phenomena of caste, with all the spell-binding and reactionary group phantasies they bring in their train.[48]

Transversality acknowledges the material-relational kernel of transference while shelling the concept of its individualism, professionalism, and familism. It arises from understanding that "in the transference there is never any actual dual relation."[49]

The concept of transversality came to life at La Borde where Guattari was absorbed in developing a praxis of "splitting up the doctor."[50] This meant destabilizing the hierarchies of medical power by dispersing the doctor-function across different nodes in the collectivity.[51] Doctors could take days off, and patients could take turns playing the doctor, just as they could play the cook, the nurse, or any number of improvisatory social roles made possible by the grounds of the clinic.[52] A sense of performativity saturated its organization, so that daily activities and movement profiles took on the existential weight of relational experiments in recomposing group subjectivity. An intended consequence of these exercises in transversality was the dissolution of identities, as the lived performance of work, love, and leisure across emergent existential territories chipped away at ossified senses of self reinforced by the medical apparatuses of standardization. The clinic's modelization as a "space of existence" created the conditions for Guattari's working definition of transversality as "the unconscious source of action in the group, going beyond the objective laws on which it is based, carrying the group's desire."[53]

Guattari elaborates on the idea of transversality in the group and how it differs from institutional transference by explaining that it "(a) is opposed to verticality, as described in the organogramme of a pyramidal structure (leaders, assistants, etc.); and to (b) horizontality, as it exists in the disturbed wards of a hospital, or, even more, in the psychiatric wards; in other words a state of affairs in which things and people fit in as best they can with the situation in which they find themselves."[54] Guattari then goes on to provide an operative illustration of the concept. He writes:

> Think of a field with a fence around it in which there are horses with adjustable blinkers: the adjustment of their blinkers is the "coefficient of transversality." If they are adjusted to make the horses totally blind, then presumably a certain traumatic form of encounter will take place. Gradually, as the flaps are opened, one can envisage them moving about more easily.... In the hospital, the "coefficient of transversality" is the degree of blindness of each of the people present.[55]

As an unconscious source of action, transversality moves analysis off of the couch, out of the hospital grid, and into the social field. Guattari also boldly believed in the therapeutic potential of cinema. He even claimed that it was "possible for a film to upset our whole existence."[56] To upset existence is both an aim of La Borde's psychotherapeutic experiments, and a possibility of transversality's carrying of group desire at the juncture of the cinema's spectatorial situation. Recomposing subjectivity, at the cinema, becomes an option when the standardizations of the apparatus are made to stutter by a machine for transversality which stages singular relational encounters of spectators and images in germ, understood as "non-exchangeable and non-substitutable singularities."[57]

When it comes to the materiality of the "film object,"[58] each film composes a singular "mixed semiotics" which creates a pure experience that is qualitatively more than the sum of its component parts.[59] In the essay "Cinema of Desire," Guattari expands upon Metz's *Film Language: A Semiotics of the Cinema* to enumerate the cinema's "matters of expression":

(1) the phonic fabric of expression, which refers to spoken language (signifying semiology);
(2) the sonorous but non-phonic fabric that refers to instrumental music (asignifying semiotic);

(3) the visual and colored fabric that refers to painting (mixed, symbolic, and asignifying semiotic);
(4) the noncolored, visual fabric that refers to black-and-white photography (mixed, symbolic, and asignifying semiotic);
(5) the gestures and movements of the human body, etc. (symbolic semiologies).[60]

The cinema is a machine that "installs itself transversally" to these five layers of mixed semiotics and "will or will not give these levels an existence, an efficiency, a power of ontological auto-affirmation."[61] While the bulk of commercial films share signaletic patterns of intensity and duration, as well as signifying tropes corresponding to their category of generic belonging, art cinemas harbor an infinitely broad range of mixed semiotics. There is a differential relation between the five layers of semiotic matter immanent to each film, meaning that no two films are the same. Each film is a singular, polyvalent composition of semiotic registers. The theoretical consequence of acknowledging the cinema's mixed semiotics of immanent differentials is that its subjectifying effects are no longer unified by an "imaginary signifier." In the words of Guattari, which he penned after his essay "Machine and Structure" was rejected by Lacan's Freudian School in 1969, the Lacanian signifier "which stems from structural linguistics forbids us from entering the real world of the machine."[62]

François Dosse relays the break between Lacan and Guattari as follows: "In 1969, when Guattari addressed the Freudian School of Paris, he had already rejected Lacan's tendencies toward formalism and logic. His topic that day was 'Machine and Structure,' but it might just as well have been entitled 'Machine Against Structure.' He was no longer the master's designated successor. Lacan had anointed his son-in-law Jacques-Alain Miller who, with his colleagues from the rue d'Ulm, had just begun publishing Cahiers pour l'Analyse (Analysis Notebooks)."[63]

This historical background helps to explain why the autonomist theorist Maurizio Lazzarato turns to Guattari, rather than Lacan, in his effort to differentiate the cinema's oneiric, brute reality from the language of prose. In *Signs and Machines: Capitalism and the Production of Subjectivity*, Lazzarato cues into the cinema's unique ability to produce effects of de-subjectification and re-subjectification, particularly through the signaletic, asignifying cusp of its mixed semiotics. He writes:

> Images (symbolic semiotics) and intensities, movements, intervals, temporalities, and velocities (asignifying semiotics) reintroduce ambiguity, uncertainty, and instability into denotation and signification. Expression

once again becomes polyvocal, multidimensional, and multireferential.... The intensities, movements, and duration of film images can produce effects of desubjectivation and disindividuation in the same way that childhood, drugs, dreams, passion, creation, or madness can strip the subject of its identity and social functions.[64]

Not only, then, is every film's semiotic blend unique, but no two encounters with the cinema are the same either. So, to shift attention from the film object as an assemblage of mixed semiotics back to cinema as a machine for transversality, it must be said that the de-subjectifying and re-subjectifying effects of a given film's mixed semiotics are highly contingent on the singular existential constellation that each spectator-in-flux brings to the cinematic encounter: the refrains, desiring investments, movement patterns, and rhythmic tendencies that give shape and movement to subjectivity.

The encounter with cinema is also a collective event, even if in an empty theater, or alone on a personal device. This is because the cinema machine free indirectly assembles a virtual collectivity out of all of the actual historical and potential future encounters with a given film, and this innate collectivity of the art amplifies the singularity and contingency of encounters with filmic iterations of mixed semiotics. Conversely, apparatus theory conceives of the spectatorial subject as an individual subject. In this sense, it reinforces what the ethnopsychoanalyst Tobie Nathan has criticized as the defining tenet of scientific psychotherapy: that "the human is alone."[65] What apparatus theory omits from its diagram of subjectivity production is the relationality that the cinema offers—a relationality unbounded by the place made for the individual spectator by the apparatus, and one which plays out between virtual interlocutors distributed spatially across different spectatorial architectures and geographies (cinemas, private homes; cities, continents, etc.), as well as fragmented over the crystal edge between past and future.

The cinema does not just put people into relation, it puts existential constellations into relation. It thus acts as a transversal immediator, machinically conjuncting alterious existential horizons which may have previously only shared mass cultural references, or perhaps even no mutual references at all.[66] When two or more spectators-in-flux go to the cinema, no matter how separated they are in space and time, and how different their relationship to that film may be, they share a drop of pure experience in common. At that terminus of pure experience which is habitually called "a film" these two strangers are gifted with the chance— that one day, potentially—they could come to the epistemological *jouissance* of knowing, at least in part, the play of impersonal desires out of which the other's personality has been temporarily constituted.[67] Machinically more than human, metastable, and certainly never alone, spectators animated by cinephilia are thus afforded the potential emergence of a novel relational subjectivity which recomposes existence as they know it.

The cinema's putting into relation of disparate existential constellations is nothing less than the production of an intensive therapeutic alliance whose analytic material is nothing other than the pure experiences of the film's mixed semiotics. The relationship that these two spectators-in-flux could come to share is transversal rather than transferential because the third "object" through which their respective existential constellations enter into relation and offer each other up for recomposition is the pure experience of a film's singular mix of semiotics, rather than the Oedipal mediator of the imaginary phallus which structures parental imagos. The cinema is a machine for a transversal relationality of anoedipal transferences that effectively accomplishes the first positive task of schizoanalysis: schizophrenizing the perverse transference of psychoanalysis.[68]

There is a scene in *Paris Awakens* when everything changes. Louise loses herself on a dance floor in a crowded nightclub. The scene activates the five layers of mixed (symbolic, signifying, and a-signifying/signaletic) semiotics.

1) The lyrics of the song are an ode to Luis Buñuel and Salvador Dalí's *Un Chien Andalou*, which the songwriter Black Francis wrote to capture the surrealist spirit of that film.
2) The Pixies' 1989 song "Debaser" blasts through the scene, creating its acoustic tenor and contributing to its affective tonality.
3) Fashions in motion. Louise wears a leather jacket over a pink top which accentuates her short light-brown hair and earrings. Her clothes brush up against a palette of denims, gold rings, a striped nautical top, festive hands, and the peering faces of onlookers. Bodies, clothes and faces jumble into a composition of lures for perception.
4) The camera pans left, then right, then back again and again, approximating her movements which spill outside of the mobile frame. An image made out of the commotion of desire.
5) Louise dances the music, shaking her head back and forth, convex to her body which slides between the crowd of dancers. Her movements come against the friction of other bodies in the space, creating kinetic and ultimately erotic tension.

FIGURES 2.8 AND 2.9. Louise dances in *Paris Awakens* (Olivier Assayas, 1991).

FIGURE 2.10. Louise rides off on the back of a motorcycle in *Paris Awakens* (Olivier Assayas, 1991).

Immersed in the middle of this semiotic storm, Louise is irreversibly changed. She comes off the dance floor, winds up in a dispute with Clément, and abandons him by riding off on the back of a motorcycle with another man. This scene marks the turning point in the love triangle where Louise and Adrien move out of Clément's apartment to begin a relationship together away from his paternal presence. This momentous change inflects the characters' play of affections and opens onto a previously unforeseen existential territory for Louise and Adrien, one where their relationship blossoms outside of the eyes of the father, and they become relationally constituted as a subject that could never have otherwise been. No longer will they relate through the Oedipal mediator of the father as stepmother and stepson, and subsequent scenes mix semiotics anew to create the affective tonality of their *amour fou* and the line of flight it takes from the paternal gaze.

How all this affects a flesh-and-blood spectator, as D. N. Rodowick points out, remains speculative.[69] Yet it is the speculative nature of how a film can upset one's whole existence which lends the cinema its therapeutic value. The dance floor scene with Louise may have shown one shy spectator how it is possible to move in a group. It may have offered another a fashion sensibility for expressing a more assertive side of herself. Perhaps it exposed another to a new song to get oneself out of bed in the morning. And perhaps, just perhaps, the effect of the film will be such that if these three hypothetical spectators were to one day meet through a life of cinephilia, then the transferences which are vectorized by their meeting will have the pure experience of the film's images as their unconscious content, rather than parental imagos. The singular, contingent, and collective cinephilic relationship machinically conjuncted in such an encounter would be the ground for a praxis of lay therapeutic activity, of bringing novel qualities of relation into existence—past the internal limit of a given lived problematic. A life of cinephilia is a life of producing a machinic unconscious, and we do not yet know what the machinic unconscious of a group subject in the transversal making can do. The therapy of cinema, like its beauty, lies as much in its transversal conjuncting of existential horizons as in its images.

[CHAPTER THREE]

A Cinephilia of Existential Adventure

A life of cinephilia embraces the existential adventure of producing a collectively inhabitable machinic unconscious made up of cinematic images which potentialize transversal vectors of subjective recomposition. One film that encapsulates the stakes of cinephilia is *Clouds of Sils Maria* (Olivier Assayas, 2014), which stages the crossroads at which the star actress Maria Enders (Juliette Binoche) finds herself when—jaded by decades in the film industry—the cinema has been evacuated of all meaning in her eyes. The film's second half opens with a sequence of picturesque landscape shots depicting the Swiss Alps while "Largo from Xerxes" by George Frideric Handel plays for the first time on the soundtrack. Maria and her personal assistant Valentine (Kristen Stewart) drive into the small mountain town of Sils Maria, where the celebrated playwright Wilhelm Melchoir had lived as a recluse during his later years. In the opening of the film, Maria has learned of Wilhelm's death just as she is about to accept a lifetime achievement award on his behalf. Now that the gala commemorating Wilhelm's life has concluded, she decides to visit his hometown and meet with his widow Rosa (Angela Winkler), with the aim of better understanding the man who inaugurated her illustrious career by casting her as the young Sigrid in his play *Maloja Snake*. In spite of her deep reservations, Maria has nominally been convinced by the promising theater director Klaus (Lars Eidinger) to accept the role of the aging Helena opposite Sigrid in his London remake of the play. Upon arrival, Rosa takes Maria on a hike up the mountainside to the secret location where Wilhelm took his own life. As they sit on a mountain slope looking at the vista before them, Rosa tells Maria of a rare, unexplained cloud formation known as the "Maloja snake" after which Wilhelm's play is named. She explains that the snakelike cloud seldomly appears, but that when it does, it comes from Italy and has a reputation for sloping through the mountain pass ahead as a harbinger of inclement weather.

The film then cuts to a self-reflexively cinephilic moment that ruptures the diegetic world's realism. A black-and-white sequence from the short film *Das Wolkenphänomen von Maloja*, or *Cloud Phenomena of Maloja* (Arnold Fanck, 1924) appears on screen, complete with the original silent-era title cards. This poetic nature documentary is comprised of still shots which emphasize landscape movements: flowing rivers, canoeing mountaineers, and magnificent clouds. The most impressive moments capture the Maloja snake cloud phenomenon from amidst the mountain heights. A sound bridge from the previous scene on the mountainside continues to play Handel over the silent images of Fanck's film, which were shot in the very same mountains of Sils Maria some ninety years prior.

After presenting a minute-long excerpt from Fanck's silent short, *Clouds of Sils Maria* cuts to a reverse-shot of the three women, Maria, Rosa, and Valentine, watching *Cloud Phenomena of Maloja* on a television set in the living room of Rosa's home. Rosa explains that Wilhelm was fascinated by this film because he felt that through it "the true nature of the landscape revealed itself." Maria replies with the qualifying statement, "But the black and white creates a distance, since the passing of time." To which Rosa responds, "It is almost essentially old. Actually, it comes from very far away. That is the beauty of it." Emotionally overwhelmed at having rewatched one of her late husband's favorite films, Rosa tears up as Valentine looks on, both of them demonstrably affected by the film to a much greater degree than Maria. Rosa then entrusts the mountainside villa to her visitors so that Maria can rehearse her lines with Valentine in preparation to go on stage for Klaus's London posthumous production of Wilhelm's celebrated play.

The brief dialogue between Rosa and Maria about *Cloud Phenomena of Maloja* captures the tension between the two intellectual traditions which have historically theorized cinephilia: the revelatory and the fetishistic, which can also be divided along the lines of the Bazinian and the psychoanalytic, or when translated into aesthetic orientations, the realist and the modernist. Rosa evokes Wilhelm's cinephilic fascination with the short film's capacity to reveal a truth of the natural world. Maria's cunning reply suggests that the matter is more complicated. She does not believe in the cloud phenomenon which the film reveals, and instead picks up on how the conventions of film style have shifted with the passing of time, heightening her sense of the film's formalism and obscuring the veracity of the weather-event embalmed by its cinematography. For Maria, the images of the nature documentary are denaturalized, and their revelatory capacity is clouded by the excess of form. The same image which stands for Rosa as an endearing revelation of a faraway truth appears to Maria as another's uninteresting fetish.

However, as the film progresses, the existential significance of this image from *Cloud Phenomena of Maloja* will, upon being unexpectedly revealed to her, catalyze a dramatic change in the course of Maria's life and career.

FIGURE 3.1. Rosa and Maria looking over the pass in *Clouds of Sils Maria* (Olivier Assayas, 2014).

FIGURES 3.2 AND 3.3. *Cloud Phenomena of Maloja* (Arnold Fanck, 1924).

FIGURES 3.4 AND 3.5. The three women of *Clouds of Sils Maria* (Olivier Assayas, 2014) watch one of Wilhelm's favourite films, *Cloud Phenomena of Maloja* (Arnold Fanck, 1924).

FETISHISTIC CINEPHILIA

Christian Metz's psychoanalytic film theory opened the discourse of political modernism which advanced a militant Brechtian aesthetics of distanciation rooted in the denunciation of spectacle. Touchstone essays from the canon of modern film theory build on Metz's dialectical relationship to cinephilia quoted in the previous chapter, wherein the film theorist is tasked with "winning the Imaginary for the Symbolic" to establish a distanciated form of cine-love marked by the maturity of secondarization. A contemporary reader unfamiliar with the personal viewing habits of modern film theorists could thus be forgiven for falsely assuming that these theorists universally repudiated cinephilia. The title of a section of Laura Mulvey's essay "Visual Pleasure and Narrative Cinema" entitled "Destruction of Pleasure as a Radical Weapon" certainly gives that impression.[1] However, Mulvey's aim of effectuating a "break with normal pleasurable expectations" was accomplished "in order to conceive a new language of desire," and in their attempts to come to articulate this desire, London-based, psychoanalytically inspired film theorists never gave up on the practice of going to the cinema.[2]

Recent years have seen an upsurge of scholarly interest in cinephilia, leading to interviews with prominent figures of modern film theory about the intricacies of their historical viewing practices. For instance, Peter Wollen has shared autobiographical details of his life which express a deep-seated cinephilic tendency. "For a number of years," he explains,

> I used to watch around ten to twenty films a week, week in, week out.... So each week, with my friends, I would plot our course around London, calculating the time it would take to get from one cinema to another, without missing the end of one film, *Run of the Arrow*, perhaps, in the Electric, or the beginning of the next, *The Tall T*, in the Ben Hur, on the other side of town.

In a 2007 conversation between Peter Wollen and Laura Mulvey, Mulvey underscores how cinephilia enabled her psychoanalytic critique of commercial cinema: "If it had not been for the background of cinephilia," she says, "the 'Visual Pleasure' critique would never have been possible. It was a critique that was enabled by cinephilia and a deep love of Hollywood."[3]

Mulvey was also featured in *Framework* journal's 2009 special issue on cinephilia, where she advances a noticeably different perspective from the 1975 "Visual Pleasure" essay. "To my mind," she writes,

> the aesthetic and political pendulum has now swung back from the 1970s revulsion against the intrinsic reality of the cinema, in revulsion against the triumph of the symbolic over the indexical. [Digital cinema] allows a cinephilic meditation on the cinema's relation to reality: not only to find in it a completely new political significance, unlike those of earlier epochs, but also to continually rediscover the beauty, that Bazin compared to the flower or snowflake, of the indexical sign.[4]

No longer does Mulvey advance the theoretical destruction of illusionist pleasure, but in a twenty-first-century embrace of Bazin, she discovers the beauty of the cinema's indexical relationship with the reality beyond representation. There are innumerable reasons that could be offered for this shift in Mulvey's thinking and the broader intellectual sensibility it represents. Mulvey herself mentions the erosion of Hollywood cinema as a two-pronged source of inspiration and critique after the Vietnam War, as well as the discovery of world cinema, as turning points in her intellectual trajectory.⁵ The renewed scholarly interest in Bazin which has reconstructed him to be much more complete—and "darker"—than the original "naive realist" that he was made out to be in structuralist Anglophone scholarship based on the Hugh Gray translations, likely also contributed to the rapprochement.⁶ Regardless of the personal motives and macrotrends in the history of ideas responsible for this remarkable change in attitude over a lifetime of cinephilia, the development represents an olive branch outstretched from the political modernist tendency towards the Bazinian tradition—a genuine interest in the cinema's revelatory capacity.

As if in mirror movement to this intellectual development, the recent interest in cinephilia from a Bazinian orientation has found one key concept of political modernism instrumental to its operations: the concept of fetishism. The most comprehensive monograph to date devoted entirely to the topic of cinephilia is Christian Keathley's *Cinephilia and History, or The Wind in the Trees*. It lends special importance to "the cinephilic moment," defined by Keathley as

> the fetishizing of fragments of a film, either individual shots or marginal (often unintentional) details in the image, especially those that appear only for a moment. . . . Whether it is the gesture of a hand, the odd rhythm of a horse's gait, or the sudden change in expression on a face, these moments are experienced by the cinephile who beholds them as nothing less than an *epiphany, a revelation*.⁷

Much like Mulvey's late turn to the beauty of the indexical image in her appraisal of contemporary cinephilia, the convergence of the revelatory and the fetishistic as key concepts in Keathley's text on cinephilia could be read as a gesture of openness from the Bazinian lineage to embrace certain psychoanalytic tenets of film spectatorship.

The fervent passion of 1950s *Cahiers*-style cinephilia has been tempered by institutional demands for a dispassionate professorial attitude,⁸ and the militancy of 1970s *Screen* theory has been softened by the dystopic turn of communist experiments.⁹ If the Bazinian lineage of film studies is willing to incorporate the fetishistic as a theoretical descriptor of the way that cinephiles relate to revelatory moments of film realism, and the political modernist sensibility acknowledges the "pendulum having swung back from the 1970s revulsion against the intrinsic reality of the cinema," studies on cinephilia can now swiftly embrace empirical work into sociological and industrial networks based on the assumption that the asperity of conceptual difference between these intellectual tendencies has been dulled by the generalized equivalence of postmodern relativism. However, a closer look at the discursive consolidation of the revelatory and the fetishistic conceptualizations of cinephilia discloses that their historic compromise is fraught with underlying tension. After all, can fetishism sincerely admit revelation into its structure of desire?

With regard to the logic of fetishism, the degree to which high-profile cinephiles such as Peter Wollen and former *Cahiers* editor Serge Daney are apt to invoke the term "fetishism" to pathologize and infantilize themselves is astonishing, as if in shame for their artistic passions. In Wollen's "Alphabet of Cinema" he devotes the letter "C" to an entry on cinephilia:

> C, then, is for Cinephilia. . . . By "cinephilia" I mean an obsessive infatuation with film, to the point of letting it dominate your life. To Serge Daney, looking back, cinephilia seemed a "sickness," a malady which became a duty, almost a religious duty, a form of clandestine self-immolation in the darkness, a voluntary exclusion from social life. At the same time, a sickness that brought immense pleasure, moments which, much later, you recognized had changed your life. I see it differently, not as a sickness, but as the symptom of a desire to remain within the child's view of the world, always outside, always fascinated by a mysterious parental drama, always seeking to master one's anxiety by compulsive repetition. Much more than just another leisure activity.[10]

If cinephilia is the symptom of a desire to remain within a child's view of the world, it is only insofar as the cinephile is figured as a fetishist, for it is the fetishist whose subjectivity is circumscribed within an infantile drama. The cinephile-as-fetishist's phantasy is propped up by the disavowal of traumatic knowledge and the threat contained therein—a disavowal that returns the fetishist to the scopic position of the child's-eye view and to a time of innocence before the revelation of sexual difference. Wollen's framing of cinephilia within the paradigm of fetishism is based on Metz's modelization of spectatorial subjectivity and reflects political modernism's distrustful attitude towards the cinema's conventions of realism as illusory and ideological. Under these schemas, the spectator's suspension of disbelief mirrors the fetishist's disavowal. Together they whisper, "I know, but all the same"[11] in their reenactment of a childhood perspective on a veiled reality: their gazes move upward, toward the truth of difference disavowed by phantasmic substitution.[12] The fetish "object" of the cinephile-as-fetishist is none other than the "impression of reality" which is compulsively revisited in piecemeal attempts to master castration anxiety.[13]

Compulsive repetition is a symptom of subjective petrification. If, as Daney suggests, life can really be changed by cinephilia, if subjectivity can sincerely be recomposed at the cinema, then it is because as much as a fetishistic structure of desire may account for a selection of film viewing habits—perhaps even the viewing habits of some people liable to be identified (or to self-identify) as cinephiles—a non-fetishistic cinephilia of existential adventure endures. There is no sense of adventure guiding the movements of the fetishist: substitute objects can be traded and cycled across positions in the signifying chain, but they ultimately represent the same missing object and unfailingly reify its determinative position and causative function in the structuring of desire. There is only one destination for the fetishist to reach, and only one conclusion for a fetishist's analyst to arrive at: that of primordial lack. Whether this lack is confronted or avoided, the desiring relation of fetishism is overdetermined by its structuring absent-presence.

In her "Visual Pleasure" essay, Mulvey cues into the subjective petrification of fetishistic spectatorship wherein the "intrinsic force" of the audience's look "is denied." She writes:

> As soon as fetishistic representation of the female image threatens to break the spell of illusion, and the erotic image on the screen appears directly (without mediation) to the spectator, the fact of fetishization, concealing as it does castration fear, *freezes the look, fixates the spectator* and prevents him from achieving any distance from the image in front of him.[14]

When the unity of narrative cinema's diegesis as well as the spectator's ego are threatened with rupture by the immediate presentation of woman-as-spectacle (as in the series of collaborations between Josef von Sternberg and Marlene Dietrich), they hold together precisely because the spectatorial look is frozen and spectatorial subjectivity is fixated by fetishistic disavowal of the real corporeal threat her spectacle conceals. Anxiety occurs at the limit of fetishism, the point where the fetishist's subjective petrification begins to come undone. Narrative cinema's spectatorial scene masters this anxiety through unconscious disavowal.

The cinephile-as-fetishist is frozen and fixated in relation to the fetish "object" (here, in Mulvey, "Woman," or in film theory more broadly, the "impression of reality") erected as a permanent memorial to an originary experience of anxiety-horror. Hence when political aesthetics is tasked with producing unpleasure, it refers to a specific type of anti-fetishistic unpleasure brought about by dismantling the cinematographic techniques which scotomize this original discovery and thus foreclose the fragilization of an ideal ego constructed upon the denial of lack and the substitutional cathexis of a fetish object. The fetish, even when presented immediately, as is Mulvey's Woman-as-fetish in much of classical

Hollywood cinema, recalls a past event in psychic organization, the contours of which remain consistent through repetition.[15] This event is capable of being rediscovered through analysis, and for the fetishist who is unconscious as to the ontogenetic event structuring fetishistic desire, such a discovery may even impart the affective tonality of a genuine revelation. However, this discovery is at most an archeological discovery, and the image, whether pleasurable fetish or unpleasurable threat, is an image of the past; not a revelation of novelty, but rather an undoing of denial which readmits to consciousness a past revelation, the knowledge of which had since been repressed. If a fetishistic model of film spectatorship is maintained, then cinephilia is condemned not only to a dialectic of pleasure and unpleasure, disavowal and knowledge, but even more constraining, to a style of melancholic attachment to a lost object—one which is impossible to mourn, since it never existed in the first place. The cinephile-as-fetishist is frozen in place and fixated on the past. Given this degree of regression to the Oedipal theater of childhood, it is hardly surprising that Daney was apt to characterize cinephilia as a disease.

Returning full circle to the apparent reconciliation between fetishistic and revelatory theories of cinephilia, we encounter a historic compromise. This accord, which displays fidelity to the revelatory quality of the cinema so celebrated by Bazin and his interlocutors, all while admitting a fetishistic character to cinephilia, effectively abnegates the sense of adventure that accompanies existential creation. After all, fetishism is sustained by the foreclosure of novel revelations, paired with a repetitive return to the originary discovery of a difference since disavowed. A revelation within the scope of fetishization is a remembering of universal and unchanging form. The fetishist's remembering, a quasi-revelatory coming to consciousness, effectively misrecognizes the complex eventfulness of the cinephilic moment, congealing it into a substitutional film object. Fetishism transduces the event of revelation into a privileged cathetic object around which subjectivity is ritually consolidated—"a form of clandestine self-immolation in the darkness, a voluntary exclusion from social life." When the occurrent art of cinema—an art of mixed semiotics in motion—is frozen in movement and fixated in time, so too is the potential for subjective recomposition through a cinephilia of existential adventure.

THE CINEPHILIC MOMENT

The cinephilic moment is not a fetish.[16] Fetishes conceal, while revelations reveal. The cinephilic moment is a flash of revelation along an existential adventure which potentializes the recomposition of subjectivity. The reason why a cinephilic moment invites the recomposition of subjectivity is precisely because it stages an encounter with an image of existential significance to the spectator, the percept of which creates a legitimate, indexical link to the world. By offering such a percept of existential significance to the spectator, the cinephilic moment reveals something about the spectator's own desiring life which can be acted upon. A cinephilic moment of revelation doubles as a therapeutic insight into the meaning of a given constellation of subjectivity, and how it could be willfully modified.

The kernel of cinephilia's revelatory capacity to recompose subjectivity is found in none other than the work of André Bazin. The following excerpt from his essay "In Defense of Rossellini" attests to the power of revelation freed from the logic of fetishism to which it has been handcuffed in the decades since Bazin's passing. Bazin has the following to say of Rossellini's *Voyage to Italy* (1954):

> The world of Rossellini is a world of pure acts, unimportant in themselves but preparing the way (as if unbeknownst to God himself) for the sudden dazzling revelation of their meaning. Thus it is with the miracle of *Voyage to Italy*: unseen by the two leading characters, almost unseen even by the camera, and in any case ambiguous (for Rossellini does not claim that it is a miracle but only the noise and crowd movements that people are in the habit of calling a miracle), its impact on the consciousness of the characters is such, nonetheless, as to prompt the unexpected outpouring of their love for one another.[17]

Bazin's description of Rossellini's world as being one of pure acts preparing the way for revelation anticipates the way that Christian Keathley, Paul Willemen, and Noel King all describe the cinephilic moment as occurring in seemingly unexceptional moments. In the cinephilic moment, "what is being seen is in excess of what is being shown," says King.[18] Both in Rossellini's world and in the cinephilic moment, a quotidian banality can take on extraordinary significance.

At the conclusion of *Voyage to Italy*, an embittered married couple has decided to divorce once and for all, only to have their car stuck in traffic caused by the San Gennaro procession, which takes place annually in Naples and is known for the miracle of liquefied blood which protects the city's residents from calamities such as the nearby volcano, Mount Vesuvius. As the couple gets out of the car to take a look at the commotion, the husband ponders aloud, "How can they believe in that? They're like a bunch of children." The participants in the parade begin to shout

"Miracolo! Miracolo!" and Ingrid Bergman's character is swept away by the crowd of bodies moved by religious affects. She then calls out to her husband, who frantically enters the procession, and they romantically reconcile with one another as the film concludes on a divinely inspired happy ending.[19]

Voyage to Italy's conclusion is one of the most remarked-upon endings in film history. Commentators have contemplated with curiosity whether Rossellini sincerely believed in the supernatural implications of his own ending, since it deviates from the rest of the film up until that point, which is neorealist in style and faithful to the laws of material reality. However, the dichotomy implied by parsing out the possibility of revelation from a materialist worldview misrecognizes their mutual presence in the neorealist canon. What Rossellini offers in this concluding scene is a secular image of a materialist revelation of concern to a relational subjectivity which finds itself spontaneously recomposed without causation—a miracle, and a miracle which arises out of the way it matters to the subjective singularity of the parties involved without sacrificing its objective existence.[20] The "pure acts" lead to a revelation precisely because of their significance to the two characters on screen. The material movements of the crowd could be just that—pure movement—and yet the movements take on the spirit of a revelation tailored to the singular existential situation of this couple; the life circumstances, desires, and conflicts which make them who they are and make their relationship what it is. The miracle of San Gennaro matters to this couple, and yet it also exists independently of them. The proof of its objective independence is that it affects the other people in the crowd differently. For instance, the final scene of the couple's reconciliation is intercut with a man in the procession waving crutches in the air. The miracle of San Gennaro reveals its healing power differently to the person with a physical disability than it does to the strife-filled marriage.

Willemen and King's cinephilia discussion rightly emphasizes how the revelatory nature of the cinephilic moment hinges on the singularity of subjectivity. In Willemen's words, "one can draw two general conclusions concerning the discourse of cinephilia in relation to what it points to. One is the moment of revelation. Secondly, what is being revealed is subjective, fleeting, variable, depending on a set of desires and the subjective constitution that is involved in a specific encounter with a specific film."[21] Willemen suggests that the moment of revelation experienced in an encounter between spectator and cinema "may be different from the person sitting next to you, in which case you have to dig him or her in the ribs with your elbow to alert them to the fact that you've just had a cinephilic moment."[22] Willemen expresses a well-placed sensitivity towards how a cinephilic moment of revelation occurs through a specific encounter with a "set of desires and subjective constitution," unique to each pairing of spectator and film.

If the conclusion of *Voyage to Italy* can serve as a model for the cinephilic moment, it is because it affirms how revelations are precipitated by the singularity of an engaged subjectivity that comes to the encounter with cinema and how such revelatory cinephilic moments are profoundly transformational.[23] Prakash Younger cues readers into the transformational force of cinephilic moments by proposing a definition of cinephilia, firmly against the fetishistic orientation, as "something that always dispossesses us of the knowledge we have, the world we (really) love transforming the world we (think we) know.... One identifies cinephilia not by the repeated manifestation of positive characteristics but by the way it ruptures existing patterns of expectation."[24]

To flesh out this proposition, Younger draws on a remarkable passage from Simone Weil's *The Need for Roots* where she describes a hypothetical scenario wherein a husband comes face to face with a painful truth that alters his view of the world and of himself. Weil writes:

> If a man surprises his wife whom he loves and in whom he has perfect confidence being flagrantly unfaithful to him, he is suddenly brought into brutal contact with a piece of truth. If he happens to hear that some woman whom he doesn't know, whose name he hears mentioned for the first time, in a town he doesn't know either, has deceived her husband, that fact doesn't alter his relationship to truth in the slightest. The latter example furnishes the key. The acquisition of knowledge causes us to approach truth when it is a question of knowledge about something we love, and not in any other case.[25]

Love is an expression of existential significance, perhaps the utmost sign of it. Once the husband reconsiders his situation in light of this uncomfortable truth, he "discovers that he has a better understanding of all the parties concerned; everything remains the same but at the same time it all looks different. Though the problem he started with has not been solved, it no longer seems to matter, he has difficulty remembering why it bothered him and, finally, it is simply gone."[26] Going to the cinema and living a life of cinephilia is an art of creating the conditions for revelations to appear—revelations which offer new ways of seeing problems of existential concern to a cinephile's subjective singularity, to the point that the problems which led the cinephile to the cinema in the first place begin to fade away, no longer seeming to matter.

LOVE OF ADVENTURE

Cinema distinguishes itself from still photography by indexing the "elusive passage from one state to another," or mummifying change.[27] In a display of remarkable ontological congruency from filming through to spectatorship, the cinema offers such elusive passages to the cinephile as well. Every encounter with the cinema giving rise to a cinephilic moment is a singular "praxial crossroads" which stages an existential dilemma impatient with the suspension of its irresolution.[28] The "philia" in cinephilia can be described as a love of reality (Bazin), a love of truth (Younger), and a love of world (Andrew). What warrants addition to these well-founded portrayals of cinephilia is the love of adventure. If adventure begins with the formulation of a problem, as Isabelle Stengers suggests in *Thinking with Whitehead*, then the love of adventure encapsulated by the cinephilic spirit can be thought of as an intimate embrace of the search for analytic revelations along a non-causal series of praxial crossroads inviting the existential re-creation of subjectivity, so as to dissolve problems through the discovery of their newly assembled lived formulations.[29]

When Maria Enders of *Clouds of Sils Maria* finds herself before Arnold Fanck's film *Cloud Phenomena of Maloja*, she is in the midst of negotiating whether or not she can assume the role of the aging Helena across from a new Sigrid now played by the young Hollywood star and paparazzi favorite Jo-Ann Ellis (Chloë Grace Moretz). Maria's choice is a praxial crossroads between different universes of value, for as she herself claims in the scene where Klaus first tries to convince her to play Helena in his restaging of *Maloja Snake*: "Somehow, I am still Sigrid . . . Sigrid is free, beyond everything, and most of all she is destructive, unpredictable. And right or wrong I have always identified with that freedom." For Maria, the role of Helena embodies the very opposite. "If you are telling me I am Helena's age now, it is true. But that doesn't mean I can play her," she asserts. Klaus attempts to get Maria to see the roles his way: "There's no antagonism. . . . Sigrid and Helena are one and the same person. That is what the play is about. And because you were Sigrid, only you can be Helena," he says with a wryly convincing smile.

On the surface, Maria's hesitation over her new role as Helena can be read as a narrative about the need to come to terms with aging and the loss of youth. In interviews about the casting of Juliette Binoche alongside Kristen Stewart (who is twenty-six years her junior), Olivier Assayas has himself pointed to this as one of the film's central themes.[30] However, the complexity of the praxial crossroads differentiating universes of value comes to the fore when we consider that Assayas has also confirmed that *Clouds of Sils Maria* is a "condensed, brutalized version" of Rainer Werner Fassbinder's *The Bitter Tears of Petra von Kant* (1972).[31]

Clouds of Sils Maria is a highly palimpsestic work which destabilizes the coherence of its fictional characters' subjectivities through a plethora of intricate intermedial references. These references include Fassbinder's film *The Bitter Tears of Petra von Kant* as well as his play of the same name, upon which the film version was based and which served as the inspiration for the Fassbinder film's flamboyantly theatrical mise-en-scène. They also include Wilhelm's fictional play *Maloja Snake* in which Maria performed twenty years prior according to the filmic diegesis, as well as Wilhelm's remake of *Maloja Snake* taken over by Klaus and in which Maria contemplates performing once again. Furthermore, *Clouds of Sils Maria* puts the real-life biographies of the star actresses who play Maria and Valentine into the picture. In 1985, a practically unknown Binoche had her first starring role in what was also the first feature film that Assayas wrote for the screen, *Rendez-Vous* (directed by André Téchiné). Their renewed collaboration in 2014 mirrors the diegetic relationship between the actress Maria and the writer Wilhelm. *Clouds of Sils Maria* also restages scenes from Stewart's off-screen life, such as her 2012 relationship with director Rupert Sanders that was sensationalized by the tabloid press and which churns the film's most dramatic sequence where the characters attempt to escape a paparazzi blitz to preserve the secrecy of their artistic collaboration and avoid scrutiny over Jo-Ann's recent indiscretions. Stewart felt such a deep affinity for the character of Valentine that she decided to make permanent Valentine's fictional tattoo of Picasso's *Guernica*.[32]

Clouds of Sils Maria leverages the palimpsestic composition of the film's intermedial referentiality to confound the distinction between performance and authenticity. On three separate occasions, Valentine aids Maria in reciting her lines for *Maloja Snake*. The more they recite, the more the distinction between the biographical personas of Binoche and Stewart, the diegetic characters of Maria and Valentine, and the dramatic figures of Helena and Sigrid (themselves nods towards Petra and Karin from *The Bitter Tears of Petra Von Kant*) become indecipherable and deliberately confused. During the first recital of the lines, Valentine is shown picking up a paper copy of Wilhelm's play, *Maloja Snake*. She opens the book and begins to rehearse the part of Sigrid across from Maria, who reluctantly attempts to incarnate Helena for the first time with visible discomfort.

At first, it is unmistakable that the two women are rehearsing theater. The book in Valentine's hand is held clearly within the frame and she even reads aloud the staging directions embedded in the text of the play. Then, very subtly, the lines of dialogue from the play begin to sound as if they belong to Maria and Valentine instead of Sigrid and Helena. This destabilizing effect is in part produced by the scene's thematics: in the scene from the play, Sigrid asks Helena how they are to maintain professionalism in their office setting once their relationship has turned personal. (Maria and Valentine are themselves navigating a similar grey zone in their professional relationship). Assayas's fluid camera accentuates the confusion by drifting between the women and perpetually inching closer to Valentine so that the book she holds—the visual reminder that she is reading her lines—falls out of the frame. A pattern develops out of the book being in the frame, and then falling out of the frame, as this happens four times in this one rehearsal scene alone. In one of the most intense moments when Sigrid confronts Helena with the fact of her desire, and the characters' subjectivities overlap with the characters of the theater play, Maria's body obscures the book yet again.

FIGURES 3.6 AND 3.7. Maria and Valentine rehearse the play *Maloja Snake* in *Clouds of Sils Maria* (Olivier Assayas, 2014).

FIGURES 3.8 AND 3.9. As Maria and Valentine rehearse the play *Maloja Snake* in *Clouds of Sils Maria*, sight of the book is repeatedly obscured as the distinction between Maria and Helena, and Valentine and Sigrid, is increasingly blurred.

The distinction between the palimpsestic levels of semiosis becomes exceptionally obfuscated during Valentine and Maria's final rehearsal in Rosa's home. At this point, the scene they rehearse is one where Helena begs the younger, rebellious Sigrid not to leave her and her fledgling company for a business opportunity in Japan. Maria, reciting the role of Helena, enters into a frenzied outburst about being abandoned by the person she is hopelessly dependent upon. As much as she tries, Maria resists fully embodying the role, snaps out of it, and laments it all to Valentine, even making disparaging comments about the play. Valentine challenges her and dares her to see the role differently. When this fails, it appears as if Maria will refuse to take the role, even after all the effort she has made to prepare for the performance. Upset that her perspective does not seem to be getting through to Maria, and that she has trouble articulating herself, Valentine proposes that she leave Maria alone and go her own way. Maria's immediate authentic response then mimics that of Helena and she breaks down, begging Valentine not to leave her.

At the film's apex, Valentine and Maria hike up the mountainside at daybreak in search of the Maloja snake cloud phenomenon which they had first witnessed together in Arnold Fanck's short film. They bicker as they move higher, with their disagreement about Maria's ability to play Helena coming to a head. Valentine tries to break out of the negative cycle of their conversation by suggesting, "We should go, we are going to miss the snake." Maria replies stubbornly, "There is no snake," to which Valentine resigns herself and says, "Fuck it." They venture along the path towards a lookout point atop rolling heights. The film then cuts to an empty frame of the plateau, and just when one would expect the characters to climb up into the shot, only Maria appears. She sits down, looks straight ahead of her into the clouds stirring in the distance. She waffles back and forth between whether or not she is bearing witness to the Maloja snake. "There! Is that the snake? No, it's just mist. . . . Or maybe it is the snake. . . . No, it's not the snake. . . . Oh yes, I think it is turning into the snake! How about you?" she asks aloud, on the assumption that Valentine is right behind her. She then turns around only to find that Valentine has disappeared without a trace. The soundtrack begins playing Handel once again as the film cuts to a montage sequence depicting the awesome Maloja snake cloud formation, with some of the shots identically re-creating Fanck's 1924 documentary.[33]

It is in this climactic scene where the Maloja snake appears to Maria that everything changes. At this very moment, Maria comes to believe in the snake whose existence she had previously doubted, she loses her relationship with Valentine (who is replaced by a new personal assistant), and she finally decides with conviction to assume the role of Helena, without a hint of the resistance which caused her so much emotional turmoil and confusion during the recitals. She now looks forward to performing as Helena in front of a full house. When an up-and-coming director appears in her dressing room right before the show offering her a starring role in his new film, she turns it down and suggests that the younger Jo-Ann would be the better fit. Maria had ventured up the mountain and brought her existential constellation to the snake, and her subjectivity was recomposed by a revelatory encounter with a previously unforeseen truth. Much like the husband in the example offered by Weil via Younger, her previous problems are dissolved and no longer seem to matter. What is it about Maria's encounter with the Maloja snake that leads to the epiphany that she indeed can and should finally assume the role of Helena?

FIGURES 3.10 AND 3.11. Maria discovers the Maloja snake in *Clouds of Sils Maria* (Olivier Assayas, 2014).

In the encounter with the snake, and what Bazin would call the ontological ambiguity of its reality,[34] Maria overcomes her skepticism to realize what the others around her all know and have been trying to get her to see the whole time: that the cloud phenomenon embalmed by Fanck's 1924 documentary points to a reality which is more than what is represented on the screen.[35] Once she sees the snake herself, she comes to believe in the indexical veracity of the documentary which so fascinated Wilhelm and inspired his writing of the eponymous play. The snake reveals to Maria that the cinema shares an existential bond with the world—one which those around her believed in all along. If only she had experienced this revelation sooner, if only she had believed in the cloud phenomenon which inspired Wilhelm's play, then her relationship with Valentine might have taken a different course. In this moment, she realizes retroactively that if she had experienced a cinephilic moment earlier on, she and Valentine would have shared anoedipal cinematic material in common, and an existential territory for mutual exploration.

Maria effectively has a retroactive cinephilic moment once she encounters the cinema's referent in the world, but by then Valentine is gone, no longer to be seen again. Perhaps in being an actress—herself the referent of the films that she starred in—she forgot the cinema's power to "bear away one's faith."[36]

In the same vein as the concluding scene of *Voyage to Italy*, Maria's encounter with the Maloja snake can be taken as a model for cinephilia. Both films put into play a spirit of adventure, and climax in a moment of revelation. It is no coincidence that travel figures prominently in them both. Whether it be an English couple's journey to the south of Italy or Maria and Valentine's trip to the Swiss Alps, these characters are in motion, carrying predicaments and impasses with them into new encounters, speculatively and pragmatically experimenting with creating the conditions for a dazzling revelation to occur, against all the odds.

Adventure is at the core of the cinephilic mode of existence, and for this reason, the cinephile is better thought of as a companion to the figures of the explorer and the flâneur as opposed to the fetishist.[37] Through the spirit of adventure productive of the revelatory cinephilic moment where subjectivity is recomposed, a distinctively non-fetishistic desire reenters the spectatorial scene. The practice of cinephilia is not one of assuaging the anxiety of the fetishist through spectacle, or of encouraging perverse fixations on substitutional objects, but rather a practice of cultivating adventurousness, a generalized disposition of openness towards encounters with alterity facilitated by the art of cinema.

Film may be an object, and even at times and for some, a fetish object, but cinema is an experience, an event.[38] The philia in cinephilia is a love of the adventure of encountering what the event of cinema has to offer: the potential for singular constellations of subjectivity to transversally conjunct through anoedipal semiotic material of common experience which points to a world beyond the screen that is populated with alterious existential horizons ripe to be explored in the production of lay analytic knowledge.

In other words, it could be said that cinephilia is a type of desire for the event, which happens to be how Giorgio Agamben thinks of adventure. He writes:

> Desiring the event simply means feeling it as one's own, venturing into it, that is, fully meeting its challenge, but without the need for something like a decision. It is only in this way that the event, which as such does not depend on us, becomes an adventure; it becomes ours, or, rather, we become its subjects. . . . If Eros and adventure are here often intimately entwined, this is not because love gives meaning and legitimacy

to adventure, but, on the contrary, because only a life that has the form of adventure can truly find love. . . . The subject does not pre-exist the adventure.[39]

Cinephiles carry desiring constellations into the event of cinema, creating the conditions for cinephilic moments where insights of existential significance reveal themselves, dissolving cumbersome praxial impasses and recasting scales of value in the process.

The non-fetishistic philia for cinema known as cinephilia expresses a repeated willingness to make an adventurous leap into the cinema, and to take the chance, upon exiting the aesthetic event, of stepping out into a novel existential territory indexed by its imagery, where the objects around which desire was previously organized are unfixed, and the potential for relational experimentation in the recomposition, and unfreezing, of subjectivity is semiotically enriched.

[CHAPTER FOUR]

Seeing Intrusive Images

The existential adventure of cinephilia takes place in conjunction with the cinema, a machine for transversality which intends an unnatural alliance with the sick. Having now proposed adventure and transversality as active principles that unmoor a spectatorial subjectivity generated by identification with Oedipal imagos and frozen by fetish objects which conceal anxiety, it is worth looking at a case study, again furnished by the intercessional material of Assayas's oeuvre, which elucidates the cinema's invitation for those who meet its challenge to become visionaries, or seers. In her introduction to *Nocturnal Fabulations*, a collective book inspired by the film director and expanded cinema artist Apichatpong Weerasethakul, Erin Manning aptly writes that "Apichatpong's films make us visionaries. This is perhaps their first act of intercession. In doing so, they force us to ask not what we've seen, but what we have not yet been able to see. And they invite us to see it with the eyes of an other, more-than real, more-than human."[1] Apichatpong's invitation to see with the eyes of another is anchored by his diegetic inclusion of characters like ghosts, shape-shifters, and dreamers, but the transversality across modes of perception and individuated perspectives that his oeuvre affords is best read as an intensification of a tendency harbored by the cinema more generally, and one which Assayas, among others, also happens to tap into.

The invitation to see with the eyes of another draws the spectator out of the position of the voyeur, and into the experiential activity of the visionary who sees in excess of what is shown. In this regard, the cinephilic spectator can be posited as a type of artist, for it is the artist who "goes beyond the perceptual states and affective transitions of the lived. The artist is a seer, a becomer."[2] As a practician of the healing art of seeing, the cinephilic spectator embarks on transformative adventures in analytic discovery which render moot the diagnosis of modern film theory's third major spectatorial pathology after transference neurosis and fetishism, that of voyeurism.[3]

It has been proposed thus far that the cinema as a machine for transversality overruns the Oedipal logic embedded in the theory of identification, and that the spirit of adventure at the heart of cinephilia is irreducible to the logic of fetishism. It is now the moment to affirm that the cinephilic spectator is not a voyeur but a visionary, and the existential problematics indexed by the cinema's images act not as objects of a gaze, but as sensuous monuments populated with a multiplicity of entryways which catalyze a play of vision capable of detaching from the visual refrains of neurotic obsession.

The film *Personal Shopper* (Olivier Assayas, 2016) offers prime intercessional material for thinking about how the pluralism of modes of perception spawned by the cinema can have therapeutic value, particularly in light of the psychic phenomenon known as intrusive imagery. The reason why intrusive imagery warrants such a focus is because it is frequently symptomatic of and comorbid with what Freud termed obsessional neurosis, and the subjectivity of the obsessional neurotic who suffers from intrusive images is structured by voyeurism. In looking at how the cinema offers the opportunity for the sufferer of intrusive images to become a seer and reenvision what troubles them so deeply, the limitations of film theories which trade on a conceptualization of the cinephilic spectator as a voyeur will become ever more apparent.

Personal Shopper is a thrilling ghost story, complete with a murder plot that unfolds amidst the luxurious world of A-list celebrities and their proclivity for high fashion. The protagonist Maureen, played by Kristen Stewart in her second Assayas appearance two years after *Clouds of Sils Maria*, is deeply affected by the mental images she has of the people in her life. She is a visionary who is able to see what others cannot. The film opens with Maureen entering an abandoned house that is for sale. She is about to undertake work as a psychic medium for prospective buyers who want to know whether or not the house is haunted. Once inside, she makes contact with a menacing ghost which terrifies her and leaves her stricken with curiosity as to whether or not the ghost is in fact her recently deceased twin brother Lewis.

At first, she is sure of what has taken place, but then doubt begins to unsettle her certainty. Did she indeed contact a ghost, or is she losing touch with reality? Does she have psychic abilities, or is she entering psychosis? She isn't sure, and even though Assayas's imagery seems to confirm her visions by presenting the viewer with ghostly appearances, the film's imbrication with her psychological processes plants a seed of doubt in the fabric of the image. What Maureen sees can no longer be taken at face value, and the mental images she has of her experiences can no longer be trusted.

FIGURES 4.1 AND 4.2. Maureen face-to-face with a ghost in *Personal Shopper* (Olivier Assayas, 2016).

The ghastly content of the images certainly carries the power to shock, but it is the uncertainty of the images which renders them obsessional and intrusive. Maureen finds herself in a situation of indecisiveness, wherein her belief in reality carries an untrustworthy claim to truth. It triggers an obsessive process that consumes her mental life by confining it to endlessly entertaining the dichotomous possibilities of the images' truth or falsity. Perhaps Maureen saw the ghost, or perhaps she did not. Perhaps her vision is a solipsistic distortion, or perhaps she has visual access to a plane of reality obfuscated to most. Without being certain as to which of the options is true, her freedom to act in the world is grossly delimited, because her mode of existence is predicated on a promise which requires the accurate discernment of these contradictory possibilities.

Maureen and her brother Lewis were both practicing spiritualists who shared the same congenital heart defect. They made a pact to contact one another across the divide between life and death in case one of them should pass away from the defect before the other. Now that Lewis has died, Maureen is committed to fulfilling her promise. As the film progresses, she grows increasingly weary. The bags under her eyes deepen as she toys with the dark side. Her existence becomes increasingly obsessional, and she loses the ability to focus on anything but her brother. Her mind is racked by doubt in her extraordinary perceptual powers, and the memory of the ghost she has perceived develops an intrusive quality because she is compelled to constantly bring it into her awareness so as to test its veracity. The image of her confrontation with her ghost-brother is consistently up for inspection and inquiry, an object of endless study which produces no new knowledge. If only the image of her brother as a ghost could be believed, then her promise would be fulfilled, and she could use the image as a platform for acting in and on the world. Instead she finds herself stuck in a state of subjective paralysis, dominated by an image which demands almost all of her psychic resources and forecloses creative development in areas of work, love, and leisure. For Maureen, work has become a trivial chore, her boyfriend is far off in the Middle East working on an IT project, and all of her spare time is devoted to futile attempts at contacting her deceased brother yet again. This closed psychological loop of bringing an image to mind, only to tear it down, before bringing it back up again, exemplifies the classical structure of obsessional neurosis.

In Freud's famous 1909 case study of the Rat Man which was published as "Notes upon a Case of Obsessional Neurosis," he touches on the proto-cinematic nature of the psychological phenomenon of "intrusive images" and anticipates contemporary psychotherapeutic developments which harness the projector-like qualities of the psychic apparatus to accomplish a therapeutics of "imagery rescripting." Revisiting the Rat Man case and putting it into dialogue with contemporary psychological research on intrusive imagery will show that cinephilic practices of film spectatorship—or the pragmatics of perceiving, passionately—are decisive interlocutors in the tragic interplay between health and illness, in which the film image assumes the role of a *pharmakon*: a potential force capable of being actualized as either a remedy or a poison.[4]

Jean-Luc Nancy figures "intrusion and its rejection" as foundational to suffering,[5] and modern psychiatry recognizes intrusive images as essential to the propagation of various disorders, particularly post-traumatic stress disorder (PTSD), obsessive-compulsive disorder (OCD), and major depressive disorder.[6] Intrusive images are defined as involuntary mental pictures that interrupt ongoing mentation. Clinicians describe them as "unselected, unexpected, uninvited, often unwelcome"[7] and pinpoint their dominant themes as being "death and decay, illness and injury, violence and disaster, and sex and blasphemy."⁸ According to Stanley Rachman, their distinctive properties

> are that they are primarily visual, and tend to emerge fully formed and complete, rather than as a splash of disconnected and ambiguous visual patches and strands. The images tend to be brief, often less than a minute in duration, unlike obsessional thoughts which can persist for hours on end. The images change very little from occasion to occasion. They display remarkable stability and consistency, as if they are preserved images or preserved memories. The images tend to be vivid, and can have a significant impact. They can be extremely upsetting and bewildering, and the person learns to dread their re-appearance.⁹

Descriptions such as these make clear the clinical import of intrusive images. What warrants elaboration is how intrusive images relate to the cinema as a machine for the transversal production of subjectivity.

The psychology literature on intrusive images makes a common trope of the analogy which it constructs between intrusive imagery and the cinema. Emily Holmes is one of the world's leading scholars of intrusive thoughts and images, and it is not by coincidence that she has explicitly chosen the vocabulary of film to describe the phenomenon. "Intrusive recollections," she explains, "can take the form of 'film clips' of part of the trauma, single images, sounds, smells, somatosensory sensations or thoughts."¹⁰ The affinity between intrusive images and the cinema is deepened by psychology researchers' material dependence on the cinema in conducting many of their experiments.¹¹ In numerous experiments into the etiology of intrusive images, "trauma films" are used to artificially create intrusive images in experimental test subjects. Contrary to what the term "trauma films" may connote to humanities researchers in the field of trauma studies whose canon of such films might include *Shoah* (Claude Lanzmann, 1985), *Night and Fog* (Alain Resnais, 1956), or *Ararat* (Atom Egoyan, 2002), the "trauma films" used in these experiments feature documentary or newsreel-style imagery of graphic violence designed to provoke an intensely uncomfortable physiological response. In a couple of experiments viewers were asked to sit through images of fatal car crashes, while in another they were faced with the scene of a ritual circumcision. Participants were followed in the days and weeks after the screenings to determine how often intrusive images of the films involuntarily disrupted their normal mentation. The researchers were then able to propose hypotheses about the etiology and therapy of intrusive images depending on what kinds of viewing conditions, follow-up exercises, and biographical factors led to increases or decreases of intrusive images from the trauma film in the period of time following its viewing.

Why specific images become intrusive for select individuals remains scientifically inconclusive. Most research points to an intense traumatic event and peri-traumatic emotions surrounding that event as being the main factors in the development of intrusive images. At present, psychological theories are still highly indebted to psychoanalysis's hypothesis regarding the compulsion to repeat traumatic experiences, and they tend to theorize that memories of the traumatic event—"untamed memories," as Freud once referred to them[12]—have been inadequately processed and hence return involuntarily, prompting adverse physiological responses and pathological repetitions.[13] What the case of the Rat Man has the benefit of showing, much like Maureen's dilemma in *Personal Shopper*, is that intrusive images may arise outside of classical examples of trauma wherein an individual personally experiences or otherwise witnesses death, serious injury, sexual violence, or the threat thereof. Intrusive images can also dominate the psychic life of someone who has never been personally subjected to a traumatic event, and is thus free from traumatic memories, but who encounters an image—whether via imagination, art, or otherwise—which carries such existential weight that it begins to dictate the refrains of their life, becoming a veritable obsession.

If intrusive images do indeed have a cinematic quality to them, then it is fair to say that psychoanalytically-informed film theories of subjectivity production, particularly those which articulate the perversity of voyeurism, can elucidate the intrinsic qualities of intrusive images and inflect the psychological discourse on the phenomenon in a way that reintroduces the question of desire and affirms the existential significance of reconfiguring the ways by which clinical subjects relate to the images which grip them. By revisiting the case of the Rat Man with the analogy between intrusive images and cinematic images in mind, it is possible to understand his obsessive neurosis as maintained by the positionality of a cinematic voyeurism turned inside out; where, instead of giving scopic pleasure according to either a sadistic or masochistic aesthetic regime, voyeurism creates an obsessive refrain of intrusive images which generate negative affects and delimit a corresponding field of petrified subjectivity.[14]

The Rat Man case follows the free associations and analytic insights of a lawyer named Ernst Lanzer who was ridden with debilitating fears and obsessive rituals. His obsessions revolved around one particular intrusive mental image of a cruel torture technique that he heard described by a fellow military officer. According to the story which was relayed to him, the torturers would subdue a prisoner face-down and then place a pot with a rat inside of it over the prisoner's buttocks, leaving the vermin to gnaw its way out through his anus and internal organs. The image impacts the Rat Man so greatly because he fears that this most horrifying of fates will befall his father. In Freud's analysis of the case study, he isolates the Rat Man's paternal cathexis to show the absurdity of the obsessional idea's content, since the Rat Man's father had passed away many years earlier. Freud posits that the irrational fear stems from the patient's infantile sexual development, a period when he harbored the wish that if some calamity were to befall his father, then he might become wealthy and obtain the material means necessary to marry. Thus the Rat Man's unconscious identification with the rat's penetrative prowess, which satisfied the aims of his libido, came accompanied by the sentiment that he was in some way opening his father to grave danger and that he would be guilty of causing his father's treacherous debasement. This constitutive contradiction prompted the Rat Man to embark on a series of pathological rituals designed to avow and then disavow his desire, such as setting a rock on the street only to momentarily remove it, and pulling his penis out of his pants in the mirror before returning it to its place. For Freud, "true obsessional acts such as these are only made possible because they constitute a kind of reconciliation, in the shape of a compromise, between the two antagonistic impulses."[15] In bringing the antagonistic conflict between the Rat Man's unconscious wishes and their prohibition to light over the course of their brief analysis together, Freud claimed to have restored the patient's personality via the psychoanalytic cure.

What is easily overlooked in Freud's "Notes upon a Case of Obsessional Neurosis" is the mise-en-scène of the Rat Man's "ideational content," the way that its scopic organization parallels the voyeuristic positionality of the cinematic spectator, and how this positionality can be identified as a decisive factor in the maintenance of the obsession. These apparatus-like elements can be said to contribute to the pathology beyond the role Freud explicitly designated for them as ideational content. In recounting the Rat Man's early erotic experiences with his babysitters, Freud exhibits a passing awareness of the voyeuristic component in the intrusive image around which his analysand's obsession develops:

> The child, as we have seen, was under the domination of a component of the sexual instinct, the desire to look, as a result of which there was a constant recurrence in him of a very intense wish connected with persons of the female sex who pleased him—the wish, that is, to see them naked.... Nevertheless, opposition to this wish from some source or other was

already in activity, for its occurrence was regularly accompanied by affect. A conflict was evidently in progress in the mind of the young libertine. Side by side with the obsessive wish, and intimately associated with it, was an obsessive fear: every time he had a wish of this kind he could not help fearing that something dreadful would happen.[16]

The originary antagonism to the Rat Man's desire which enables the appearance of his later neurosis after the completion of the latency period is a prohibition against his infantile voyeuristic proclivities.

Might it be possible that the image of torture which persistently and severely intrudes upon his mental processes can be attributed to the uniquely voyeuristic quality of the Rat Man's childhood desire—for images—that became the object of repression? According to the Freudian model, the voyeuristic position of the Rat Man vis-à-vis the torture scene, as well as the scene's appearance as a mental *image*, are of secondary importance. These aspects are deemed to be substitute ideational content; false culprits whose affective magnitude is attributable to other unconscious reasons altogether. Freud writes:

> A layman will say that the affect is too great for the occasion—that it is exaggerated—and that consequently the inference following from the self-reproach (the inference that the patient is a criminal) is false. On the contrary, the [analytic] physician says: "No. The affect is justified. The sense of guilt is not in itself open to further criticism. But it belongs to some other content, which is unknown (unconscious), and which requires to be looked for. The known ideational content has only got into its actual position owing to a false connection. We are not used to feeling strong affects without their having any ideational content, and therefore, if the content is missing, we seize as a substitute upon some other content which is in some way or other suitable, much as our police, when they cannot catch the right murderer, arrest a wrong one instead. Moreover, this fact of there being a false connection is the only way of accounting for the powerlessness of logical processes to combat the tormenting idea." I concluded by admitting that this new way of looking at the matter gave immediate rise to some hard problems; for how could he admit that his self-reproach of being a criminal towards his father was justified, when he must know that as a matter of fact he had never committed any crime against him?[17]

In the case of the Rat Man, a false connection is made between conjugal eroticism and overwhelming guilt due to the simultaneous emergence in the analysand's biography of the possibility of genital love with the necessity of the father's death. This biographical development neatly mirrors the archetypal cathexis of the primal horde, and Freud's presentation of the case grounds the Rat Man's obsessive neurosis in the horde's originary guilt, modeled as the Ur-unconscious of all humankind.[18] Unlike Culture, whose prohibitions are deemed productive of sociality through the creation of extensive alliances, the inhibitions of the neurotic are posited as a "caricature of a religion" which seek to "accomplish by private means what arose in society through collective labour"—a flight from social institutions to private fantasy, and consequently a "withdrawal from human companionship."[19]

According to Freud's Oedipal phylogenesis of civilization and the Rat Man's neurotic maladjustment to it, the vicious torture scene that torments the Rat Man is little more than the misleading ideational content of a formal, archetypal cathexis, namely, the repressed wish to kill the father. Through framing the intrusive image as content in a "parental image,"[20] or imago, Freud's father-thesis effaces the image's complex existence as a sign.

In a turn of unintended irony that only the perspective afforded by historical hindsight can reveal, this implicit expunging of the intrusive image's significance anticipates the attitudes embedded in the cognitive behavioral therapies which have eclipsed psychoanalysis in terms of institutional authority and medical application. Stanley Rachman sums up how the CBT approach to OCD is predicated on an explicit dismantling of the intrusive image's significance. He writes:

> If an unwanted image is catastrophically misinterpreted as being of great and negative personal significance, as revealing a serious personal flaw and/or a serious threat, it is likely to turn into an obsessional image—a distressing, repugnant recurring image.[21] The recommended treatment for OCD is cognitive-behavior therapy with or without medication. Patients are informed that virtually everyone experiences some unwanted and unwelcome images and thoughts, and the best way to tackle the intrusions is to de-toxify them, to replace the catastrophic misinterpretations with benign explanations.[22]

According to this perspective on intrusive images informed by the CBT school of thought, the hermeneutic impulse of psychoanalysis is predestined to fail, since it is the very task of interpretation which is understood to grant intrusive images their obsessive character. Hence, CBT repudiates the significance of the intrusive image altogether in the therapeutic aim of rendering it benign, equally evacuating the prospect that the intrusive image matters as a sign.[23]

The pressing question which is skirted by CBT's intentional banalization of the intrusive image and Freud's framing of the scene as the ideational content of a parental image is precisely the question of why this particular image develops intrusive qualities and takes on existential significance. The image's designation as either haphazardly benign or a "false culprit" evades the pressing question of why it, and not some other image, matters so intensely to the patient. The details of the case study show that the Rat Man had encountered many erotic sights during his childhood, and yet none of them acquired the obsessive interest of the rat-torture scene. He had probably also heard a variety of gruesome tales during his military service, but only one of them became a point of obsession. The torture scene's captivating mix of blatant sexual denigration combined with brash violence likely contributed to its being unconsciously chosen as the intrusive image. Another fundamental component, however, is that unlike the purely erotic images of his childhood which he discovered via his own eyes, the Rat Man was not present at the scene of the torture, and thus the image is a product of his imagination. The Rat Man is inclusively excluded from the image: he is present as a voyeur, but an absent one who wasn't really there at the scene of the torture, and yet knows the torture to have taken place, without having been able to verify its details in person. The obsessional character which this precise image acquires is inextricable from the positionality of the Rat Man as an absent presence, a special type of voyeur who cannot make recourse to the physical organs of his eyes since they were materially cut off from the scene, leading him to repetitively overcompensate through the imaginative faculty.

Christian Metz shows that this frustrating predicament of thwarted voyeurism shares positional commonalities with the situation of the cinematic spectator who is also absent from the reality presented to his eyes as an image. Metz explains: "As opposed to other sexual drives, the 'perceiving drive' concretely represents the absence of its object in the distance at which it maintains it and which is part of its very definition."[24] He then goes on to assert:

> The voyeur is very careful to maintain a gulf, an empty space, between the object and the eye, the object and his own body: his look fastens the object at the right distance, as with those cinema spectators who take care to avoid being too close to or too far from the screen. The voyeur represents in space the fracture which forever separates him from the object; he represents his very dissatisfaction (which is precisely what he needs as a voyeur), and thus also his "satisfaction" insofar as it is of a specifically voyeuristic type. To fill in this distance would threaten to overwhelm the

subject, to bring him to orgasm and the pleasure of his own body, hence to the exercise of other drives, mobilising the senses of contact and putting an end to the scopic arrangement.²⁵

Unlike in the theater, the cinema's voyeurs and the exhibitionists fail to coincide. "They have missed one another," says Metz.²⁶

Three fundamental qualities of intrusive images that overlap with cinema spectatorship can be established so as to articulate the cinema's therapeutic value via its status as mediatic *pharmakon* in symbiotic relation with the imagistic material of psychic life. The first of these qualities is the voyeuristic dynamic of absent presence, a unique type of voyeurism which distinguishes the cinema from the theater. The second is the physical immobility of the voyeuristic subject, and the third pertains to the way that intrusive images and the cinema both raise the question of believability, or adequate indexicality.

First of all, the fact of the Rat Man having "missed" the torture scene is key to its maintenance as an intrusive image. The Rat Man's case history is filled with stories of him having witnessed fascinating scenes, and yet none of them absorb the same level of attention because he was present at the same time and in the same space of what was being exhibited. These scenes were played in a theatrical rather than cinematic mode. It is one thing to be fascinated by what one has perceived in person. It is quite another to be fascinated by what one can only imagine, but knows that another person has perceived and experienced firsthand. The Rat Man case indicates that it is this free indirect relational paradigm of transpersonal visual experiences that structures the etiology of intrusive images. To be a voyeur under such conditions is to be restrained against one's will by the vicissitudes of time, by the misfortune of having lived one's own life, and the necessity of having been partial to it. It is a form of bondage to one's self and the collection of memories it archives, and consequentially a form of deprivation from all that others have themselves seen and hold as unshareable memories in their own personal collection. The voyeuristic will to scopic knowledge is left frustrated by the inaccessibility of other experiences that have perished into memory beyond the scope of the voyeur's field of vision.

This dynamic of an absent presence at work in the voyeuristic scene of the Rat Man may at first glance only seem to be active in cases of intrusive images where the patient was not actually present at the scene which intrudes upon mentation. Upon closer inspection, there are indeed many cases where people who experience intrusive images were in fact present at the scene which provides the intrusive material. This is especially true in cases of PTSD where an individual was violently victimized or caught in an accident, only to experience flashbacks of the traumatic event.[27] Nevertheless, a certain absence asserts itself. Rather than an absence of physical presence, what commonly occurs in instances of PTSD is an absence of memory; specifically an absence of what is called "narrative memory" or "verbally accessible memory."[28]

One famous case of Pierre Janet's from the Salpêtrière Hospital demonstrates such an absence with remarkable vividness. A 23-year-old woman named Irène was traumatized by her mother's untimely death at the hands of tuberculosis. After caring for her ailing mother so intently that she hardly slept for over sixty straight nights, all while suffering the abuses of her alcoholic father, her mother died. Irène could not process the reality of the event and painstakingly attempted to revive her deceased mother. Eventually, when her extended family intervened and made funeral arrangements, they discovered that Irène had no memory of her mother's death even though she had been by her mother's side as she passed away.[29] Even when Irène's family and Janet himself confronted her with the undeniable fact, she could only consciously relate to the image as a product of her imagination but not of her memory. The image of the death would then intrude upon her in a dissociative state, leading her to involuntarily reenact her futile attempts to revive her mother's corpse. Her "narrative memory system" was amnesiac, whereas her "traumatic memory system" was hyperactive—it "remembered too much."[30] While Irène's situation differs significantly from the Rat Man, what they have in common is being perceptually removed from the scene which troubles them, either through a twist of fate or through the dissociative power of trauma rendering the memory inaccessible. In both cases the inaccessibility of the scene to memory prompted severely debilitating rituals, and the dynamic of frustrated perception cemented the voyeur in a paralyzing position of being caught in a cyclical imaginative search for an impossible image whose reliability could satiate the obsession.

In addition to the failure of perception and memory, either due to absence or trauma, another quality which intrusive images share with the cinematic experience is physical immobilization. Apparatus theory has made a point of including the immobility of the spectator into its formulation of the cinema's essential characteristics.[31] Recent psychological studies have intensified this quality of the cinematic experience when inquiring into the etiology of intrusive images. One joint study alluded to earlier had test subjects screen a "trauma film" under different settings, one of which allowed for movement and another which enforced immobility. The study demonstrated a strong correlation between physical immobility and the heightened severity of intrusive images: "Participants in non-movement conditions reported more intrusive images than participants in a free-to-move control condition."[32] That tonic immobility in instances of trauma increases the likelihood and severity of intrusive flashbacks is well established, and unfortunately, traumatic events such as car accidents or childhood sexual abuse often by their very nature induce immobility in the victim.[33]

What a consideration of the Rat Man case and its similarities with cinematic spectatorship reveals is that a positional immobility vis-à-vis the imagined scene contributes to the maintenance of intrusive images. Because the Rat Man has missed the scene and was absent from it in space and time, he is precluded from entering it, breaking it up, or modifying it. The time has come and passed and he is destined to remain an imaginary witness to a mental image which exists only in the memory of others. His impotence over the matter is positionally paralyzing, as the happenstance of his life consolidates his role as a frustrated voyeur leaning on the inaccurate substitutions of his imagination. Something similar can be said for trauma victims whose manner of dissociation during the traumatic event routinely leads to them being perceptually positioned in their memories as helpless voyeurs of their own abuse, unable to intervene and as if they were not actually present. In the words of trauma researchers van der Kolk and van der Hart, "many trauma survivors report that they automatically are removed from the scene; they look at it from a distance or disappear altogether, leaving other parts of their personality to suffer and store the overwhelming experience."[34] When someone is perceptually severed from a traumatic event and is placed into a voyeuristic perspective on the scene either through dissociation (as in the case of trauma survivors like Irène) or through imagination (as in the case of patients with obsessional neurosis like the Rat Man), they are then confronted with the prospect of whether or not to believe the image they have of the event.

In the case of Irène at the Salpêtrière, the gravity of her dissociation meant that she literally could not believe that her mother had died even though it had transpired right in front of her eyes. The intrusive image from which the Rat Man suffers turns on a similar crisis of belief, because he knows that the image he has created out of the faculty of his imagination does not index the event in question. Hence, he is presented with a binary gamut of futile options: either to abandon the image of involuntary intrigue altogether, or conversely to tear it down and re-create it all over again in a quest for the lost knowledge, the elusive truth of the event which he failed to perceive, not through any failure of his imaginative faculty, but by virtue of his not having been present at the scene of the crime. His obsession develops around this inadequacy of his imagination to index a real historical event which exceeds mental representation. Obsession develops because the Rat Man is never satisfied with the image that he has created, precisely because he knows that it is a creation of his own mind. His faculty of judgment deems it to be inadequate, and the image is torn down in the psychic effort to build another one in its place—an image that might suffice to satisfy his voyeuristic curiosity and his desire to know. The pattern of creation and destruction continues, involuntarily, without end. Such is the infernal spiral of the obsessional neurotic who thinks in images, and whose thinking is impeded by images.

Psychotherapy responds with an experiential technique called "imagery rescripting" to find a way out of the inhibiting cycle. Imagery rescripting has its roots in Pierre Janet's "imagery substitution" technique which influenced many clinicians over the course of the twentieth century, and today finds itself at the forefront of treatment for conditions such as PTSD, depression, and OCD.[35] The technique works by using the faculty of imagination to deliberately alter the content of intrusive images with the aim of mitigating their severity and reducing the frequency of their reoccurrence. The technique is based on the "bi-directional axiom: 'Emotional memory is perceptual,' and conversely, 'perceptual-imagery is emotional.'"[36] Since emotional memory is perceptual and vice versa, perceptually rescripting distressing imagery modifies the automatic emotional response which accompanies it. In practical terms, when psychotherapists embark on imagery rescripting procedures with their clients, they attempt to replace the intrusive image with a beautiful one, reshape it, shrink it in size, or dramatize it into a happy ending.[37] Some therapists also encourage their clients to approach the intrusive image as if through another pair of eyes. For example, if a client is troubled by scenes of childhood abuse, they can imagine entering the scene as an adult with the perspective, knowledge, and compassion that they now possess and use this acquired wisdom to comfort the image they have of themselves as a child.[38]

What these various approaches to imagery rescripting have in common is that they break the sufferer out of a voyeuristic position and restore the capacity for entering into relational movement with the intrusive image.[39] In other words, they actively reconfigure the arrangement of physical paralysis and the sensation of having missed the event in question. Imagery rescripting encourages clients to develop an imaginative power over the image and to move through it as if one were endowed with omnipotent agency. The scientific literature supports the claim that such techniques are powerful therapeutic tools. On the one hand, empirical support for the imagination's capacity to alleviate the symptoms of mental illness is highly encouraging. Imagery rescripting requires few resources, comes without side effects, and eludes the capture of the pharmaceutical industry's monetization schemes. However, the nature of the Rat Man's intrusive images and their affinity with cinematic spectatorship indicate that one final ingredient must be supplied for the techniques to be at their most effective, and that is a quantum of indexicality. Imagery rescripting de-paralyzes the spectator and puts her back into touch with an event she feels she has missed, but these imaginary modifications do not index such an event. They are merely imaginary "rescriptings" of it.

Conversely, the cinema's indexical images really put its spectators into touch with events that they may have missed, and the ontological ambiguity of these images enables spectators to become visionaries and see more than what is shown on screen. Much has been made of the indexicality of the photographic relationship between the image and the world, and of indexicality as the ontological basis of cinema.[40] Unlike imagery rescripting, where images are conjured up in the mind of the client with the guidance of a psychotherapist, the cinema maintains an existential link to the world by virtue of its indexical signs. Thus, a cinematic image which speaks to the existential predicament underlying a clinical case of intrusive images may very well present itself as indexical evidence, grounded in material reality, of another way to grasp the problem.[41] And if the index is turned on its side, and viewed not only as operating between the image-as-sign and profilmic reality, but in the virtual realm of collective spectatorial sociality, then its second advantage over client-therapist imagery rescripting appears. Whereas imagery rescripting between client and therapist indexes their collective work, that work is subject to the protocols and economics of professional relationships. The alliance may be therapeutic, yet it is also an alliance whose contours are remarkably overdetermined and confined to the logic of the clinic. In addition to indexing a profilmic reality, the cinematic image also indexes the multiplicity of virtual perspectives, of entryways, which lend the film its unique constitution as a material monument of collective significance.

Personal Shopper exemplifies how a given film's aesthetic composition can make the cinema into a crystal territory for transversal perceptual participation capable of loosening the individualizing and immobilizing grip of intrusive images that hinge on obsession and voyeurism. At a turning point in the film, Maureen begins to receive provocative text messages from an unknown source asking her about her relationship to Kyra (Nora von Waldstätten), the celebrity for whom Maureen is a personal shopper.

The familiarity with which the message's sender seems to know Maureen's most intimate desires, combined with the sender's ability to pinpoint her whereabouts, leads Maureen to wonder if her brother Lewis may have found a way to communicate with her from the realm of the dead. The anonymous text messages incite Maureen to violate Kyra's specific instructions to never try on any of the clothes that she is tasked with purchasing on her behalf. After some convincing, the unknown texter persuades Maureen to enter Kyra's apartment while she is away, wear her most luxurious clothes, and fantasize about what her life could be like if she were rich and famous. Maureen goes through with the plan, spurred by the possibility that she is communicating with her brother.

The scene plays out as if it were an imagery rescripting session. Maureen imagines what it would be like if she had the life she wanted: one where her brother was still alive, or at least available for communication through spiritualism, and where she is relieved from her duties frantically shuffling around Paris buying clothes that she will never wear for someone who she does not even like. Encouraged by the intuition that she has made contact with her brother this time, she musters the confidence to become someone else entirely for a night. Maureen falls asleep in Kyra's empty bed and then leaves the next morning to return to her daily shopping routine. When she comes back to the apartment at night to drop off the new purchases, she finds Kyra gruesomely murdered in her bed, the very same one where Maureen had just fallen asleep the previous night when fantasizing about having Kyra's life.

Maureen is briefly considered a suspect, but a few scenes later Kyra's spurned lover Ingo (Lars Eidinger) runs out of a hotel chased by police who apprehend him and charge him with murder. The case is solved. Maureen is liberated from her duties as a personal shopper and can now go visit her boyfriend in Oman, grateful that she did not in fact have Kyra's life after all. In spite of all these positive developments, Ingo's culpability for the murder and the anonymous text messages put Maureen back into her original position of not believing in her psychic visions of her brother. The film concludes with Maureen in an Omani cave dialoguing with the spirit rappings of yet another ghost who she hopes is Lewis. She wants to know if he is at peace. The reply she receives is ambiguous, but one thing is certain, and it's that she is not. If only Maureen could break out of her voyeuristic perspective on her situation and see with another pair of eyes; if only she could see her psychically intrusive image as a cinematic image, visible to so many others. Then she would find the peace that she is looking for.

At two key moments towards the end of the film, Assayas offers the spectator scopic hints as to the veracity of the ghosts. Right before Ingo bolts out of the hotel, the film cuts to a long take of the hotel's glass

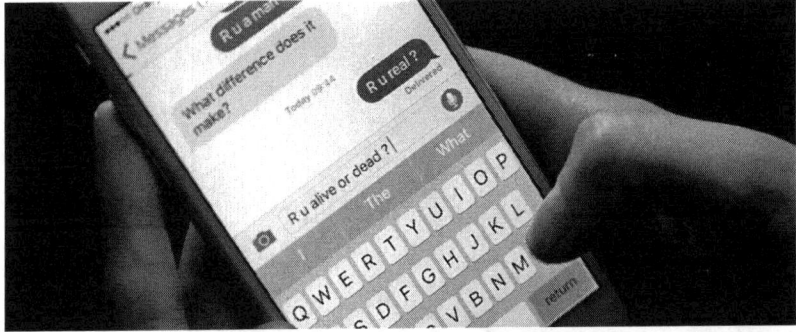

FIGURES 4.3, 4.4, 4.5. Encouraged by text messages from an unknown sender, Maureen tries on Kyra's clothes in *Personal Shopper* (Olivier Assayas, 2016).

entrance doors inconspicuously sliding open, which raises a doubt about the police having nabbed the correct murder suspect. The sliding doors could be a purely formalist insert, or the shot could be read as a suggestion that the murderer was in fact a spirit, whose presence was picked up by a sensor on the doors, and who escapes through them completely invisible and unnoticed.

FIGURE 4.6. The sliding doors at the hotel open on their own in *Personal Shopper* (Olivier Assayas, 2016).

Then in the penultimate scene, Maureen sits outside with Erwin (Anders Danielsen Lie), the new partner of her brother's widow Lara (Sigrid Bouaziz). They speak with one another while seated on outdoor patio furniture shot in shallow focus, leaving the background softly blurred but visible. Over Maureen's shoulder a ghost with a male silhouette appears. Presumably, it is Lewis haunting his old home. He picks up a glass of water and drops it to the floor, smashing it, offering proof of his presence. Maureen cleans up the pieces not knowing what had just transpired behind her back and outside of her field of vision.

FIGURE 4.7. Maureen contemplating her deceased brother as a ghost looms in the background in *Personal Shopper* (Olivier Assayas, 2016).

What *Personal Shopper* accomplishes is the creation of a non-intrusive cinematic image of Maureen's non-cinematic intrusive image. It exteriorizes a realm of vision that she thinks only she can perceive, and offers itself up as a pure experience for a multiplicity of perspectives which index a scopic polyphony of singular existential coordinates. In *Personal Shopper*, the intrusive image becomes a territory for the conjunction of a multiplicity of perceptions, a conjunction which re-singularizes the intrusive image's existential significance, transforming its personal intrusivity into a collective monument, and the paralytic immobility of its voyeurism into a chance to see the predicament through the intensive commotion of relational movement. Cinema brought images from consciousness into the world.[42] As material images in the world, the cinema acts as a vital archive of perspectives on lived existential problematics. The images it leaves behind propose themselves as reactivatable percepts with latent potential for triggering new processes of scopic knowledge production. It is in this sense that Deleuze and Guattari conceive of art as a monument. They write: "It is true that every work of art is a monument, but here the monument is not something commemorating a past, it is a bloc of present sensations that owe their preservation only to themselves and that provide the event with the compound that celebrates it. The monument's action is not memory but fabulation."[43] Following their line of thought, it can be said that the cinema turns the individual-focused and ephemeral endeavor of imagery rescripting into a collectively cohabitable existential territory which is enduring and monumental.

In this therapeutic mode as a nexus of transversal perceptions, the cinematic image invites experiential engagements which imbue it with sense and enter into mutual affection. The therapeutic value of the cinema in the face of intrusive images lies in its ability to cultivate novel entryways, unique to each film, of coming to the cinema and entering into relation with the multiplicity of unconscious investments vectorized by the percepts folded through its aesthetic composition. For a sufferer of intrusive images who is locked in a position of frustrated voyeurism, who is physically immobilized, and whose own mental images are unbelievable in their lack of an indexical link to the world, the cinema extends an overture: it gifts the aesthetic composition of a multiplicity of perspectives, a transversality which undoes positionality, and an indexically verifiable encounter with reality. As it turns out, the qualities of the cinema which mirrored those of intrusive images were but one expression of the seventh art, one side of the pharmakon's Janus-face.

Despite the efforts of CBT-informed approaches to categorize intrusive images as meaningless, the intrusive image is indeed a sign, and imagery rescripting at its most adventurous is a practice of imaginative re-signification. The cinematic image is a material sign. At its most adventurous, going to the cinema is a practice of entering into relation not only with the image, but with all of the image's virtual interlocutors, and the singular way that the image composes with their difference. Therefore, the cinematic image is an indexical sign whose aesthetic assembling of autonomous streams of experience points to its myriad openings for perceptual engagement that imprint it with an expanded meaning beyond the immediate fact of its occurrence. The cinematic image, while remaining material, actual, and real, opens the chords of a virtual fabulatory creation, an assemblage of re-singularizing enunciation. It ultimately invites voyeurs to become seers—visionaries who see more than what is shown, and for whom the act of seeing imbues the image with meaning by partaking in an asynchronous and disjunctively collective project of existential co-creation. Imagery rescripting, for all its demonstrated therapeutic efficacy, is but an apprenticeship for going to the cinema and becoming the artist that the spectator in search of existential health most certainly is.

[CONCLUSION]

Existential Health contra Public Health

What is existential health?

When first generating the concept of existential health in 2019, in what has since proven to be an epoch ago, my initial intention was to expound the value of existential health by placing it in contradistinction to the widespread concept of mental health. This exploration grew out of my writing of the book *Cinemas of Therapeutic Activism: Depression and the Politics of Existence*, wherein clinical depression is framed as a global pandemic which auteurs from disparate regions of the world all sought to make sense of through the artistic resources of cinema. *Cinemas of Therapeutic Activism* expresses the conviction that these auteurs' styles of endowing depression with meaning offer up images which complicate the dominant narratives of depression couched in medical perception. Thinking and writing from a contemporary vantage point, this avenue of exploration holds up, and it seems likely that future developments in cinema will continue to enact serious arts-based research into related topics, particularly if the current era of widespread mental illness is prolonged.[1] What *Cinemas of Therapeutic Activism* did not fathom in 2019, in what must be acknowledged as a mix of naivete and short-sightedness, is the extent to which the default signification of the word "pandemic" would be upended, perhaps for the rest of the twenty-first century.

It is now hard to imagine writing about a pandemic of mental illness without qualification, something that was only possible prior to 2020; the coronavirus pandemic which originated in Wuhan, China, has usurped all other pandemics in the contemporary cultural imagination, and certainly in common parlance. Instead of contrasting the concept of existential health with the well-established notion of mental health, this new pandemic of infectious disease has pushed a more urgent, and likely an even more fruitful foil to the fore—that of public health. To answer the question, "What is existential health?" it is crucial to consider what was negated from the social field by state-imposed public health mandates from 2020 to 2023. Beginning in March 2020, existential health was systematically extinguished in the name of public health. Not coincidentally, for the first time since the Second World War, most of the world's cinemas were also forcibly closed. The ability to take risks, to encounter alterity, to express embodied desire, to live collectively, to incarnate a spirit of adventure, and to constitute a subjective singularity were all uniformly suppressed. Existential health depends on all of these vocations. In its search for maximum security from the novel coronavirus, society failed to confront the stark political and philosophical repercussions of sacrificing the conditions that make existential health possible.

As the heavily mediatized saying goes, the impoverishment of social life during the politicization of the global pandemic was accepted by the majority of the population as a "new normal."[2] In early 2022, the situation was as dire as ever: the mass media and its Big Tech social media corollaries had primed the populace for the acceptance of total biopolitical governance, best represented by vaccine passports which grant freedoms based on compliance with public health protocols. The implementation of this strategy was bolstered by the calculated rise of a severe secular moralism which exalted safety as the most supreme of all values and shamed divergences from the newly established norms. Though these pandemic norms were unfamiliar to the populations that practiced them, the sacrificial ethos which guided them has a very long history. As Herbert Marcuse writes: "Western civilization has always glorified the hero, the sacrifice of life for the city, the state, the nation. It has rarely asked the question whether the established city, state, nation were worth the sacrifice."[3]

The cultural logic of public health is intolerant of critical difference, and the reign of public health from 2020 to 2023 saw to it that opposition to the administration of lockdowns was shadow-banned and de-platformed, leading to an inertia of thought in the public sphere and a gross standardization across the entire spectrum of political parties. Consequently, the insuppressible desire for embodied relations operating at the nucleus of subjectivity production fell under the purview of police states emboldened by emergency decrees which did not hesitate to condemn the old to die alone, unaccompanied in their final moments of life, incinerated without a funeral, and the young to live alone, as mutilated orphans of the new scapegoat: Eros.

Public health is the statist command of uniform docility. Existential health is an anarchic pursuit of singular potency. What left-wing politics reneged in their panicked acquiescence to public health and its totalizing managerial logic, is precisely the freedom and autonomy which processes of singularization lay claim to.

The modern history of critical theory is haunted by the living specter of authoritarianism. One need only think of Bertolt Brecht making his final pact with the East German government, György Lukács's recurrent Stalinism, or the espoused Maoism of Jean-Luc Godard's filmmaking, which was representative of broader currents within France's May 1968 movement criticized by Assayas in the film *After May* and the related book, *A Post-May Adolescence: Letter to Alice Debord*. It was also with these totalitarian impasses in mind that Félix Guattari and Antonio Negri wrote their 1985 tract, *Communists Like Us*, which sought to reimagine a communism of singularities, that is, an anti-totalitarian communism of "liberated possibilities."[4] This autonomist vein of communism proposes the freedom and the autonomy for singular processes of subjectivity-production to develop according to the desires immanent to them, rather than in accordance with duties to the state, party, or other some transcendent apparatus. After announcing their project to "rescue 'communism' from its own disrepute," Guattari and Negri write:

> Make no mistake about it: communism is not a blind, reductionist collectivism dependent on repression. It is the singular expression for the combined productivity of individuals and groups (collectivities) emphatically not reducible to each other. If it is not a continuous reaffirmation of singularity, then it is nothing—and so it is not paradoxical to define communism as the process of singularization.[5]

Singularity is such an indispensable part of Guattari and Negri's political project precisely because it is what totalitarianism cannot tolerate. To participate in valorizing pluralistic processes of singularization is to enter a process of becoming anti-authoritarian. Throughout the era of coronavirus pandemic restrictions, the medical authorities used the media apparatuses to discursively construct singularity as an antisocial tendency. The pandemic proved to be an exercise in subjectification, and the intensified logic of biopolitical governmentality has set a new precedent.

In "The Proliferation of Margins," one of Guattari's two written contributions to *Autonomia: Post-Political Politics*, a collection of primary texts from the Autonomia Operaia movement in 1970s Italy, he theorizes the administered social order of post-Fordism as being based on the repression of desire. Guattari writes: "Social production, under the control of capitalist and technocratic 'elites,' is more and more cut off from the interests and desires of individuals and leads . . . to the flattening out and repression of desires in their singularity, that is, to the loss of the meaning of life."⁶ In response to what he and the Italian autonomists saw in 1970s integrated world capitalism as the standardization of worker subjectivity (in both capitalist and socialist countries), Guattari privileges singularity as the principle of dissent from the real economy's surplus repression, and as a struggle for the freedom to recompose subjectivity according to a collectivity's immanent machinations of desire, machinations which—if the collective has not come to desire its own repression—unavoidably break from the requirements of the labor market. Peter Pál Pelbart carries Guattari's thinking into contemporaneous times, and points to how the free marketeering of subjectivity erodes existential health. He writes: "Our era revolves around this pathology: market-ready modes of existence."⁷ After the recent public health crisis, his statement could be extended to include a new range of pandemic-ready subjectivities.

The praxis of recomposing subjectivity to produce novel singularities is a specifically existential praxis because it articulates difference as a lived mode of existence. It is a creative act of differentiation from the mediatized mold of standardized subjectivities, an act which gives meaning to a singular constellation of desire. If, as Sartre has proposed, "everything has been figured out, except how to live," existential philosophies appear at the juncture where experimentations in collective life break from the subjective coordinates already given by the established norms of the social field, perpetually asking, "What are we?" and "What shall we do?"⁸ If there is one thing that existential philosophies demand, it is to be lived out, in the creative recomposition of a subjectivity that is never given in advance.⁹

At La Borde, one of the therapeutic aims was to recompose the standard group subjectivity of the psychiatric institution, with its clearly defined social roles, entrenched hierarchies, and stifling regimentation. The directors of the institute theorized that a permissive, non-directive atmosphere could allow qualitative changes in group relations to take place. Pelbart describes the approach: "As La Borde director Jean Oury highlights, along with Guattari, that is the condition for something to happen—nothing 'must' happen—since it's precisely when something must happen that the most impalpable happenings run the risk of being aborted."¹⁰ La Borde's working formulation for prompting recompositions of subjectivity holds much pertinence for an analysis of the erosion of existential health in an age of mental illness that has been exacerbated by the impositions of public health authorities. When Guattari and Oury say, "Nothing 'must' happen," the meaning of that allowance is very different from the commands of the public health officials when they utter, "Nothing must happen." The former is a way of saying that nothing is obliged to happen, but that a happening may emerge spontaneously. The latter indicates that there is an obligation to ensure that nothing ever happens. One is a relational technique for fostering existential health, while the other is a strategy for eradicating it in the name of public health.

The creative capacity to make something happen, without compelling something to happen, all the while resisting institutional or market demands which would either prevent something from happening or oblige something predetermined to happen, is a potency. In Franco "Bifo" Berardi's essay on the coronavirus pandemic, he activates the autonomist tradition to reaffirm the importance of the struggle for autonomy in today's political climate where the traditional orientations between left- and right-wing politics have been confused, particularly as they relate to the upholding or the transgression of the law. Berardi writes:

> Since the first days of the pandemic, and since the beginning of the ensuing lockdowns, public opinion has been split between those who reject any limit to their personal freedom, and those who support a more or less strict regulation of social interaction. The very borders between the political fronts—the classical distinctions between right-wing and left-wing ideology—have been blurred on this point: opposition to state-enforced lockdowns and health regulations has been taken over by right-wing libertarians. How can we explain the fact that some anarchists and many other leftists are respecting health rules dictated by a "state of exception," while fascists are the ones reclaiming their freedom to do whatever they like? There is a comedic exchange of roles, whereby fascists proclaim themselves as the "defenders of freedom" and progressives emerge as the defenders of the law. This, too, signals the dissolution of the twentieth-century political landscape.[11]

In this disorienting political climate where the concept of freedom is co-opted by libertarianism to justify the market's saturation of subjective life, and where a range of left-wing positions not only accept, but actively demand extravagant state intervention over a widening purview of everyday life, the need for autonomy is increasingly apparent.

Autonomy encompasses the refusal of work, freedom from toil, dissent from party politics, and ultimately, an affirmation of the unconscious and desire's creative potency for singular auto-poesis. In other words, autonomist politics seek to re-create on the societal scale the atmosphere of indeterminacy and non-compulsory activity that Oury and Guattari cultivated at La Borde: a society in which "nothing 'must' happen." When unceasingly confronted with the threat of subjugation to the motivations of capital, autonomy is only realizable through potency, and Berardi situates it at the heart of the autonomist movement:

> Since action happens in the physical world, where physical forces are at play, freedom depends on our potency to overcome these forces. We are free to do what we have the potency to do. Only to the extent of our potency are we "free" to choose and act. . . . In the end, freedom is the dimension that we can access by strenuously pursuing autonomy, and depends only on our potency. In fact, autonomy can be defined as the potency of imagination and of action.[12]

Berardi's definition of political autonomy as the potency of imagination and action turns attention back to the question of health, and specifically the distinction that can be drawn between its "existential" and "public" varieties.

Existential health can be thought of as the quantum of potential active in a given event for the transformational emergence of a group subject which enriches all who have a lived stake in it, and in proportion to that lived stake, through attunement to values such as knowledge and passion which are animated by encountering the experimental significations of art.

Experiments in participatory art can give existential health a chance, especially when they overturn the social norms of the art gallery, or leave it entirely, as the Brazilian artist Lygia Clark is known for having done. Over the first half of her career from around 1944 to 1966, Clark was associated with the neo-concrete movement and her frame-breaking paintings. Her output of this period culminated in the abstract, mutable sculptures called *Bichos* (*Beasts*), made out of foldable aluminum sheets which could be reconfigured by audiences and displayed in a variety of ways. As time went on, Clark transitioned away from her practice of producing art objects, and ultimately from the commercial gallery system altogether. By the late 1970s, Clark was in a phase of her career known as "Estruturação do self" (Structuring the Self) where she designed *Objetos relacionais* (*Relational Objects*) to explore what could ostensibly be described as art's therapeutic value, if only the habitual meanings of art and therapy are liable to revision.[13]

In her article "Molding a Contemporary Soul: The Empty-Full of Lygia Clark," Suely Rolnik offers a compelling vision of how art can push therapy past its limits in the stimulation of an existential health which in turn overruns the limits of art. Rolnik writes:

> Clark's proposition surmounts in the work itself the separation between the artistic domain and psychotherapy. She creates a territory, situated

neither in the sphere of art as a department of social life specializing in semiotic activities, where access to the creative power of life is confined; nor in the sphere of therapy, specialized in treating a subjectivity separated from this power; nor in the border between the two—an entirely new territory.[14]

This entirely new existential territory, irreducible to the teleologies of both institutionalized art and therapy, where the "creative power of life" is liberated from "specialized semiotic activities" and the "treating of subjectivity," is a vitality, a health. Rolnik asks why Clark's relational objects healing practice was not simply "a matter of replacing art with therapy, or using therapy as a form of opposition to art." Because "therapy as practiced," posits Rolnik,

> was merely the corollary of art as a separate sphere: it created the conditions for listening to the vibrating body which had become necessary since the end of the nineteenth century, but so as to integrate them into the experience of the psyche, through the interpretation of fantasies/ghosts, looking toward constructing an individual history in order to reconstitute an identity, with this reconstitution as the goal of treatment.... Why was it also not a matter of a boundary or fusion between art and therapy in a kind of conciliatory "holistic" totality? Because the existence of each of these spheres cannot be dissociated from the division of functions that have as their basis the de-eroticizing of human life in its creative force.[15]

Rolnik offers a vision of health as existentially significant aesthetic production attuned to the quivering of Eros, which may contribute to the aims of fine art or clinical therapy, but which is irreducible to their specific teleologies. This line of flight from the logic of the clinical is entirely consistent with Rolnik's intellectual orientation; along with Peter Pál Pelbart and others, she is a torch-bearer of the schizoanalytic tendency in psychoanalysis, which has made an enormous contribution to Brazilian political culture. After the fall of the military dictatorship in Brazil in the 1980s, Rolnik guided Guattari on a tour of the country to meet with activist groups associated with the Partido dos Trabalhadores (the then-burgeoning Worker's Party, which would eventually win the elections of 2002 and 2022 when its leader Luiz Inácio Lula da Silva became president), an adventure chronicled in the astounding book *Molecular Revolution in Brazil*.

The way in which Rolnik, who is a psychoanalyst, distances Lygia Clark's therapeutically driven art from the psychoanalytic technique of "constructing an individual history in order to reconstitute an identity, with this reconstitution as the goal of treatment" warrants attention, particularly for the degree to which this technique of identification has shaped the cinema's relationship to existential health. Film studies has changed dramatically over the past fifty years, shifting from the psychoanalytically inspired theory of the 1970s to the cultural studies which are more widespread today, and yet the concept of identity persists as a common base undergirding the field. An identitarian bedrock of meaning is now a methodological given for a wide range of film scholarship. What is rarely acknowledged is how such identitarian methods unknowingly couch themselves in the model of spectatorial subjectivity figured by Christian Metz, wherein the spectator "*identifies with himself*, with himself as a pure act of perception (as wakefulness, alertness): as condition of possibility of the perceived and hence as a kind of transcendental subject, anterior to every *there is*."[16] This primary mode of unconscious identification with one's self, or with the empty place made for one's self by the cinematographic apparatus, precedes the more frequently acknowledged secondary mode of identification, whereby the spectator—thanks to having already accomplished primary identification—can then consciously identify with an on-screen character.

Ever since Steven Shaviro's *The Cinematic Body* challenged this model of imaginary identification as being at the core of the film experience, it has been possible to write about spectatorship without referring back to apparatus theory, and today most studies simply sidestep the issue altogether, opting instead for culturalist or empirical methods which ostensibly have no need for returning to film theory's founding scene of Plato's cave. Nevertheless, when such studies are built upon an identitarian ground, and when they traffic in a politics of representation based on secondary identification with on-screen characters, they inadvertently entrench the apparatus theory's central tenet: that before all else, and in order for secondary identification to occur, the cinema produces a standardized and transcendental spectatorial subjectivity through primary identification. As diverse as these secondary identifications may be, they all descend from the same taxonomic category, the ideal individual subject identical to himself.

If the art of cinema is to be endowed with a nonclinical therapeutic potency, capable of fostering existential health via the potential for recomposing subjectivity in much the same vein as Lygia's Clark's "Structuring the Self," it is because the cinema gifts its interlocutors the chance to depart from the experience different from when they arrived. When this happens, even though it never "must" happen, and certainly cannot be mandated beforehand, it does not necessarily entail that a spectator's identity has changed. In fact, that is highly unlikely, except in the most deeply unsettling of circumstances. To recompose subjectivity is not to modify identity: it is to shift the coordinates of the existential territory on which an intangible sense of self emerges through embodied negotiations with values, risks, affective intensities, and signs. The cinema can create the conditions for such a recomposition of subjectivity to occur when it is approached with a cinephilic disposition that combines the spirit of adventure with a degree of reverence that is more often found before a spread of Tarot cards apt to disclose possible avenues of action forward through a serious predicament.[17]

If therapeutic value can be attributed to the cinema, this is ultimately for three entangled reasons: (1) its function as a machine for transversality, whereby anoedipal images molecularly undercut Oedipal imagos of identification to create a common reserve of unconscious semiotic material which guides the lay creation of new analytic relations made through a life of cinephilia; (2) its status as an occurrent, relational, and non-fetishistic art, which produces revelatory cinephilic moments that matter to the singular existential constellations at stake in the encounter with its images; and (3) its aesthetic visions of lived and indexically-verifiable existential problematics which stand up as sensuous monuments ripe for inhabitation by seers who detach from the positionality of voyeurism to re-signify the intrusive images which bear most heavily on their subjective lives. These three operations together constitute the cinema's offering to the sick, its artful alliance with the collective project of curating existential health through therapeutic activism.

Perhaps it is no coincidence that during the pandemic, the cinema was shuttered for years due to having been deemed nonessential by the public health authorities. After all, the gift of existential health offered by the former is a threat to the political power of the latter. The antagonism between the suppressed struggle for existential health and the statist impositions of public health affords a critical distance to also think about how the mental health system has historically functioned mostly as a set of institutions and techniques for adapting worker subjectivity to the false necessity of toil under Capital. Psychoanalysis itself appears as a pharmakon in this regard. In some historical moments it has functioned as a grand apology for the societal superego; and yet it has also proven to be the most fertile ground for intellectual inquiry into the production of subjectivity. That is why the survival of the psychoanalytic tradition is one of the most pressing issues in mental health. Without it, the helping professions would be left with an antiseptic range of treatment options coalescing around the "evidence-based" altar of CBT, which expunges the dynamic unconscious and limits therapy to a short-term clinical intervention. Guattari legitimately critiqued psychoanalysts for being "specialists of the unconscious" at a time when psychoanalysis was a dominant cultural force in France, and often took the side of the law in order to maintain its hegemonic position.[18] Today, with psychoanalysis having been returned to its origins as a therapeutic practice marginal to the medical establishment, its foundational discovery, the unconscious, is in jeopardy of becoming an artifact of a bygone imagination, like the Egyptian art which adorned Freud's study.

The cleansing of contact with the unconscious is also prevalent in medical research into psychedelics. Much like public health, it too has difficulties accepting the high risks—but also the profound rewards—of commitment to a praxis of existential health which is sensitive to the dynamism of the unconscious. In the first half of the 2020s, psychedelic medicine companies have actively taken advantage of softening regulatory environments in countries like Switzerland, Germany, and Canada to research a new class of medical products which they are incentivized to bring to market. A publicly traded company named MindMed is among these psychedelic medicine companies with a wide range of clinical trials. Its mission includes addressing the opioid crisis in North America, and the company has undergone late-stage clinical trials to determine whether 18-methoxycoronaridine (18-MC), a "novel iboga alkaloid congener," can act as an addiction inhibitor.[19] If successful and approved by regulators, 18-MC could mark an extraordinary clinical breakthrough that dramatically improves the mental health of countless people, to the point of even saving them from premature death. However, the perceived significance of this medical achievement diminishes considerably when the psychedelic origins of 18-MC are taken into account.

18-MC is a derivative of the highly psychoactive substance ibogaine, which is found in the roots and bark of the sacred *Tabernanthe iboga* (iboga) plant that grows primarily in Gabon, though production also occurs in some other West African countries such as Cameroon. Indigenous medicinal knowledge from the region has already proven the therapeutic benefits of iboga according to its own radically empirical methods. The Bwiti religion reveres iboga as the fruit of knowledge described in the book of Genesis, and initiation into Bwiti takes place through the plant's ritual ingestion.[20] Iboga is possibly the most powerful psychedelic medicine on the face of the earth, and a full "flood" dose can produce a high-intensity altered state of consciousness complete with visions lasting up to eight hours, with heavy residual effects continuing for more than seventy-two hours afterwards.[21] Stanislaw Świderski, an anthropologist of the Bwiti, describes the significance of the visions prompted by the iboga experience: "For the initiate, the visions are indeed a process of revelation of the beyond by audio-visual means, paired with an immediate, intuitive understanding. . . . As the initiates say, it is through vision that everything is understood."[22]

The reason why MindMed has opted to invest in the commercializing of 18-MC as a possible consumer pharmaceutical, rather than simply promoting the cultivation and supervised use of iboga, even though the latter already has a history of medical uses both among the Bwiti and in alternative clinics and retreat centers, is because iboga, to invoke the standard medical terminology, is highly "hallucinogenic." A full dose of iboga is almost certain to render someone incapable of walking or sleeping for days, and during the first six to eight hours after ingestion, that person is likely to experience vivid, overpowering visual images inside their mind's eye. With 18-MC, MindMed strips the hallucinogenic properties out of the iboga, while attempting to retain its anti-addictive properties, thus producing what the company markets as an "antibiotic of addiction" and a "safer," "next-gen version of Ibogaine."[23] MindMed takes pride in this intention, and it boasts very straightforwardly: "We are pioneering medicines that have the potential to maintain the therapeutic benefits of psychedelics, without the hallucinogenic effects." In sum, MindMed wants to make psychedelically derived medicine, without the psychedelics. If this company is successful in bringing its opioid treatment to market, 18-MC will be available for microdosing in pill form and would be consumed daily without any alteration of a patient's routine. Yet again, this time in the realm of psychedelically derived mental health care, "nothing must happen."

Another way to describe what MindMed is doing is that it is seeking to eliminate the unconscious images of existential significance which iboga brings to vision. The company believes that mental health outcomes can be improved without grappling with the presence of the unconscious, and taking on the risks of pursuing existential health. The strategy of this psychedelic medicine company is thus entirely consistent with the general trend, since the publication of the *DSM-III*, of evacuating the unconscious from the clinical scene. It remains to be seen what kind of impact 18-MC may play in quelling North America's opioid crisis. Perhaps it could very well change the landscape of treatment options and provide patients with better results than current medicines such as methadone.[24] Nevertheless, no matter how much of an evidence base scientists may build up around 18-MC, it could never prove to be as transformative as iboga in its unadulterated state (or in its total alkaloid format), precisely because the authentic reception of iboga is capable of bringing the initiatory subject into an encounter with an unconscious image of existential significance. People who have ingested a full dose of iboga report seeing the very reason why they have an addiction in the first place.[25] Unlike

18-MC, iboga doesn't cure a brain disease named addiction. It reveals to a genuine truth-seeker unconscious images which index unaddressed root trauma, and allows the patient to heal that trauma right then and there, in the psychedelic realm, by responding to the unconscious images revealed to them and then incorporating these images into a novel composition of subjectivity.

To be certain, there is a real risk involved in embarking on the iboga adventure. The Bwiti make no attempt to hide the fact that on rare occasions, some initiates do not survive the ritual, and yet this has never deterred them from exalting iboga. On the contrary, it has deepened their conviction because the Bwiti see the value in every death. Before every Bwiti initiation, the candidates are required to make a full and complete confession to a ceremonial guide, and they are warned that intentionally leaving out any wrongdoings could lead to the most severe of repercussions during the ritual. For some, their initiation is merely aborted due to having failed to receive iboga with a clean conscience. Others die. According to Bwiti beliefs, every death from iboga corresponds to an insincere confession.[26]

If and when MindMed or another pharmaceutical company is successful in the distribution of 18-MC, it will have managed to poach the iboga plant's therapeutic efficacy, but without the pragmatics of seeing-knowing which come along with it, and certainly without the risks of a disingenuous confession leading to death. 18-MC could very well have a positive impact on global mental health and play a major role in mitigating the opioid crisis. However, it also attests to a broader tendency within both the mental health-industrial complex and the recently emboldened public health sector to govern moments of crisis through risk-management strategies which foreclose an adventure of existential health where the production of subjectivity is at stake. MindMed's approach to psychedelic medicine and government reactions to the coronavirus pandemic are but iterations of wider trends in which the institutions responsible for both mental and public health attempt to extinguish any last yearning for existential health.

After all, this should come as no surprise. As Tobie Nathan suggests, "healing is always an act of pure violence against the order of the universe."[27] A praxis of creating the conditions for existential health to bloom, and of anarchically pursuing the potency of singularity, throws the reactive forces of society's reigning superego into question—an act which can attract the most severe of responses in return. Against a backdrop of persistent threat and systemic deprivation, the cinema's playful significations percolate, providing common transferential material for the creation of lay analytic relationships which offer a bridge out of the alienation of being a sovereign individual responsible for one's own mental health, and the isolation of bearing the burden for the entire public's physical health. In this sensuous aesthetic zone of transversal experimentation once relegated to the far margins of social life and outlawed by the state of exception, the unconscious pulses and vibrates, machining clandestine images, open to being inhabited and given a new meaning in the living out of their tenuous significance by analytic adventurers who are not afraid of being irreversibly changed by a singular relational process of mutual discovery.

Acknowledgments

I would like to extend heartfelt thanks to Erin Manning, Thomas Lamarre, D. N. Rodowick, and Brian Price, whose combined and lasting support created the conditions for this book to emerge.

Cinephilia and the Adventure for Existential Health: Recomposing Subjectivity at the Cinema is supported in part by funding from the Social Sciences and Humanities Research Council of Canada. Additionally, this research was supported by the Fonds de recherche du Québec—Société et culture (FRQSC) and was funded by the Horizon 2020 Marie Skłodowska-Curie Actions FRIAS COFUND Fellowship Programme for Junior and Senior Researchers. Grant number 754340.

Notes

INTRODUCTION

1. Nico Baumbach, *Cinema/Politics/Philosophy* (New York: Columbia University Press, 2019), 90.
2. "Literature is a health. These problems mark out a set of paths. The texts presented here, and the authors considered, are such paths. . . . Every work is a voyage, a journey, but one that travels along this or that external path only by virtue of the internal paths and trajectories that compose it, that constitute its landscape or its concert. Gilles Deleuze, *Essays Critical and Clinical*, trans. Daniel W. Smith and Michael A. Greco (London: Verso, 1998), lv–lvi.
3. The concept of subjectivity is a leitmotif throughout Guattari's oeuvre and it takes on different emphasis depending on the context in which it appears. The following two quotations from *Schizoanalytic Cartographies* and *Chaosmosis* serve to provide an initial sense of Guattari's approach to conceptualizing subjectivity:

> Rather than returning constantly to the same, supposedly foundational, structures, the same archetypes, the same "mathemes," schizoanalytic meta-modelling will choose to map compositions of the unconscious, contingent topographies, evolving with social formations, technologies, arts, sciences, etc. (Félix Guattari, *Schizoanalytic Cartographies*, trans. Andrew Goffey [London: Bloomsbury, 2013], 22)

> In a more general way, one has to admit that every individual and social group conveys its own system of modelizing subjectivity; that is, a certain cartography—composed of cognitive references as well as mythical, ritual and symptomatological references—with which it positions itself in relation to its affects and anguishes, and attempts to manage its inhibitions and drives. (Félix Guattari, *Chaosmosis: An Ethico-Aesthetic Paradigm*, trans. Paul Bains and Julian Pefanis [Bloomington: Indiana University Press 1995], 11)

The specific term "recomposition of subjectivity" originated in the book *New Lines of Alliance, New Spaces of Liberty* by Félix Guattari and Antonio Negri, and appears very sparingly in Guattari's oeuvre. The original French-language text from 1985 is entitled *Les Nouveaux Espaces de liberté* and was subsequently published in English under the title *Communists Like Us* in 1990. In that text, Guattari and Negri discuss the failures of the twentieth century's left-wing political movements that led to the expansion of deadening bureaucracy, increased centralization, and ultimately, totalitarianism. They also heavily criticize the "terrorist interlude" in countries such as Germany and Italy where Leninist-inspired groups took up arms and militarized. The authors alternatively advocate for a proliferation of peaceful social movements whose multidimensional alliance-building across lines of segmentation imposed by the state activates a "molecular effervescence and maturation of new revolutionary subjectivities" (68). Guattari and Negri give the example of how the anti-nuclear and ecology movements built a new alliance to revitalize both movements and reorient them towards a new horizon of common action. They also cite how the working class in developed economies "found itself objectively associated with the suppression of the proletariats of the Third World" because of how elevated inflation and unemployment in the United States and the Latin American debt crisis obliged workers in these different regions to compare their situations: "This is a clear example of what we mean when we speak of the 'materiality of the passageways of the recomposition of subjectivity.'" Félix Guattari and Antonio Negri, *New Lines of Alliance, New Spaces of Liberty*, trans. Michael Ryan, Jared Becker, Arianna Bove, and Noe Le Blanc (Brooklyn, NY: Autonomedia, 2010), 74.

4. Félix Guattari, "The Poor Person's Couch," in *Chaosophy: Texts and Interviews 1972–1977*, trans. David L. Sweet, Jarred Becker, and Taylor Adkins, ed. Sylvère Lotringer (Los Angeles: Semiotext(e), 2009), 266–67 (translation modified).

5. Herbert Marcuse, *One-Dimensional Man* (London: Routledge, 2002), 18.

6. Alternative terms in circulation also include the "therapeutic relationship" and the "working alliance."

7. John C. Norcross and Michael J. Lambert, *Psychotherapy Relationships That Work, Volume 1: Evidence-Based Therapist Contributions*, 3rd ed. (Oxford: Oxford University Press, 2019), 4–8, 48. Norcross's appraisal of the importance of the therapeutic alliance builds on the "person-centered" approach to therapy developed by Carl Rogers, best represented by the latter's works *The Therapeutic Relationship and Its Impact* and *Client-Centered Therapy*. Flückiger et al.'s meta-analysis supports the correlation that Norcross draws between the strength of the therapeutic alliance and treatment prognosis. See C. Flückiger et al., "The Alliance in Adult Psychotherapy: A Meta-Analytic Synthesis," *Psychotherapy* 55, no. 4 (2018): 316–40.

8. John C. Norcross, "The Therapeutic Relationship, Individualized Treatment and Other Keys to Successful Psychotherapy," Kanopy.

9. "Recent years have witnessed the emergence of two powerful, and seemingly contradictory, visions of what most fundamentally causes change in psychotherapy. One of these visions emphasizes the primacy of therapist technique. . . . The second vision instead focuses on the patient-therapist relationship and so-called therapist-offered relationship qualities as the sine qua non of therapeutic effectiveness." Efforts at reconciliation between the camps are "based on the notion that

what matters most in psychotherapeutic treatments is the interplay of the two, of techniques and the therapeutic relationship." Charles J. Gelso, "The Interplay of Techniques and the Therapeutic Relationship in Psychotherapy—Introduction to Special Issue," *Psychotherapy* 42, no. 4 (2005): 419–20.

10. As John Norcross likes to say, "Different strokes for different folks." John C. Norcross and Bruce E. Wampold, "Compendium of Treatment Adaptations," *Psychotherapy in Australia* 19, no. 3 (2013): 34.

11. External factors include the compatibility of cultural underpinnings and religious beliefs in the therapist and the client. For the different types of factors that go into shaping a compatible therapeutic alliance, see Norcross and Lambert, *Psychotherapy Relationships That Work*, chapters 16–20.

12. Adam O. Horvath, A. C. Del Re, Christoph Flückiger, and Dianne Symonds, "Alliance in Individual Psychotherapy," *Psychotherapy* 48, no. 1 (2011): 9.

13. Advocates of the "dodo bird effect" have even gone so far as to question the importance of the treatment method and suggest that the therapeutic alliance is in itself a sufficient condition to spur gains in psychological health. A review of the controversy around the postulate of the dodo bird effect is available in David H. Barlow, ed., "Special Section on the Dodo Bird Verdict," *Clinical Psychology: Science and Practice* 1, no. 9 (March 2002): 2–34.

14. Some early examples of this nascent development from the late 2010s include the Michael Phelps-sponsored Talkspace (https://www.talkspace.com/), and the AI-powered chatbot app WoeBot (https://woebot.io/).

15. The best examples of this push are found in the United Kingdom in the time since Tony Blair mandated the National Health Service (NHS) to provide mass psychotherapy covered under public health insurance. Richard Layard and David Clark's *Thrive: The Power of Evidence-Based Psychological Therapies* charts the course of its implementation. Bennion et al., in "E-Therapies in England for Stress, Anxiety or Depression," provide an overview of common "e-therapies" used by the NHS.

16. Louise Gaston and Charles R. Marmar's "Manual of California Psychotherapy Alliance Scales," http://www.traumatys.com/wp-content/uploads/2017/09/CALPAS-Manual.pdf.

17. The WAI-Tech figures prominently in Kiluk et al., "Only Connect: The Working Alliance in Computer-Based Cognitive Behavioral Therapy," *Behaviour Research and Therapy* 63 (2014): 139–46; and Loree et al., "Comparing Satisfaction, Alliance and Intervention Components in Electronically Delivered and In-Person Brief Interventions for Substance Use among Childbearing-Aged Women."

18. Kiluk et al., "Only Connect," 141.

19. "For example, Bickmore et al.'s 'Establishing the computer-patient working alliance in automated health behavior change interventions' reported that a computerized intervention for physical activity adoption that included a 'relational agent' (e.g., animated computer character that simulated face-to-face conversation using social-emotional behaviors) produced higher working alliance ratings than a comparison intervention without the relational qualities." Kiluk et al., "Only Connect," 140.

20. Timothy W. Bickmore, Lisa Caruso, Kerri Clough-Gorr, and Tim Heeren, "'It's Just like You Talk to a Friend': Relational Agents for Older Adults," *Interacting with Computers* 17, no. 6 (2005): 711–35.

21. "For Foucault, the shift toward the sovereign family (the nuclear family emerging through the dismantling of the extended family) is the key to understanding psychiatric power: psychiatric power assembles disciplinary power (the closed sites of production) and sovereign power (displaced onto the shrinking family)." Thomas Lamarre, *The Anime Ecology: A Media Theory of Animation* (Minneapolis: University of Minnesota Press, 2009), 176.

22. "Transference is the sine qua non of a successful treatment." Gary Genosko, *Guattari: An Aberrant Introduction* (London: Continuum, 2002), 69.

23. Claude Lévi-Strauss, *The Elementary Structures of Kinship*, trans. John Richard von Sturmer and James Harle Bell, ed. Rodney Needham (Boston: Beacon, 1969), 481.

24. Claude Lévi-Strauss, *The Elementary Structures of Kinship*, 496.

25. This inexhaustible reserve of relationality that remains in spite of extensive systems which yoke relationality to signs of exchangeability is what Gilbert Simondon calls the "preindividual": "To understand the passage from preindividual being to individuated being, we must not embark on a search for a principle of individuation. This is where traditional ontology has gone astray: in privileging the constituted term, it has ignored the operation constituting the individual, that is, individuation as process." Muriel Combes, *Gilbert Simondon and the Philosophy of the Transindividual*, trans. Thomas Lamarre (Cambridge, MA: MIT Press, 2013), 2. "The preindividual is the phaseless excess—the more-than that envelops yet exceeds the newness of the process in its unfolding. The preindividual is the germ of potential in every activity. It can be thought as the force of becoming akin to the pull of the Deleuzo-Guattarian virtual where it combines with the actual. The preindividual is real and it is felt, but only in its effects." Erin Manning, *Always More Than One: Individuation's Dance* (Durham, NC: Duke University Press, 2013), 16–17.

26. Or a "surplus value of life," to use Brian Massumi's turn of phrase in *99 Theses on the Revaluation of Value: A Postcapitalist Manifesto* (Minneapolis: University of Minnesota Press, 2018), 16.

27. "The first task of the revaluation of value is to *uncouple value from quantification*. Value must be recognized for what it is: irreducibly qualitative." Massumi, *99 Theses*, 5.

28. "All arts are occurrent arts. That's another phrase from Susanne Langer (*Feeling and Form*, 121). All arts are occurrent arts because any and every perception, artifactual or 'natural,' is just that, an experiential event. It's an event both in the sense that it is a happening, and in the sense that when it happens something new transpires. There is eventfulness in art, just as there is artfulness in nature. And there is creativity across the board. Because every event is utterly singular, a one-off, even though with and through its one-offness a 'likeness' is necessarily thought-felt to a whole population of other events with which it forms an endless series of repeated variations." Brian Massumi, *Semblance and Event: Activist Philosophy and the Occurrent Arts* (Cambridge, MA: MIT Press, 2011), 82–83.

29. In turn, the social contract of cinema spectatorship demands a degree of discipline in exchange for visual pleasure. See Linda Williams, "Discipline and Fun: *Psycho* and Postmodern Cinema," in *Reinventing Film Studies*, ed. Linda Williams and Christine Gledhill (London: Arnold, 2000), 351–78.

30. The work of art "is a bloc of sensations, that is to say, a compound of percepts and affects." Gilles Deleuze and Félix Guattari, *What Is Philosophy?* (New York: Columbia University Press, 1994), 164. Ironically enough, the mental health disciplines whose authority is so frequently derived from the medical visions of neuroscience systematically eschew molecular perceptions of mutations in subjectivity in favor of collecting aggregate statistical data.

31. The work of Maurizio Lazzarato builds on that of Guattari and is particularly attentive to the cinema as a liminal site of subjectivization. Lazzarato writes: "A political battle has unfolded and continues to unfold around cinema for control of the effects of subjectivation and desubjectivation that the 'non-human' semiotics of the cinematographic image produce on the individuated subject. The three preverbal senses of self, the sense of a verbal self, and semiotics (at once asignifying, symbolic, and signifying) are mobilized by cinematographic machinisms which by deterritorializing the image and perception (the 'film-eye') risks undoing, in its way, the unity of the subject." Maurizio Lazzarato, *Signs and Machines: Capitalism and the Production of Subjectivity*, trans. Joshua David Jordan (Los Angeles: Semiotext(e), 2014), 108. Additionally, Lazzarato states: "The cinema machine is completely inside the real. But what makes it an apparatus for subjection and enslavement can also be turned into new processes for subjectivation provided that one recognize the nature of machinic assemblages, that one abandon the anthropological and humanist perspective that imbues so much of critical thought." Lazzarato, *Signs and Machines*, 138.

32. Eduardo Viveiros de Castro, "Intensive Filiation and Demonic Alliance," in *Deleuzian Intersections: Science, Technology, Anthropology*, ed. Casper Bruun Jensen and Hjetil Rödje (New York: Berghahn Books, 2010), 232.

33. "The relation with the anomalous is one of alliance." Gilles Deleuze and Félix Guattari, *A Thousand Plateaus: Capitalism and Schizophrenia, Vol. 2*, trans. Brian Massumi (Minneapolis: University of Minnesota Press, 2009), 246.

34. Viveiros de Castro, "Intensive Filiation and Demonic Alliance," 239. The unnatural alliance is further articulated in Deleuze's essay on Herman Melville in the *Critical and Clinical* book, where Ahab becomes Moby-Dick. "One can say rather that a zone of indistinction, of indiscernibility, of ambiguity, establishes itself between two terms, as if they had attained the point immediately preceding their respective differentiation: not a similitude, but a slippage, an extreme vicinity, an absolute contiguity; not a natural filiation, but an unnatural alliance. . . . It is no longer a question of Mimesis, but of becoming. Ahab does not imitate the whale, he becomes Moby-Dick, he enters into the zone of proximity where he can no longer be distinguished from Moby-Dick, and strikes himself in striking the whale." Deleuze, *Essays Critical and Clinical*, 78.

35. "Guattari collaborated beginning in 1960 on group projects dedicated to developing this radical 'institutional psychotherapy,' and later entered an uneasy alliance with the international antipsychiatry movement spearheaded by R.D. Laing in England and Franco Basaglia in Italy. As Lacanian schools of psychoanalysis gained ground against psychiatry, the contractual Oedipal relationship between the analyst and the transference-bound analysand became as much of a target for Guattari as the legal bondage of the institutionalized patient in the conventional State

hospital. He came to occupy the same position in relation to psychoanalysis as he had all along in relation to the parties of the left: an ultra-opposition within the opposition." Brian Massumi, "Translator's Foreword: Pleasures of Philosophy," in Deleuze and Guattari, *A Thousand Plateaus: Capitalism and Schizophrenia*, xi.

36. "If '[t]he expression "difference of intensity" is a tautology' (Deleuze, *Difference and Repetition*, 281), 'becoming-other' is another, or perhaps the same, tautology." Viveiros de Castro, "Intensive Filiation and Demonic Alliance," 250.

37. For example, John P. Wilson, *The Posttraumatic Self: Restoring Meaning and Wholeness to Personality* (New York: Routledge, 2006); and Jennifer Radden, *The Philosophy of Psychiatry: A Companion* (Oxford: Oxford University Press, 2004), 74, 323, 409.

38. Guattari, *Chaosmosis*, 21.

39. "Or could it be conceivable an intense, anOedipal alliance that comprises only 'prepersonal variations in intensity'? In a few words, the problem is that of imagining a concept of alliance as disjunctive synthesis." Viveiros de Castro, "Intensive Filiation and Demonic Alliance," 235. "The disjunctive synthesis of becoming is not possible in the terms of the formal combinatorial rules that engender structures; it is born in the far-from-equilibrium fields of real multiplicities." Manuel DeLanda, *Intensive Science and Virtual Philosophy* (London: Continuum, 2002), 75. Quoted in Viveiros de Castro, "Intensive Filiation and Demonic Alliance," 236.

40. On artfulness, Erin Manning writes: "Artfulness, the aesthetic yield, is about how a set of conditions coalesce to favor the opening of a process to its inherent collectivity, to the more-than of its potential. Erin Manning, *The Minor Gesture* (Durham, NC: Duke University Press, 2016), 58.

41. J. Moussaieff Masson, *Against Therapy: Emotional Tyranny and the Myth of Psychological Healing* (New York: Atheneum, 1988), 84.

42. Ferenczi is today best known for his famous essay on father-daughter incest, "Confusion of Tongues between Adults and the Child: The Language of Tenderness and of Passion." *Contemporary Psychoanalysis* 24, no. 2 (1988): 196–206.

43. Masson, *Against Therapy*, 85.

44. Such a pure alliance, or durationally expansive therapeutic alliance, would also live up to the aspirations of Félix Guattari and Antonio Negri's "new lines of alliance": "Perpetually recomposing subjectivity and praxis is only conceivable in the totally free movement of each of its components, and in absolute respect of their own times—time for comprehending or refusing to comprehend, time to be unified or to be autonomous, time of identification or of the most exacerbated differences." Guattari and Negri, *New Lines of Alliance*, 86.

CHAPTER I

1. On the mental health crisis, specifically as it concerns clinical depression, see my chapter "Perceiving the Pandemic" in *Cinemas of Therapeutic Activism: Depression and the Politics of Existence*.

2. Franco "Bifo" Berardi, *The Soul at Work: From Alienation to Autonomy*, trans. Francesca Cadel and Guiseppina Mecchia (Los Angeles: Semiotext(e), 2009), 140.

3. Manning, *The Minor Gesture*, 170, 119.
4. Josep Rafanell i Orra, *En finir avec le capitalisme thérapeutique: Soin, politique, communauté* (Paris: Éditions la Découverte, 2011), 284. My translation.
5. Félix Guattari and Suely Rolnik, *Molecular Revolution in Brazil*, trans. Karel Clapshaw and Brian Holmes (Los Angeles: Semiotext(e), 2008), 41.
6. A form of cinema which is instrumentalized by medical institutions and professionals can be defined as "useful cinema." According to Haidee Wasson and Charles Acland, the term "useful cinema" refers to the use of film as a tool for various purposes and functions in institutional contexts. They write: "Useful cinema does not so much name a mode of production, a genre, or an exhibition venue as it identifies a disposition, an outlook, and an approach toward a medium on the part of institutions and institutional agents." In other words, useful cinema is not defined by its formal characteristics, but by a capacity for instrumentalization by different actors and agendas. Wasson and Acland explore how film has been used for education, propaganda, entertainment, art, and social change in various settings such as museums, libraries, schools, factories, and military bases. They argue that useful cinema challenges the notion of cinema as a commercial and theatrical medium, and that it reveals the diversity and complexity of film history and culture. Haidee Wasson and Charles Acland, eds., *Useful Cinema* (Durham, NC: Duke University Press, 2011), 4.
7. Martha Nussbaum, *The Therapy of Desire: Theory and Practice in Hellenistic Ethics* (Princeton, NJ: Princeton University Press, 2009).
8. Tobie Nathan and Isabelle Stengers, *Doctors and Healers*, trans. Stephen Muecke (London: Polity, 2018), 105. My translation.
9. Brian Massumi, *Parables for the Virtual: Movement, Affect, Sensation* (Durham, NC: Duke University Press, 2002), 230, 246.
10. Cardinal Joseph Ratzinger, *Truth and Tolerance: Christian Belief and World Religions*, trans. Henry Taylor (San Francisco: Ignatius, 2004), 31.
11. Brian Massumi offers the following definition of speculative pragmatism: "The speculative aspect relates to the character of potential native to the world's activity, as expressed eventfully in the taking place of change. The pragmatic aspect has to do with how, in the taking-definite-shape of potential in a singular becoming, the relational and qualitative poles co-compose as formative forces." Massumi, *Semblance and Event*, 12.
12. Oliver Burkeman, "Therapy Wars: The Revenge of Freud," *The Guardian*, January 7, 2016, https://www.theguardian.com/science/2016/jan/07/therapy-wars-revenge-of-freud-cognitive-behavioural-therapy.
13. Jonathan Shedler, "Bamboozled by Bad Science: The First Myth about Evidence-Based Therapy," *Psychology Today*, October 31, 2013, https://www.psychologytoday.com/us/blog/psychologically-minded/201310/bamboozled-bad-science.
14. Institutional reaction to countercultural approaches such as art therapy, naturopathy, and Indigenous healing techniques can be even stronger, particularly when controlled substances are involved. A good example of this witch-hunt mentality is reflected in the persecution of Dr. Gabor Maté, who uses ayahuasca in his treatment of people with drug addictions in Vancouver, Canada. For more on this story, see Michael Posner, "B.C. Doctor Agrees to Stop Using Amazonian Plant to Treat

Addictions," *The Globe and Mail*, November 9, 2011, https://www.theglobeandmail.com/life/health-and-fitness/bc-doctor-agrees-to-stop-using-amazonian-plant-to-treat-addictions/article4250579/.

15. Jules Evans, "David Clark on Improving Access for Psychological Therapy (IAPT)," Philosophy for Life, May 31, 2013, http://www.philosophyforlife.org/david-clark-on-improving-access-for-psychological-therapy-iapt/.

16. The fact that the IAPT began in 2008, the year of the financial collapse, is more than a mere coincidence. The IAPT's implementation was bolstered by the arguments which David Clark and the "happiness economist" Richard Layard made to the British government with regard to the program's economic function. In their coauthored book *Thrive: The Power of Evidence-Based Psychological Therapies*, they repeatedly make the case that the program would pay for itself by lifting mentally ill people off of welfare and disability insurance, reducing unemployment, and cutting health care costs for physical illnesses which are aggravated by mental illness. See Richard Layard and David Clark, *Thrive: The Power of Evidence-Based Psychological Therapies* (London: Allen Lane: 2014), 4.

17. Lawton and Clark, *Thrive*, 194.

18. Darian Leader, "A Quick Fix for the Soul," *The Guardian*, September 9, 2008, https://www.theguardian.com/science/2008/sep/09/psychology.humanbehaviour.

19. Cathy Malchiodi, "Foreword," in *Video and Filmmaking as Psychotherapy: Research and Practice*, ed. Joshua L. Cohen and J. Lauren Johnson (New York: Routledge, 2015), xiii–xvi.

20. Only a minority (1 percent) reported them as potentially harmful. Georgios K. Lampropolous, Nikolaos Kazantzis, and Frank P. Deane, "Psychologists' Use of Motion Pictures in Clinical Practice," *Professional Psychology: Research and Practice* 35, no. 5 (2004): 535.

21. The authors of an article in 2000 in the *American Journal of Family Therapy* argue: "In spite of its usefulness, bibliotherapy may be losing some of its appeal in light of new technology. The use of motion pictures is emerging as a useful alternative to bibliotherapy." Shannon B. Dermer and Jennifer B. Hutchings, "Utilizing Movies in Family Therapy: Applications for Individuals, Couples, and Families," *American Journal of Family Therapy* 28 (2000): 164.

22. Malchiodi, "Foreword," xiv.

23. Zur Institute, "Using the Power of Movies in the Therapeutic Process: Cinema Therapy," Zur Institute: Online Continuing Education for Mental Health Professionals, https://www.zurinstitute.com/cinematherapycourse.html.

24. Birgit Wolz, *E-Motion Picture Magic: A Movie Lover's Guide to Healing and Transformation* (Centennial, CO: Glenbridge, 2005), 42.

25. Wolz, *E-Motion Picture Magic*, 36.

26. Gary Solomon, *The Motion Picture Prescription: Watch This Movie and Call Me in the Morning* (Santa Rosa, CA: Aslan, 1995), 11.

27. John W. Hesley and Jan G. Hesley, *Rent Two Films and Let's Talk in the Morning: Using Popular Movies in Psychotherapy* (New York: John Wiley and Sons, 1998), 4–5.

28. For a wider sense of the literature in the cinematherapy field, see the following publications: Kevin Duncan, David Beck, and Richard Granum, "Ordinary People: Using a Popular Film in Group Therapy," *Journal of Counselling and Development* 65

(September 1986): 50–51; Melissa L. Heston and Terry Kottman, "Movies as Metaphors: A Counseling Intervention," *Journal of Humanistic Education & Development* 23, no. 2 (December 1997): 92–99; Lindsey Joiner, *The Big Book of Therapeutic Activity Ideas for Children and Teens: Inspiring Arts-Based Activities and Character Education Curricula* (London: Jessica Kingsley, 2012); and Gary Solomon, *Reel Therapy: How Movies Inspire You to Overcome Life's Problems* (New York: Lebhar-Friedman Books, 2001).

29. Hesley and Hesley, *Rent Two Films*, 78.

30. Esra Yazici, Fuat Ulus, Rabia Selvitop, Ahmet Bülent Yazici, and Nazan Aydin, "Use of Movies for Group Therapy of Psychiatric Inpatients: Theory and Practice," *International Journal of Group Psychotherapy* 64, no. 2 (2014): 254–71.

31. Yazici et al., "Use of Movies," 256.

32. For the full list of sixteen points, see pp. 261–64 of Yazici et al., "Use of Movies." Page 265 includes a list of the five challenges which the authors identified in administering the program.

33. Michael Fleming and Ericka Bohnel, "Use of Feature Film as Part of Psychological Assessment," *Professional Psychology: Research and Practice* 40, no. 6 (2009): 641–47.

34. Fleming and Bohnel, "Use of Feature Film," 644.

35. "The road has come to a dead end at symptom relief," he writes. "Every single drug on the shelf of the psychopharmacopeia is cosmetic. There are no curative drugs and no drug is in development that I know of that aims at cure." Martin Seligman, *Flourish: A Visionary New Understanding of Happiness and Well-Being* (New York: Free Press, 2011), 46.

36. "Positive psychology is the study of the conditions and processes that contribute to the flourishing or optimal functioning of people, groups, and institutions." Shelly L. Gable and Jonathan Haidt, "What (and Why) Is Positive Psychology?" *Review of General Psychology* 9, no. 2 (June 2005): 103–10.

37. Ryan M. Niemiec and Danny Wedding, *Positive Psychology at the Movies: Using Films to Build Character Strengths and Well-Being*, 2nd ed. (Boston: Hogrefe, 2014), 15.

38. Nikolas Rose, "Brain, Self and Society," Andrew F. Holmes Dean of Medicine Distinction Lectures, McGill University, Montreal, Canada, October 27, 2016.

39. Florence W. Kaslow, "Foreword," in *The Cinematic Mirror for Psychology and Life Coaching*, ed. Mary Banks Gregerson (Leavenworth, KS: Springer, 2009), v. Birgit Wolz is the one soft exception to the rule, since she does promote patient-led cinematherapy groups, assuming that they follow the guidelines laid out in her book. Wolz, *E-Motion Picture Magic*, 179.

40. Michel Foucault, *Discipline & Punish: The Birth of the Prison*, trans. Alan Sheridan (New York: Vintage Books, 1995), 170–94.

41. Michel Foucault, *Psychiatric Power: Lectures at the Collège de France 1973–1974*, ed. Jacques Lagrange, François Ewald, Alessandro Fontana, and Arnold I. Davidson, trans. Graham Burchell (Basingstoke, UK: Palgrave Macmillan, 2006), 3.

42. Martin Seligman, *Authentic Happiness: Using the New Positive Psychology to Realize Your Potential for Lasting Fulfillment* (New York: Free Press, 2002), 129.

43. Seligman, *Authentic Happiness*, 127 (my italics added for emphasis).

44. Seligman has also faced controversial accusations of being linked to the development of advanced psychological torture techniques in Abu Ghraib. See Martin

Seligman and Tamsin Shaw, "'Learned Helplessness' & Torture: An Exchange," *New York Review of Books*, April 21, 2016, http://www.nybooks.com/articles/2016/04/21/learned-helplessness-torture-an-exchange/.

45. Martin Seligman and Mihaly Csikszentmihalyi, "Positive Psychology: An Introduction," *American Psychologist* 55, no. 1 (2000): 5. This universalist attitude is also reflected in the Wedding and Niemiec manual. The very first section of the book is entitled "The Language of Film Is Universal."

46. For a summary of the critiques which have been leveled at positive psychology by other psychologists, see the following anthology section devoted to essays on the topic: "Criticism of Positive Psychology," in *The Routledge International Handbook of Critical Positive Psychology*, ed. Nicholas J. L. Brown, Tim Lomas, and Francisco Jose Eiroa-Orosa (London: Routledge, 2018), 11–192.

47. The *Afflictions: Culture & Mental Illness in Indonesia* film series consists of six short documentaries which are listed on the official website: http://www.afflictionsfilmseries.com/. Tobie Nathan's scholarly output in the field of ethnopsychiatry is extensive and has not been fully translated into English. *L'Influence qui guérit* offers readers a look into his ethnopsychiatric work with West African healers and advances the idea that the efficacy of therapeutic modalities is culturally and situationally contingent. Tobie Nathan, *L'Influence qui guérit* (Paris: Odile Jacob, 2009).

48. In *Eros and Civilization*, Marcuse defines surplus repression as follows: "Surplus-repression: the restrictions necessitated by social domination. This is distinguished from (basic) repression: the 'modifications' of the instincts necessary for the perpetuation of the human race in civilization." Herbert Marcuse, *Eros and Civilization* (Boston: Beacon, 1974), 35.

CHAPTER 2

1. For instance, *L'Eau froide* (1994) ends with the dissolution of a young couple, possibly due to suicide. *Fin août, début septembre* (1998) concludes with the death of the main character and the termination of his hidden romantic relationship, while *Désordre* (1986) depicts the breakup of a rock band. Similarly, *Après Mai* (2012) unfolds with the progressive detachment of a group of friends once united in their passion for revolutionary politics.

2. The Barthes quotation reads as follows: "Death of the Father would deprive literature of many of its pleasures. If there is no longer a Father, why tell stories? Doesn't every narrative lead back to Oedipus? Isn't storytelling always a way of searching for one's origin, speaking one's conflicts with the Law, entering into the dialectic of tenderness and hatred? Today, we dismiss Oedipus and narrative at one and the same time: we no longer love, we no longer fear, we no longer narrate. As fiction, Oedipus was at least good for something: to make good novels, to tell good stories (this is written after having seen Murnau's *City Girl*)." Roland Barthes, *The Pleasure of the Text*, trans. Richard Miller (New York: Hill and Wang, 1975), 47.

3. Barthes's question found particular resonance with film analysis through the pioneering work of Raymond Bellour, who cites Barthes in the epigraph to his chapter "Symbolic Blockage (on *North by Northwest*)." In this essay, a palimpsest of (narrative

and representational) "blockages" are interpreted as castration threats for a protagonist who is on an Oedipal-style quest to discover the truth behind his mistaken identity. Raymond Bellour, *The Analysis of Film*, ed. Constance Penley (Bloomington: Indiana University Press, 2000), 77–192.

4. Paul Willemen, "Through the Glass Darkly: Cinephilia Reconsidered," in *Looks and Frictions: Essays in Cultural Studies and Film Theory* (Bloomington: Indiana University Press, 1994), 225.

5. Deleuze and Guattari offer a compelling account of how psychoanalysis has historically sided with social repression: "As to those who refuse to be oedipalized in one form or another, at one end or the other in the treatment, the psychoanalyst is there to call the asylum or the police for help. The police on our side!—never did psychoanalysis better display its taste for supporting the movement of social repression, and for participating in it with enthusiasm. Let it not be thought that we are alluding to the folkloric aspects of psychoanalysis. The fact that there are some, around Lacan, who are developing another conception of psychoanalysis, does not mean that we should take no notice of the dominant tone in the most respected associations: consider Dr. Mendel and the Drs. Stephane, the state of fury that is theirs, and their literally police-like appeal at the thought that someone might claim to escape the Oedipal dragnet. Oedipus is one of those things that becomes all the more dangerous the less people believe in it; then the cops are there to replace the high priests. The first profound example of an analysis of double bind, in this sense, can be found in Marx's *On the Jewish Question*: between the family and the State—the Oedipus of familial authority and the Oedipus of social authority." Gilles Deleuze and Félix Guattari, *Anti-Oedipus: Capitalism and Schizophrenia, Vol. 1* (Minneapolis: University of Minnesota Press, 1986), 81.

Janet Walker's book *Couching Resistance: Women, Film, and Psychoanalytic Psychiatry* builds on the premise that psychoanalysis has often been used as a conformist tool to quell the actions of women who are perceived as deviant. In the introduction to her book, she writes: "The chapters that follow delineate some of the specific discursive operations of what I will call 'adjustment psychiatry,' following social critic Russell Jacoby, who has used the term 'conformist psychology' to characterize the orientation of neo-Freudian and post-Freudian psychology, and following feminist film scholar Diane Waldman, who has used the term 'adjustment therapy' when characterizing the gender-specific ramifications of American psychoanalysis and its thematic portrayal in certain Hollywood films." Janet Walker, *Couching Resistance: Women, Film, and Psychoanalytic Psychiatry* (Minneapolis: Minnesota University Press, 1993), xvi.

6. "Under the influence of this increase in consciousness of the physician, who has developed from the medicine man, sorcerer, charlatan, and magic healer, and who at his best often remains somewhat an artist, will develop increasing knowledge of mental mechanisms, and in the same sense, prove the saying that medicine is the oldest art and the youngest science." Sándor Ferenczi and Otto Rank, *The Development of Psychoanalysis* (New York: Dover, 1956), 68.

7. Jean-Louis Baudry, "Ideological Effects of the Basic Cinematographic Apparatus," in *Narrative, Apparatus, Ideology: A Film Theory Reader*, ed. Philip Rosen (New York: Columbia University Press, 1986), 295.

8. Christian Metz, "The Imaginary Signifier," *Screen* 16, no. 2 (1975): 48–49.

9. Kaja Silverman's concept of suture is particularly relevant here as it sought to expound how the classical text made an empty space for—sutured—the spectatorial subject who primarily identified with the apparatus and its use of the camera as a relay. She writes: "The viewer of the cinematic spectacle experiences shot 1 as an imaginary plenitude, unbounded by any gaze, and unmarked by difference. Shot 1 is thus the site of *a jouissance* akin to that of the mirror stage prior to the child's discovery of its separation from the ideal image which it has discovered in the reflecting glass. However, almost immediately the viewing subject becomes aware of the limitations on what it sees—aware, that is, of an absent field. At this point shot 1 becomes a signifier of that absent field, and *jouissance* gives way to unpleasure." Kaja Silverman, *The Subject of Semiotics* (New York: Oxford University Press, 1983), 203.

10. On the technical determinism of apparatus theory and the need for a media theory of under-determination, see Thomas Lamarre, *The Anime Machine: A Media Theory of Animation* (Minneapolis: University of Minnesota Press, 2009), xxvi–xxxi.

11. The language of *impression* also connotes a certain plasticity of the spectatorial psyche, anticipating the plastic turn in the neurosciences which influenced Deleuze's thinking on cinema. Gilles Deleuze, "The Brain Is the Screen: An Interview with Gilles Deleuze," in *The Brain Is the Screen: Deleuze and the Philosophy of Cinema*, ed. Gregory Flaxman (Minneapolis: University of Minnesota Press, 2000), 365–73.

12. Conversely, Phil Rosen invites a bi-directional rereading of apparatus theory through the work of Jean-Louis Comolli, which Daniel Fairfax has revived and compiled anew for an Anglophone readership. Rosen suggests that what Comolli meant by his use of the term "impression of reality" is akin to "activation of the spectator." Rosen writes: "For Comolli, the cinematic impression of reality never entails a simple submission of the spectator to an illusion, but an activation of the spectator. In his view, the cinematic impression of reality is always inadequate to the task of transmitting reality in any absolute sense. This is why the impression of reality can only be completed by spectatorial investment, which means spectatorship is an activity." Philip Rosen, "Preface," in Jean-Louis Comolli, *Cinema Against Spectacle: Technique and Ideology Revisited*, trans. and ed. Daniel Fairfax (Amsterdam: Amsterdam University Press, 2015), 9.

13. The quotation in its entirety reads as follows: "Cave, grotto, 'sort of cavernous chamber underground,' people have not failed to see in it a representation of the maternal womb, of the matrix into which we are supposed to wish to return. Granted, but only the place is taken into account by this interpretation and not the apparatus as a whole; and if this apparatus really produces images, it first of all produces an effect of specific subjects—*to the extent that a subject is intrinsically part of the apparatus*; once the cinema has been technically perfected, it produces this same effect defined by the words 'impression of reality'. . . . This impression of reality appears as if—just as if—it were known to Plato. At the very least, it seems that Plato ingeniously attempts and succeeds in fixing up a machine capable of reproducing 'something' that he must have known, and that has less to do with its capacity for repeating the real . . . than with reproduction and repetition

of a particular condition, and the representation of a particular place on which this condition depends." Jean-Louis Baudry, "The Apparatus: Metapsychological Approaches to the Impression of Reality in Cinema," in *Film Theory and Criticism*, 7th ed., ed. Leo Braudy and Marshall Cohen (New York: Oxford University Press, 2009), 177–78 (my emphasis).

14. Mary Ann Doane, "Remembering Women: Psychical and Historical Constructions in Film Theory," in *Femmes Fatales: Feminism, Film Theory, and Psychoanalysis* (New York: Routledge, 1991), 83.

15. "We must still avow that the process of identification is one of denying the difference between self and other." Anne Friedberg, "A Denial of Difference: Theories of Cinematic Identification," in *Psychoanalysis and Cinema*, ed. Ann Kaplan (New York: Routledge, 1990), 40.

16. Mary Ann Doane picks up on the metaphor of impression and its closing of proximity when she writes: "Identification as a mechanism is conceptualized as reducing the gap between film and spectator, masking the absence upon which the cinematic representation is founded." Mary Ann Doane, "Misrecognition and Identity," *Ciné-Tracts: A Journal of Film and Cultural Studies* 3, no. 3 (Fall 1980): 25.

17. Jean Laplanche and Jean-Bertrand Pontalis, *The Language of Psychoanalysis*, trans. Donald Nicholson-Smith (London: Karnac Books, 1973), 206.

18. Metz, "The Imaginary Signifier," 50.

19. Joan Copjec, "Thriller: An Intrigue of Identification," *Ciné-Tracts: A Journal of Film and Cultural Studies* 3, no. 3 (Fall 1980): 36.

20. Jacques Aumont, Alain Bergala, Marie Alain, and Marc Vernet, *Esthétique du film* (Paris: Fernand Nathan, 1983), 180. As cited in Robert Stam, Robert Burgoyne, and Sandy Flitterman-Lewis, *New Vocabularies in Film Semiotics: Structuralism, Poststructuralism and Beyond* (London: Routledge, 1992), 153.

21. On cinema as dream and mirror, see Thierry Kuntzel, "The Film-Work," *Trivium-Estudos Interdisciplinares* 11, no. 2 (2019): 132–45; and Thierry Kuntzel, "The Film-Work, 2," *Camera Obscura: Feminism, Culture, and Media Studies* 2, no. 2 (5) (1980): 6–70.

22. Peter Wollen, "Godard and Counter-Cinema: *Vent d'Est*," *Afterimages* 4 (Autumn 1972): 7–16. *Screen* published two special issues on Brecht (in which Wollen played a crucial role)—issues 15, no. 2 (Summer 1974) and 16, no. 4 (Winter 1976). And books from the early 1980s, such as Martin Walsh's *The Brechtian Aspect of Radical Cinema* and George Lellis's *Bertolt Brecht: Cahiers du cinéma and Contemporary Film Theory*, grant Brecht an important role in their politics.

23. Christian Metz, *Psychoanalysis and Cinema: The Imaginary Signifier*, trans. Celia Britton, Annwyl Williams, Ben Brewster, and Alfred Guzzetti, ed. Stephen Heath and Colin MacCabe (London: Macmillan, 1982), 3.

24. "The psychoanalytic study of film enacts an economic conversion by which a strong object cathexis (here attraction to the cinema), initially molar and opaque, subsequently undergoes an instinctual vicissitude that bifidates it and arranges it like a pair of pliers, one pincer (voyeuristic sadism sublimated into epistemophilia) coming to meet the other in which the original imaginary dual effusion with the object is retained as a (living, surviving) witness—in short, this itinerary and the present configuration that results from it." Metz, *Psychoanalysis and Cinema*, 16.

25. Metz, *Psychoanalysis and Cinema*, 15, 79.
26. From Fairfax's glossary entry on the lure: "*Leurre* (lure). Another adoption from Lacan's idiosyncratic vocabulary, *leurre* was widely used by all the major *Cahiers* writers to denote the process of spectatorial investment in the reality of the diegetic events depicted in a film, most notably with respect to the empathetic identification with on-screen characters. They were careful, however, to insist that this credence in the 'impression of reality' is never a totalizing conviction, but is always constrained by a lack (the perceptual differences between a film screening and everyday vision), and is thus exemplary of the divided subjectivity encapsulated by the Lacanian phrase 'Je sais bien . . . mais quand même . . .' (I know very well . . . but all the same . . .). Cf., in particular, Pascal Bonitzer's 'Horschamp' (*Cahiers du cinéma*, no. 234-35, pp. 15-26)." Daniel Fairfax, "Glossary," in Jean-Louis Comolli, *Cinema Against Spectacle: Technique and Ideology Revisited*, trans. and ed. Daniel Fairfax (Amsterdam: Amsterdam University Press, 2015), 296.

Rosen develops the implications of the concept in his preface to the Comolli anthology. "It is worth considering some of the implications of the metaphor of the lure. First, a lure is designed to attract an action from its target; that is, if the target takes the lure, this means it must do something in order to take the bait. So the metaphor encompasses the idea of an activation of the spectator. But second, there is always the possibility that the target of the lure might recognize it as an artifice, as mere bait for something else. A fetishistic structure has potential knowledge value—'I know very well, but all the same.' The possibility of gaining such understanding of the nature of the lure entails the possibility of counteractivity. The lure might be refused, or even destroyed. Or there might be a kind of play with the lure, whereby structures of belief and artifice can be investigated. To put it more generally, this metaphor of the lure designates the cinematic impression of reality as a complex, contradictory process, a kind of balancing act that admits the possibility of comprehending its nature." Rosen, "Preface," 10.
27. Baudry's attitude towards cinephilia was notably more austere than Metz's. He writes: "Of course, I didn't forget that the desire to go to the movies preceded the choice of the film. Actually, that's something which ordinary discourse has also noted: we go to the movies before deciding which film we want to see. And cinephiles, among whom I did not count myself, seem just as blind in their passions as those lovers who imagine they love a woman because of her qualities or because of her beauty. They need good movies, but most of all, to rationalize their need for cinema." Jean-Louis Baudry, "Author and Analyzable Subject," in *Apparatus: Selected Writings*, ed. Theresa Hak Kyung (New York: Tanam, 1980), 68.
28. Nico Baumbach, "All That Heaven Allows: What Is, or Was, Cinephilia? (Part One)," *Film Comment*, March 12, 2012, https://www.filmcomment.com/blog/all-that-heaven-allows-what-is-or-was-cinephilia-part-one/.
29. "Analysis can have for its goal only the advent of a true speech and the realization by the subject of his history in his relation to a future." Jacques Lacan, "The Function and Field of Speech and Language in Psychoanalysis," in *Écrits: A Selection*, trans. Alan Sheridan (London: Routledge, 2015), 65.
30. In Lacan's 1964 essay "On Freud's' 'Trieb' and the Psychoanalyst's Desire," he asks the question "What then is the aim [*fin*] of analysis beyond therapeutics? It

is impossible not to distinguish the two when the point is to create an analyst." Jacques Lacan, "On Freud's 'Trieb' and the Psychoanalyst's Desire [1964]," in *Écrits: The First Complete Edition in English*, trans. Bruce Fink (New York: W.W. Norton, 2006), 724.

31. John Müller, "Lacan's Mirror Stage," *Psychoanalytic Inquiry* 5, no. 2 (1985): 249.

32. The exception to this general absence is Elizabeth Cowie's book *Representing the Woman: Cinema and Psychoanalysis*, which does in passing recognize that transference may be at play in the spectatorial relationship to on-screen characters (points of secondary identification). She writes: "Transference itself is not a structuring psychical process, but is something which is drawn into play within the analytic situation, that is, it draws on the forms of identification already in play for the subject. Moreover it always comes into play in conjunction with its answering response, the analyst's countertransference. Analysis is, after all, where we come into place in relation to the other and the desire of the other. Film, as a fictional narrative form, must however extend the 'as if' relation of the analytic transference so that the spectator can find not only figures who will play out the position of her or his dreaded and desired parental figures, for example, but also figures who can represent the spectator, that is, who 'stand-in' for the identifying spectator." Elizabeth Cowie, *Representing the Woman: Cinema and Psychoanalysis* (London: Macmillan, 1997), 113.

33. This therapeutic lacuna is reasonably attributable to Lacan's own allegiance—contra Freud and the analytic consensus—to a "higher" function of psychoanalysis. For Lacan, psychoanalysis is not essentially a therapeutic process, but rather a search for truth—the truth of desire—the discovery of which may not always be salubrious. Jacques Lacan, *Le Séminaire, Livre XVII: L'Envers de la psychanalyse, 1969–70*, ed. Jacques-Alain Miller (Paris: Seuil, 1991), 122.

34. Tobie Nathan writes: "Psychoanalysts coming after Freud—I mean especially French ones—took pains to define the status of this person. Today, they all seem to agree that it is the idea of the subject that best accounts for it: a philosophical 'subject' (Lacan, *le sujet du désir*), or even increasingly a legal 'subject' (Legendre, *le sujet de la loi*). But this subject is a synthesis of structural elements that themselves constitute a kind of organ: the psychic apparatus. This organ, just like the brain, possesses sensitive extremities; these are the affects. The instrument designed to establish interactions with the organ—I'm referring to transference—always goes via the intermediary of affects. This is why Freud constantly stresses that there can be no psychoanalysis without transference." (Translation modified.) Nathan and Stengers, *Doctors and Healers*, 36.

35. Laplanche and Pontalis, *The Language of Psychoanalysis*, 456.

36. In its primary form identification is quite simply, as Lacan points out, the process of assuming an image: "We have only to understand the mirror stage as an identification, in the full sense that analysis gives to the term: namely the transformation that takes place in the subject when he assumes an image—whose predestination to this phase effect is sufficiently indicated by the use, in analytic theory, of the ancient term imago." Lacan, *Écrits: A Selection*, 2. Quoted in Doane, "Misrecognition and Identity," 28.

37. Laplanche and Pontalis, *The Language of Psychoanalysis*, 461.

38. Deleuze and Guattari, *Anti-Oedipus*, 46 (translation modified).
39. Laplanche and Pontalis, *The Language of Psychoanalysis*, 461.
40. Sigmund Freud, "Fragment of an Analysis of a Case of Hysteria," in *The Standard Edition of the Complete Psychological Works of Sigmund Freud, Volume VII (1901–1905): A Case of Hysteria, Three Essays on Sexuality and Other Works*, trans. James Strachey (London: Hogarth, 1966), 1450.
41. Laplanche and Pontalis, *The Language of Psychoanalysis*, 457.
42. The image of Léaud's face from *The 400 Blows* was even chosen for the cover of Alan Williams's book *Republic of Images: A History of French Filmmaking*.
43. Antoine's aberrant movements along the beach in the final scene were inspired by the movement profiles of the autistic children who lived with Ferdinand Deligny. "Through his friendship with Bazin, Deligny also formed an important connection with the young François Truffaut. The two consulted as Truffaut was in the process of making his 1959 debut feature, *Les 400 coups* (*The 400 Blows*). According to their correspondence, Deligny was especially influential upon Truffaut's construction of the film's iconic final sequence, in which Truffaut's protagonist and autobiographical counterpart Antoine Doinel escapes from the rural institution for social delinquents where he has been confined, and is shown running across the countryside into the churning waves of the ocean." Leon Hilton, "Mapping the Wander Lines: The Quiet Revelations of Fernand Deligny," *Los Angeles Review of Books*, July 2, 2015, https://lareviewofbooks.org/article/mapping-the-wander-lines-the-quiet-revelations-of-fernand-deligny/.
44. "Now, 3+1 is the formula of Oedipus, because it traps all social phenomena in the triangle (mommy, daddy, me) and then subsumes that triangle into a single transcendent notion of order. This is a closed notion of the social totality twice over—first because of trapping all phenomena in the triangle and second because the triangle is subsequently reduced to a unity. [Deleuze and Guattari] oppose this closed notion of the social totality what I would call an open totality. This alternative notion 'opens to the four winds, to the four corners of the social field (not even 3+1, but 4+n)' (p. 96 mid-top)" Michael Hardt, "Anti-Oedipus: Part 2," Reading Notes on Deleuze and Guattari Capitalism & Schizophrenia, Duke University, http://people.duke.edu/~hardt/Deleuze&Guattari.html.
45. In a text entitled "From Apparatus to Machine," Thomas Lamarre brings forth Guattari's inversion of the relation between machine and technology, writing: "The machine is not an apparatus. The challenge is to find the machine on which the apparatus depends." Lamarre, *The Anime-Machine*, xxvi.
46. Guattari, *Chaosmosis*, 33. Comolli shares an affinity with Guattari's perspective in this regard, writing: "a machine is always social before it is technical." Jean-Louis Comolli, "Machines of the Visible," in *The Cinematic Apparatus*, ed. Stephen Heath and Teresa De Lauretis (New York: St. Martin's Press, 1980), 122. Cited in Lisa Cartwright, *Screening the Body: Tracing Medicine's Visual Culture* (Minneapolis: University of Minnesota Press, 1995), 6.
47. For a historical account of La Borde, see François Dosse, "La Borde: Between Myth and Reality," in *Gilles Deleuze and Félix Guattari: Intersecting Lives* (New York: Columbia University Press, 2010), 40–54.

48. Félix Guattari, "Transversality," in *Psychoanalysis and Transversality: Texts and Interviews 1955–1971*, trans. Ames Hodges (Los Angeles: Semiotext(e), 2015), 111.
49. Félix Guattari, "The Transference," in *Psychoanalysis and Transversality: Texts and Interviews 1955–1971*, trans. Ames Hodges (Los Angeles: Semiotext(e), 2015), 79.
50. Guattari, *Psychoanalysis and Transversality*, 117
51. "Transversality is a dimension that tries to overcome both the impasse of pure verticality and that of mere horizontality." Guattari, *Psychoanalysis and Transversality*, 113
52. This transversality of roles effectively built on Ferenczi and Severn's adventure of mutual analysis recounted at the end of the introduction. For a more detailed picture of life at La Borde, see Gary Genosko, *Félix Guattari: A Critical Introduction* (London: Pluto, 2009), 58–62. Emmanuelle Guattari offers an intimate portrait of her childhood at the clinic in *La Petite Borde*. Emmanuelle Guattari, *I, Little Asylum* (Cambridge, MA: MIT Press, 2014).
53. Guattari, "Transversality," 118.
54. Guattari, "Transversality," 112 (translation modified).
55. Guattari, "Transversality," 112.
56. Félix Guattari, *Chaosophy: Texts and Interviews 1972–1977*, ed. Sylvère Lotringer, trans. David L. Sweet, Jarred Becker, and Taylor Adkins (Los Angeles: Semiotext(e), 2009), 266.
57. Gilles Deleuze, *Difference and Repetition*, trans. Paul Patton (New York: Columbia University Press, 1994), 1.
58. The only condition upon which film can be admitted as an object and still retain the force of artfulness is if it is viewed as an "ecosophic object." See my essay: Adam Szymanski, "*Uncle Boonmee Who Can Recall His Past Lives* and the Ecosophic Aesthetics of Peace," in *Nocturnal Fabulations: Ecology, Vitality and Opacity in the Cinema of Apichatpong Weerasethakul* (London: Open Humanities, 2017), 48–78.
59. "The object risks remaining countable, perceived only as the sum of its parts. What is of interest to me is what techniques are necessary to activate the more-than of objectness within the artistic context, what techniques are necessary to give the object the opportunity to take on the aura, as Walter Benjamin might say, of another kind of newly invented value, a value activated in the setting that transduces the everyday object into an artful one." Manning, *The Minor Gesture*, 69.
60. Félix Guattari, "Cinema of Desire," in *Chaosophy: Texts and Interviews 1972–1977*, ed. Sylvère Lotringer, trans. David L. Sweet, Jarred Becker, and Taylor Adkins (Los Angeles: Semiotext(e), 2009), 243.
61. Guattari, *Chaosmosis*, 35.
62. Guattari, *Chaosmosis*, 48.
63. Dosse, *Gilles Deleuze and Félix Guattari*, 223.
64. Lazzarato, *Signs and Machines*, 110–11 (quotation modified).
65. "Psychotherapy that is called 'scientific' (obviously, I'm not talking about its truth value, only its method, whether Freudian, anti-Freudian or neo-Freudian, fanatical Kleinian or crypto-Lacanian, whatever . . .)—this type of psychotherapy, I was saying, always contains a single premise that is clear and explicit: humans are alone! We are alone in the universe, therefore alone in the face of Science, and

consequently also alone in the face of the state." Nathan and Stengers, *Doctors and Healers*, 3–4.

66. Pure experience is "the instant field of the present at all times; the only one primal stuff or material in the world." William James, *Essays in Radical Empiricism* (Mineola, NY: Dover, 2003), 12, 2. David Lapoujade's work is helpful for the way it emphasizes the primacy of pure experience anterior to the emergence of subjectivity. He writes: "Pure experience is experience from the point of view of the event. The event arises at the intersection where subject and object meet (if that relation is privileged), and in their in-between, but before they are there: this is why the event is not their fusion; it comes before them. Subject and object are successors to it." David Lapoujade, *William James: Empiricism and Pragmatism*, trans. Thomas Lamarre (Durham, NC: Duke University Press, 2020), 15.

67. The terminus is a common site where vectors of belief—or streams of consciousness—meet, before continuing along their respective trajectories, having shared this terminal experience "in common." To meet at a terminus is to transcend the isolating threshold of the constituted self, to arrive at "the point at which one state of mind passes into another." James, *Essays in Radical Empiricism*, 132.

68. "The essential aspect of the first positive task is to ensure the machinic conversion of primal repression, there too in an adapted variable manner. Which is to say: undoing the blockage or the coincidence on which the repression properly speaking relies; transforming the apparent opposition of repulsion (the body without organs/the machines-partial objects) into a condition of real functioning; ensuring this functioning in the forms of attraction and production of intensities; thereafter integrating the failures in the attractive functioning, as well as enveloping the zero degree in the intensities produced; and thereby causing the desiring-machines to start up again. Such is the delicate and focal point that fills the function of transference in schizoanalysis-dispersing, schizophrenizing the perverse transference of psychoanalysis." Deleuze and Guattari, *Anti-Oedipus*, 339.

69. "All claims made about the processes of identification in actual spectators, powerful and important as they may be, are speculative. . . . They can tell us nothing definitive about the forms of sexual identification, or the potential meanings, produced with respect to actual spectators. . . . One must accept fundamentally that these positions exist only as potentialities that are ultimately undecidable with respect to any given spectator." D. N. Rodowick, *The Difficulty of Difference: Psychoanalysis, Sexual Difference and Film Theory* (London: Routledge, 1991), viii.

CHAPTER 3

1. Francesco Casetti identifies in 1970s film theory a "serious return" of the cinephobia (irrational fear of cinema) that was widespread from the early 1910s to the mid-1930s as the cinema first gained in popularity and social influence. Casetti, "Why Fears Matter: Cinephobia in Early Film Culture," *Screen* 59, no. 2 (Summer 2018): 156.
2. Laura Mulvey, "Visual Pleasure and Narrative Cinema," in *Film Theory and Criticism, 7th Edition*, ed. Leo Braudy and Marshall Cohen (New York: Oxford University Press, 2009), 713.

3. Laura Mulvey and Peter Wollen, "From Cinephilia to Film Studies," in *Inventing Film Studies*, ed. Lee Grieveson and Haidee Wasson (Durham, NC: Duke University Press, 2008), 228.

4. Laura Mulvey, "Some Reflections on the Cinephilia Question," *Framework: The Journal of Cinema and Media* 50, no. 1-2 (Fall 2009): 193.

5. "It was harder to combine a political allegiance to the Left and an allegiance to the culture of the United States. The political spectrum was changing by the late '60s and early 70s. There was the Vietnam War. As our political allegiance shifted toward the Third World there were also more opportunities to see its cinema." Mulvey and Wollen, "From Cinephilia to Film Studies," 228.

6. The darker Bazin is brought to the fore in the work of Dudley Andrew. In his book *André Bazin*, Andrew writes: "The world is 'mysterious' and 'ambiguous' not because it is as yet only partly disclosed, as if we need only to wait for scientists to finish their investigations. This would be a 'naive realism' imagining the world as some self-sufficient sphere which we approach now from one side, now from another, striving to penetrate it and use it. If we attribute to Bazin the ideas of those in his milieu, of Sartre, Marcel, Mounier, and Merleau-Ponty, then 'mystery' becomes a quality of the world itself rather than a state to be overcome." Andrew, *André Bazin* (New York: Oxford University Press, 2013), 100.

In "The Ontology of a Fetish," Andrew builds on this line of articulation. He writes: "Reading his reading notes I recognize two Bazins. On the one hand stands the sunny, textbook Bazin, for whom cinema reveals reality. This is the Bazin for whom films are the monstration of the world's self-presentation, offering epiphanies to the vigilant. On the other hand, as has become increasingly evident, a darker Bazin prefigures several philosophers in the post-Sartrean French context right up to our own day (Derrida, Deleuze, Nancy, Rancière)." Dudley Andrew, "The Ontology of a Fetish," *Film Quarterly* 61, no. 4 (Summer 2008): 66.

7. Christian Keathley, *Cinephilia and History, or the Wind in the Trees* (Bloomington: Indiana University Press, 2005), 7. Keathley's definition takes its cues from the influential interview between Paul Willemen and Noel King which in the early 1990s effectuated a similar consolidation between the revelatory and the fetishistic currents of film scholarship. See Willemen, "Through the Glass Darkly," 223-57.

8. The call for a dispassionate attitude in the discipline of film studies is represented by the following passage from Haidee Wasson, which she wrote in response to a public lecture by Dudley Andrew at Concordia University: "As we know, cinephilia, like any kind of object love, is complicated. But it's important to point out that as instrumental as the love of film may be for the achievements of film study, there is also an anti-intellectual and anti-institutional side to cinephilia that does not always serve the discipline or encourage healthy debate. The politics of taste are difficult; the politics of love perhaps even more so. Thus, while I certainly have my own romance with moving images, I also find myself increasingly wary of the anti-intellectual aspects of cinephilia, especially in times when we need to work especially hard to maintain our specificity in the context of an institutional politic that would rather have us say we do everything poorly than do one thing well. I don't think that this kind of love provides by itself the kind of impersonal and dispassionate currency we need to establish a foothold in meaningful debates,

particularly those that rise above and reach out across the humanities, let alone across to all of those who practice film studies." Haidee Wasson, "Response to Dudley Andrew: Small Discipline, Big Pictures," *Synoptique*, May 2010.

9. Jean-Luc Godard is the director whose creative activity typified the political compass of 1970s film theory. From the historical perspective afforded by half a century's passing, Godard's once-celebrated Maoist phase has not aged well. China has turned into a rogue superpower state which blends the economics of late capitalism with many traits of twentieth-century authoritarianisms. In a master class that he gave at the Toronto International Film Festival in 2012, Olivier Assayas echoed this sentiment and explains how his aversion to the authoritarian impulse of certain segments of French leftism in the 1970s has influenced his filmmaking. TIFF Originals, "OLIVIER ASSAYAS | Master Class | Festival 2012," n.p.

10. Peter Wollen, "An Alphabet of Cinema," *New Left Review* 12 (November-December 2001): 119.

11. "And while the Freudian fetish includes a trace of indexicality in its function as 'memorial,' the consumer of commodities is not known to whisper 'I know, but all the same . . .'" Octave Mannoni quoted in Laura Mulvey, *Fetishism and Curiosity*, 6.

12. Kaja Silverman draws a perspicuous analogy between the male child in the phallic stage and the cinema's spectator: "Like the little boy who sees the female genitals for the first time and who disavows the absence of the penis, this viewer refuses to acknowledge what he or she knows full well—that cinema is founded on the lack of the object." Silverman, *The Acoustic Mirror: The Female Voice in Psychoanalysis and Cinema* (Bloomington: Indiana University Press, 1988), 4. For a dissection of the continuities, and especially the discontinuities, between the child's perception of phallic absence and the film spectator, see Ben Singer, "Film, Photography, and Fetish: The Analyses of Christian Metz," *Cinema Journal* 27, no. 4 (Summer 1988): 4–22.

13. "Comolli provides a much more convincing articulation of cinematic fetishism when he proposes that what stands in for the absent real is a simulated real—what he calls 'an impression of reality.'" Silverman, *The Acoustic Mirror*, 5.

14. Mulvey, "Visual Pleasure," 722.

15. In his essay on fetishism, Freud writes: "Yes, in his [the child's] mind the woman *has* got a penis, in spite of everything; but this penis is no longer the same as it was before. Something else has taken its place, has been appointed its substitute, as it were, and now inherits the interest which was formerly directed to its predecessor. But this interest suffers an extraordinary increase as well, because the horror of castration has set up a memorial to itself in the creation of this substitute." Sigmund Freud, "Fetishism," in *The Standard Edition of the Complete Psychological Works of Sigmund Freud, Vol. XXI*, trans. James Strachey (London: Hogarth, 1961), 4536.

16. Buttressing the explanation that I provided above as to why cinephilia is nonfetishistic, Prakash Younger states convincingly: "The fundamental heresy, which I hereby expose as incoherent and absurd, is that one can love films in themselves. If, as [Susan] Sontag claims, films can 'encapsulate everything,' it is only because they function as portals to reality; in the final analysis films can never be better than *metaxu*, means to an end, bridges or windows that allow contact with and reflection on the real world of human beings, living, dead and yet-to-be-born, with

whom we have erotic and ethical relations. The compulsive fixation on one's own past responses only testifies to a fear of contact and a lack of hope in reflection that are symptomatic of (what was once called) the postmodern condition. It is not that self-proclaiming cinephiles have not enjoyed this contact or reflection, but that their retrospective accounts of the phenomenon are an abusive reduction of their own experience and a criminal devaluation of the experience of others. By fetishizing cinephilic experience and making it exclusive they collapse the movement of opening and dialogue which the experience itself always inaugurates: paradoxical as it may seem, most of the current discourse on the topic is both uncinephilic and unphilosophical." Prakash Younger, "What Is Cinephilosophy? A Bazinian Paradigm, Part 1: A Philosophical Preamble, for the Love of Truth," *Offscreen* 13, no. 2 (February 2009): n.p.

17. André Bazin, "In Defense of Rossellini," in *Bazin and Italian Neorealism*, ed. Burt Cardullo (New York: Continuum, 2011), 170.

18. Willemen, "Through the Glass Darkly," 237.

19. It should be noted that while the film does end on a happy note, and the couple reconciles through an embrace in a medium-close-up shot, the final shot of the film does not conclude in the manner characteristic of classical Hollywood convention. Instead, Rossellini's camera drifts to the left of the couple through a crane shot that follows the San Gennaro procession, immersing the characters' personal drama in the Neapolitan cycles of life and death.

20. The breaking of narrative causation is a broader tendency within neorealism. See Bazin's "Umberto D: A Great Work," where he advances his vision for a cinema of duration based on Zavattini's thirteen theses on cinema.

21. Willemen, "Through the Glass Darkly," 236.

22. Willemen, "Through the Glass Darkly," 237.

23. Revelation presupposes what Slavoj Žižek calls an "engaged subjectivity" in his discussion of Saint Paul's conversion. He writes: "The engaged observer perceives positive historical occurrences as parts of the Event of the French Revolution only to the extent that he observes them from the unique engaged standpoint of revolution.... In this precise sense, an Event involves subjectivity: the engaged 'subject perspective' on the Event is part of the Event itself.... Christian revelation is thus an example (although probably *the* example) of how we, human beings, are not constrained to the positivity of Being; of how, from time to time, in a contingent and unpredictable way, a truth-Event can occur that opens up to us the possibility of participating in another life by remaining faithful to the truth-Event." Žižek, "Paul and the Truth Event," in *Paul's New Moment: Continental Philosophy and the Future of Christian Theology*, ed. John Millbank, Slavoj Žižek, and Creston Davis (Grand Rapids, MI: Brazos, 2010), 83, 94.

24. Younger, "What Is Cinephilosophy?"

25. Simone Weil, *The Need for Roots: Prelude of a Declaration of Duties towards Mankind*, trans. Arthur Willis (London: Routledge, 2002), 247, quoted in Younger, "What Is Cinephilosophy?"

26. Younger, "What Is Cinephilosophy?"

27. The vocation of transferring the passage from one state to another, even when that passage is from life to death, is what differentiates cinema from still

photography. André Bazin, "Death Every Afternoon," in *Rites of Realism: Essays on Corporeal Cinema*, ed. Ivone Margulies, trans. Mark A. Cohen (Durham, NC: Duke University Press, 2003), 30.

28. "Singularity is not given in a massive opposition with generality or universality, but as a praxial crossroads and, thus, as a choice. This ethical choice of the always possible reimmersion in questions like 'what am I doing here?' 'what am I doing right here?' 'do I have a responsibility for what I am at the moment?' but also, for what will come afterwards, not just for me but for the other, for the entirety of universes of sense that are concerned?" Félix Guattari, "The Vertigo of Immanence: Interview with John Johnston, June 1992," in *The Guattari Effect*, ed. Eric Alliez and Andrew Goffey (London: Continuum, 2011), 32.

29. "If reading Whitehead means accepting to commit oneself to an adventure whose starting point is always the formulation of a problem, without the legitimacy of the problem being well-founded, without the possibility of answering it being justified in terms of the right to think, one may rightly wonder if the formulations he attempted are still able to engage us today." Isabelle Stengers, *Thinking with Whitehead: A Free and Wild Creation of Concepts*, trans. Michael Chase (Cambridge, MA: Harvard University Press, 2011), 10.

30. "DP/30 @ TIFF: Clouds of Sils Maria, Olivier Assayas," YouTube, https://www.youtube.com/watch?v=qkZBosAanMI.

31. Oliver Whitney, "Kristen Stewart Addresses the Irony of 'Clouds of Sils Maria,'" Huffington Post, October 9, 2014, https://www.huffingtonpost.ca/entry/kristen-stewart-clouds-of-sils-maria_n_5961102?ri18n=true.

32. Whitney, "Kristen Stewart Addresses the Irony."

33. Assayas returned to the very same locations in the Swiss Alps where Fanck had shot ninety years earlier. Assayas also opted to shoot on celluloid film in the age of digital filmmaking, and thus made use of the same technological medium as Fanck as well.

34. André Bazin, "De Sica: Metteur en Scène," in *André Bazin and Italian Neorealism*, ed. Bert Cardullo (New York: Continuum, 2011), 80.

35. Dudley Andrew presents Serge Daney's "Cahiers axiom" in *What Cinema Is!* "The Cahiers axiom is this: that the cinema has a fundamental rapport with reality and that the real is not what is represented—and that's final." Olivier Assayas was a staff writer at *Cahiers du Cinéma* from 1980 to 1985, a period which overlapped with Daney's tenure as editor-in-chief.

36. André Bazin, "Ontology of the Photographic Image," in *What Is Cinema?* trans. Hugh Gray (Berkeley: University of California Press, 2005), 14.

37. On the flâneur and the explorer as prototypes for the modern cinephile, see the following two excerpts from works on cinephilia by Thomas Elsaesser and Christian Keathley: "The natural home of this cinephilia is neither the university nor a city's second-run cinemas, but the film festival and the film museum, whose increasingly international circuits the cinephile critic, programmer, or distributor frequents as flaneur, prospector, and explorer." Thomas Elsaesser, "Cinephilia or the Uses of Disenchantment," in *Cinephilia: Movies, Love and Memory*, ed. Marijke de Valck and Malte Hagener (Amsterdam: Amsterdam University Press, 2005), 36. "Unlike the rail traveler, the cinephile does not simply forsake the primary, attentive

viewing mode ... for its alternative, the panoramic. Rather, like that prototype of the modern spectator, the *flâneur*, the cinephile engages in both modes simultaneously." Keathley, *Cinephilia and History*, 44.

38. "In the theatre, a film continues to seem like an event against which one can measure oneself, and from which one can rediscover one's surroundings. Think of how there, more than elsewhere, a film is not reduced to something ordinary or habitual—it conserves a certain noteworthiness with respect to the everyday. Or think of how it obliges one to take steps in order to meet it—leave the house, buy a ticket, mix with the crowd—which give importance to the activity. Or how it makes one share it with others, as a sort of small privilege. In the theatre, more than elsewhere, a film is an event, and in this sense it becomes a small enigma that provokes the spectators, as it restitutes a consciousness of self and of one's surroundings.... This dimension of experience is really what is at stake, and as long as cinema is able to maintain this, it will survive." Francesco Casetti, "Back to the Motherland: The Film Theatre in the Postmedia Age," *Screen* 52, no. 1 (Spring 2011): 12.

39. Giorgio Agamben, *The Adventure*, trans. Lorenzo Chiesa (London: MIT Press, 2018), 72, 54.

CHAPTER 4

1. Erin Manning, "Introduction," in *Nocturnal Fabulations: Ecology, Vitality and Opacity in the Cinema of Apichatpong Weerasethakul* (London: Open Humanities, 2017), 16.

2. Deleuze and Guattari, *What Is Philosophy?* 171.

3. On the structural position of voyeurism alongside fetishism and identification in modern film theory, see Mary Ann Doane's "Film and the Masquerade: Theorising the Female Spectator," Gaylyn Studlar's "Masochism and the Perverse Pleasures of the Cinema," and Thomas Elsaesser's "Cinephilia or the Uses of Disenchantment."

In "Film and the Masquerade: Theorising the Female Spectator," Doane foregrounds the three defining themes of modern film theory which have been broached in this study: identification with an ideal ego, fetishism, and voyeurism. She writes: "It is quite tempting to foreclose entirely the possibility of female spectatorship, to repeat at the level of theory the gesture of the photograph, given the history of a cinema which relies so heavily on voyeurism, fetishism, and identification with an ego ideal conceivable only in masculine terms." Doane, "Film and the Masquerade," *Screen* 23, no. 3-4 (1982): 87.

For her part, Studlar writes: "The male spectator escapes the castration anxiety the female image evokes either by a sadistic voyeurism (demystifying the female) or through fetishistic scopophilia. The latter, a 'complete disavowal of castration,' turns the female into a fetish, the signifier of the absent phallus." Studlar, "Masochism and the Perverse Pleasures of the Cinema," *Quarterly Review of Film & Video* 9, no. 4 (1984): 274.

Elsaesser also emphasizes modern film theory's tendency to pathologize spectatorship under the categories of fetishism and voyeurism. He writes: "The Theory both covered over and preserved the fact that ambivalence about the status of

Hollywood as the good/bad object persisted, notwithstanding that the love of cinema was now called by a different name: voyeurism, fetishism, and scopophilia. But naming here is shaming; nothing could henceforth hide the painful truth that by 1975, cinephilia had been dragged out of its closet, the darkened womblike auditorium, and revealed itself as a source of disappointment: the magic of the movies, in the cold light of day, had become a manipulation of regressive fantasies and the place of the big male escape from sexual difference. Elsaesser, "Cinephilia or the Uses of Disenchantment," in *Cinephilia: Movies, Love and Memory*, ed. Marijke de Valck and Malte Hagener (Amsterdam: Amsterdam University Press, 2005), 32.

4. The concept of the *pharmakon* is best known today through Derrida's chapter "Plato's Pharmacy," where he reads the *Phaedrus* dialogues concerning writing's effect on speech, memory, and logos. Socrates compares the written texts Phaedrus has brought along to a drug (a *pharmakon*), which introduces an ambivalence: it may be a remedy or a poison. "This charm," Derrida writes, "this spellbinding virtue, this power of fascination, can be—alternately or simultaneously—beneficent or maleficent. For example, writing is a remedy because it solves the problem of forgetting, and yet it is also a poison because it weakens memory and dulls the philosopher's dialogic propensities. Writing is no more valuable, says Plato, as a remedy than as a poison.... There is no such thing as a harmless remedy. The pharmakon can never be simply beneficial." Jacques Derrida, *Dissemination* (Chicago: University of Chicago Press, 1981), 90.

5. Jean-Luc Nancy, "The Intruder," in *Extreme Bodies: The Use and Abuse of the Body in Art*, ed. Francesca Alfano Miglietti (Milan: Skira, 2003), 248.

6. "There is increasing empirical research suggesting that intrusive visual images and memories are a common feature of many disorders." C. R. Brewin, J. D. Gregory, M. Lipton, and N. Burgess, "Intrusive Images in Psychological Disorders: Characteristics, Neural Mechanisms, and Treatment Implications." *Psychological Review* 117, no. 1 (2010): 210-32. In 1909 Freud himself observed that "the most heterogeneous psychical structures can be heaped together under the name of 'obsessional ideas.'" Sigmund Freud, "Notes Upon a Case of Obsessional Neurosis," in *The Standard Edition of the Complete Psychological Works of Sigmund Freud, Volume X: Little Hans and The Rat Man*, trans. James Strachey (London: Hogarth, 1955), 220.

7. Stanley Rachman, "Unwanted Intrusive Images in Obsessive Compulsive Disorders," *Journal of Behavior Therapy and Experimental Psychiatry* 38, no. 4 (2007): 404.

8. Padmal de Silva, "Obsessional-Compulsive Imagery," *Behaviour Research and Therapy* 24, no. 3 (1986): 341.

9. Rachman, "Unwanted Intrusive Images," 405.

10. E. A. Holmes, N. Grey, and K. A. Young, "Intrusive Images and 'Hotspots' of Trauma Memories in Posttraumatic Stress Disorder: An Exploratory Investigation of Emotions and Cognitive Themes," *Journal of Behavior Therapy and Experimental Psychiatry* 36, no. 1 (2005): 4.

11. Examples include M. A. Hagenaars et al., "Intrusive Images and Intrusive Thoughts as Different Phenomena: Two Experimental Studies," *Memory* 18, no. 1 (2010): 76–84; E. A. Holmes, C. R. Brewin, and R. G. Hennessey, "Trauma Films, Information Processing, and Intrusive Memory Development," *Journal of Experimental Psychology. General* 133, no. 1 (2004): 3–22; and M. J. Horowitz, "Psychic

Trauma: Return of Images after a Stress Film," *Archives of General Psychiatry* 20, no. 5 (1969): 552–59.
12. Horowitz, "Psychic Trauma," 552.
13. Bessel van der Kolk is best known for his popular book on somatic-based trauma treatments, *The Body Keeps the Score*. The history of psychology has also shown him to be partially responsible (alongside the psycho-traumatologist Onno van der Hart) for bringing Pierre Janet into the twenty-first century and documenting Janet's working hypothesis of the subconscious, to which Freud's model of the dynamic unconscious was indebted. In "The Intrusive Past," van der Hart and van der Kolk posit intrusive images in cases of PTSD as caused by embodied memory of a traumatic event that short-circuits the narrative memory system. Van der Kolk and van der Hart, "The Intrusive Past: The Flexibility of Memory and the Engraving of Trauma," *American Imago* 48, no. 4 (1991): 433.
14. See Gaylyn Studlar's "Masochism and the Perverse Pleasures of the Cinema" on the possibility of a masochistic spectator against the sadism which Metz asserts as fundamental to the scopic drive. Studlar incorporates D. N. Rodowick's critique of Mulvey's "Visual Pleasure and Narrative Cinema" in "The Difficulty of Difference," wherein Mulvey "cannot admit that the masculine look contains passive elements and can signify submission to rather than possession of the female." Studlar, "Masochism and the Perverse Pleasures of the Cinema," *Quarterly Review of Film & Video* 9, no. 4 (1984): 274; and Rodowick, "The Difficulty of Difference," *Wide Angle* 5, no. 1 (1982): 7–9.
15. Freud, "Notes Upon a Case," 243.
16. Freud, "Notes Upon a Case," 162.
17. Freud, "Notes Upon a Case," 174.
18. "In the first place the character of compulsion neurotics shows a predominant trait of painful conscientiousness which is a symptom of reaction against the temptation which lurks in the unconscious, and which develops into the highest degrees of guilty conscience as their illness grows worse." Sigmund Freud, *Totem and Taboo: Resemblances between the Psychic Lives of Savages and Neurotics* (London: George Routledge and Sons, 1919), 115–16.

"One day the expelled brothers joined forces, slew and ate the father, and thus put an end to the father horde. Together they dared and accomplished what would have remained impossible for them singly. Perhaps some advance in culture, like the use of a new weapon, had given them the feeling of superiority. Of course these cannibalistic savages ate their victim. This violent primal father had surely been the envied and feared model for each of the brothers. Now they accomplished their identification with him by devouring him and each acquiring a part of his strength. The totem feast, which is perhaps mankind's first celebration, would be the repetition and commemoration of this memorable, criminal act with which so many things began, social organization, moral restrictions and religion." Freud, *Totem and Taboo*, 285–86.
19. Freud, *Totem and Taboo*, 123–24.
20. This formal parental cathexis constitutes what Gilles Deleuze and Félix Guattari term a "parental image." They write: "When we are invited to go beyond a simplistic conception of Oedipus based on parental images, in order to define symbolic

functions within a structure, it is in vain that the traditional daddy-mommy are replaced by a mother-function, a father-function; we don't quite see what there is to gain by this, except for the founding of the universality of Oedipus beyond the variability of images; the fusing of desire even more strongly to law and prohibitions; and the pushing of the process of oedipalization of the unconscious to its limits." Deleuze and Guattari, *Anti-Oedipus*, 82.

21. The author here builds on his earlier work, *The Treatment of Obsessions* (New York: Oxford University Press, 2003).

22. Rachman, "Unwanted Intrusive Images," 408.

23. It is important to note that Freud does admit signs into his clinic, and psychoanalysis is in fact predicated on a hermeneutics of signification, a premise which Lacan went on to structuralize. The signs in the Rat Man case are his obsessive neurotic symptoms revealed during free association, and these are interpreted according to the psychodynamics of the Oedipus complex. What Freudian psychoanalysis does not admit as a sign is the intrusive image itself, which is merely the substitutional ideational content.

24. Metz, "The Imaginary Signifier," 60.

25. Metz, "The Imaginary Signifier," 60–61.

26. Metz, "The Imaginary Signifier," 63.

27. On flashbacks as a type of involuntary memory, see Brewin et al., "Intrusive Images in Psychological Disorders," 210–32. According to the *DSM-5*'s symptomatology of PTSD, the presence of at least one "intrusion symptom" is a requirement for the diagnostic criteria to be fulfilled. Intrusion symptoms include recurrent and distressing memories of the traumatic event, nightmares, dissociative reactions, and psychological or physiological reactions to events which resemble the traumatic event. American Psychiatric Association, *DSM-5: Diagnostic and Statistical Manual of Mental Disorders* (Washington, DC: American Psychiatric Association, 2013), 271.

28. For a summary of the difference between the verbally accessible memory (VAM) system and the situationally accessible memory (SAM) system which are central to the dual representation theory of PTSD, see Hagenaars et al., "Intrusive Images and Intrusive Thoughts," 76–84. This distinction between the VAM and the SAM maps onto the earlier distinction between "narrative memory" and "traumatic memory" in Pierre Janet's work. See the subheading "Narrative and Traumatic Memory" in van der Kolk and van der Hart, "The Intrusive Past," 425–54.

29. Van der Kolk and van der Hart, "The Intrusive Past," 428.

30. Van der Kolk and van der Hart, "The Intrusive Past," 429–30. For Janet's original account of the case, consult the following French sources: Pierre Janet, *L'Amnésie et la dissociation des souvenirs par l'émotion* (Paris: F. Alcan, 1904); and Pierre Janet, *L'État mental des hystériques: Les Stigmates mentaux* (Paris: Ancienne Librairie Germer Balliere et Cie, 1911). Van der Kolk, van der Hart, and Paul Brown provide a comprehensive overview of Janet's publications on PTSD in "Pierre Janet's Treatment of Post-Traumatic Stress," *Journal of Traumatic Stress* 2, no. 4 (1989): 379–95.

31. "In the cave, the prisoner-spectators are seated, still, prisoners because immobilized: unable to move—constraint or paralysis? It is true that they are chained, but, freed, they would still refuse to leave the place where they are; and so obstinately would they resist that they might put to death anyone trying to lead them out.

In other words, this first constraint, against their will, this deprivation of movement which was imposed on them initially, this motor inhibition which affected so much their future dispositions, conditions them to the point that they prefer to stay where they are and to perpetuate this immobility rather than leave.... Forced immobility is undoubtedly a valuable argument for the demonstration/description that Plato makes of the human condition: the coincidence of religious and idealist conceptions; but the initial immobility was not invented by Plato; it can also refer to the forced immobility of the child who is without motor resources at birth, and to the forced immobility of the sleeper who we know repeats the postnatal state and even intrauterine existence; but this is also the immobility that the visitor to the dim space rediscovers, leaning back into his chair. It might even be added that the spectators' immobility is characteristic of the filmic apparatus as a whole." Jean-Louis Baudry, "The Apparatus: Metapsychological Approaches to the Impression of Reality in Cinema," in *Film Theory and Criticism* (New York: Oxford University Press, 2009), 174–75.

32. M. A. Hagenaars et al., "The Effect of Hypnotically Induced Somatoform Dissociation on the Development of Intrusions after an Aversive Film," *Cognition & Emotion* 22, no. 5 (2008): 944.

33. On the role of tonic immobility in the development of intrusive memories, see J. M. E. Kuiling, F. Klaassen, and M. A. Hagenaars, "The Role of Tonic Immobility and Control in the Development of Intrusive Memories after Experimental Trauma," *Memory* 27, no. 6 (2019): 772–79. For a description of how the sexual abuse of children induces immobility in its victims, see Aleksandar Dimitrijević's lecture "What Is Trauma and How to Avoid and Heal It: Lecture I," at Stillpoint Spaces Berlin: https://www.youtube.com/watch?v=oqZ6nILqYd4&t=957s.

34. Van der Kolk and van der Hart, "The Intrusive Past," 437.

35. "The substitution technique is one of Janet's most original contributions to psychotherapy." Van der Hart et al. archive how it has gone on to influence the work of various clinicians working in the 1970s and 1980s: Erickson and Rossi, 1979; Eichelman, 1985; Lamb, 1982, 1985; Miller, 1986; Waxman, 1982." Onno van der Hart, Paul Brown, and Bessel A. van der Kolk, "Pierre Janet's Treatment of Post-Traumatic Stress," *Journal of Traumatic Stress* 2, no. 4 (1989): 393.

Speckens et al. write: "Previous research has shown that patients with OCD and comorbid posttraumatic stress disorder might not benefit as much from standard behavioral treatment as those without. Consequently, additional therapeutic interventions such as imaginal reliving and restructuring of meaning or imagery modification of traumatic memories might be helpful in OCD patients with mental images that are linked to earlier adverse events." Anne E. M. Speckens, Ann Hackmann, Anke Ehlers, and Bea Cuthbert, "Imagery Special Issue: Intrusive Images and Memories of Earlier Adverse Events in Patients with Obsessive Compulsive Disorder," *Journal of Behavior Therapy and Experimental Psychiatry* 38, no. 4 (2007): 411.

Not coincidentally, given the similarities between filmmaking and imagery rescripting, the film director Alejandro Jodorowsky espouses very similar methods for psychological healing, which he calls "psychomagic." Alejandro Jodorowsky, *Psychomagic: The Transformative Power of Shamanic Psychotherapy* (Rochester, VT: Inner Traditions/Bear, 2010).

36. E. A. Holmes, Arnoud Arntz, and Mervin R. Smucker, "Imagery Rescripting in Cognitive Behavior Therapy: Images, Treatment Techniques and Outcomes," *Journal of Behavior Therapy and Experimental Psychiatry* 38, no. 4 (2007): 299.

37. Rachman, "Unwanted Intrusive Images," 409. Holmes et al. emphasize image transformation and substitution in their description of imagery rescripting: "The Imagery Rescripting (IR) techniques addressed are those in which either (1) a pre-existing negative mental image (IR 'Type A') is transformed into a more benign image (i.e., negative image to positive image rescripting), or (2) a new positive image (IR 'Type B') is constructed afresh to capture those positive meanings needed to counteract the key psychological concerns for a patient (i.e., using a fresh positive image to rescript negative schematic beliefs)." Holmes et al., "Imagery Rescripting in Cognitive Behavior Therapy," 298.

38. For an example of this type of approach, see the clinical psychologist Gino Medeoro's video tutorial at https://www.youtube.com/watch?v=P6UhsyzeNCI.

39. Erin Manning deploys the term "relational movement" to emphasize movement's metastable and creative qualities. For a discussion of relational movement, see Erin Manning, *Relationscapes: Movement, Art, Philosophy* (Cambridge, MA: MIT Press, 2009).

40. The touchstone defense of cinema as an indexical art in the age of digital filmmaking is Dudley Andrew, *What Cinema Is! Bazin's Quest and Its Charge* (Chichester, UK: Wiley-Blackwell, 2010).

41. Nevertheless, the fact of having "missed" the reality rendered imagistic, in the manner described by Metz, raises a justifiable suspicion and makes the case in the realm of political aesthetics for the adherence to a broader neorealist ethos capable of augmenting the indexical specificity of the medium.

42. Gilles Deleuze, *Cinema 1: The Movement-Image*, trans. Hugh Tomlinson and Barbara Habberjam (Minneapolis: University of Minnesota Press, 1986), 84.

43. Deleuze and Guattari, *What Is Philosophy?* 167–68.

CONCLUSION

1. On the epidemic of mental illness from the perspective of a psychiatrist who questions psychiatric orthodoxy, see Marcia Angell's essay "The Epidemic of Mental Illness: Why?" in *The New York Review of Books,* June 23, 2011, https://www.nybooks.com/articles/2011/06/23/epidemic-mental-illness-why/. Angell is the former editor-in-chief of the *New England Journal of Medicine* and a senior lecturer in the Department of Global Health and Social Medicine at the Harvard Medical School.

2. For an example of a high-profile engagement with this notion of the "new normal," see Richard Florida's article "The Lasting Normal for the Post-Pandemic City," Bloomberg CityLab, June 25, 2020, https://www.bloomberg.com/news/features/2020-06-25/the-new-normal-after-the-coronavirus-pandemic.

3. Marcuse, *Eros and Civilization*, xix.

4. Guattari and Negri describe their project as follows: "The project: to rescue 'communism' from its own disrepute. Once invoked as the liberation of work through mankind's collective creation, communism has instead stifled humanity. We who

see in communism the liberation of both collective and individual possibilities must reverse that regimentation of thought and desire which terminates the individual." Guattari and Negri, *Communists Like Us*, 7.

5. Guattari and Negri, *Communists Like Us*, 17

6. Felix Guattari, "The Proliferation of Margins," in *Autonomia: Post-Political Politics*, ed. Sylvère Lotringer, trans. Richard Gardner and Sybil Walker (Los Angeles: Semiotext(e), 2007), 110.

7. Peter Pál Pelbart, "Modes of Exhaustion, Modes of Existence," *Inflexions* 10 (2017): 137, https://www.inflexions.org/exhaustion/PDFs/08_Pelbart.pdf.

8. Lewis R. Gordon, *Existentia Africana: Understanding Africana Existential Thought* (New York: Routledge, 2013), 7.

9. "I regard existentialism—the popularly named ideological movement—as a fundamentally European historical phenomenon. It is, in effect, the history of European literature that bears that name. On the other hand, we can regard philosophies of existence—the specialized term that I sometimes call existential philosophies—as philosophical questions premised upon concerns of freedom, anguish, responsibility, embodied agency, sociality, and liberation. Philosophies of existence are marked by a centering of what is often known as the situation of questioning or inquiry itself. Another term for situation is the lived context of concern." Gordon, *Existential Africana*, 10.

10. Pelbart, "Modes of Exhaustion, Modes of Existence," 141.

11. Franco "Bifo" Berardi, "Freedom and Potency," *e-flux* 116 (March 2021), https://www.e-flux.com/journal/116/378694/freedom-and-potency/.

12. Berardi, "Freedom and Potency." Potency is an ontological power to recompose subjectivity. On the politics of "ontopower," Massumi writes: "Capitalist power, it was said earlier, is an ontopower: a positive power of becoming, a creative power operating relationally between the oscillatory poles of the dividual and the transindividual (its own individualist rhetoric notwithstanding; or more precisely, withstanding all too well its paradox). Ontopower, it was also said, can only be countered by ontopower." Brian Massumi, *Ontopower: War, Powers, and the State of Perception* (Durham, NC: Duke University Press, 2015), 93.

13. The 12-part DVD series of interviews about Clark's work, *Lygia Clark: Archive pour une oeuvre-événement* (*Lygia Clark: Archive for an Event-Work*) (Suely Rolnik, 2011), provides an in-depth discussion of her participatory performances from the period.

14. Suely Rolnik, "Molding a Contemporary Soul: The Empty-Full of Lygia Clark," in *The Experimental Exercise of Freedom: Lygia Clark, Gego, Mathias Goeritz, Hélio Oiticica and Mira Schendel*, ed. Rina Carvajal and Alma Ruiz (Los Angeles: Museum of Contemporary Art, 1999), 99.

15. Rolnik, "Molding a Contemporary Soul," 100.

16. Metz, "The Imaginary Signifier," 48–49.

17. This is how the Chilean filmmaker Alejandro Jodorowsky, together with the actress and poet Marianne Costa, conceives of the tarot; not as a tool for divination but as a signifier of unconscious pathways. He writes: "It seemed to me that instead of using the Tarot like a crystal ball, making it a tool that enabled exotic seers to penetrate hypothetical futures, I would put it into service for a new form

of psychoanalysis: Tarology." Jodorowsky and Costa, *The Way of Tarot: The Spiritual Teacher in the Cards*, trans. Jon E. Graham (Rochester, VT: Destiny Books, 2009), 23.

18. Félix Guattari, *The Machinic Unconscious: Essays in Schizoanalysis*, trans. Taylor Adkins (Los Angeles: Semiotext(e), 2011), 10.

19. Stanley D. Glick, Isabelle M. Maisonneuve, and Karen K. Szumlinski, "18-Methoxycoronaridine (18-MC) and Ibogaine: Comparison of Antiaddictive Efficacy, Toxicity, and Mechanisms of Action," *Annals of the New York Academy of Sciences* 914, no. 1 (2000): 369–86.

20. "You have heard what the Catholics tell us regarding a fruit that our first parents ate. What kind of fruit did our parents think they ate, Adam-Obola and Eve-Biome? What type of tree was it? They are lying because they do not want to tell us the truth. For this reason God left the iboga, so that men would see their bodies as God had made them, as He himself has hidden inside them. Therefore brothers take the iboga, the iboga plant that God gave to Adam and Eve, Obola and Biome. They take it so that the eyes and ears which were closed at the moment of the fall are opened and the clean conscience which was lost is restored, so that they can know what is hidden in their bodies." Stanislaw Świderski, "Les Récits biblique dans l'adaptation africaine," *Journal of Religion in Africa* 10, no. 3 (1979): 208–9.

21. On the three stages of the iboga experience (acute phase, evaluative phase, residual stimulation phase) and their respective durations, see The Third Wave, "The Ultimate Guide to Ibogaine," 2017, https://thethirdwave.co/psychedelics/ibogaine/.

22. Stanislaw Świderski, "Les Visions d'iboga," *Anthropos* 76, no. 3/4 (1981): 413, 404.

23. MindMed corporate website in 2022.

24. On the effectiveness of ibogaine treatments in human participants, see A. K. Davis et al., "Subjective Effectiveness of Ibogaine Treatment for Problematic Opioid Consumption: Short- and Long-Term Outcomes and Current Psychological Functioning," *Journal of Psychedelic Studies* 1 (2017): 1–9, https://doi.org/10.1556/2054.01.2017.009.

25. Or in situations where addiction is not an issue, iboga shows the reason for whatever ailment or existential impasse may have led the patient to receive the plant. While most studies into ibogaine's clinical application tend to focus on severe opioid addiction, the plant's traditional use is much more expansive, and is an intrinsic ingredient in the Bwiti way of life.

On the excavation of unconscious images, Joseph Barsuglia and coauthors have the following to say: "In individuals with substance use disorders, ibogaine stimulates heightened memory retrieval specifically related to drug abuse, the perception of one's own future with or without drug use, and visions which reveal powerful insights into the psychological factors contributing to the addiction, such as emotionally unresolved personal traumas (Schenberg et al., 2017). Several studies have shown that lifetime trauma incidence is a primary predictor of developing an addictive disorder (Konkolÿ Thege et al., 2017; Mandavia et al., 2016), and during ibogaine treatment, individuals with different forms of substance addictions consistently report therapeutic processing of autobiographical imagery, childhood experiences, and evocation of repressed traumatic memories (Davis et al., 2017; Schenberg et al., 2017; Winkelman, 2014)." Joseph P. Barsuglia et al., "A Case Report SPECT Study and Theoretical Rationale for the Sequential Administration of Ibogaine and

5-MeO-DMT in the Treatment of Alcohol Use Disorder," *Progress in Brain Research* 242 (2018): 121–58.

26. On the importance of the confession in Bwiti, see Stanislaw Świderski's "Les Visions d'iboga" and Giorgio Samorini's "The Bwiti Religion and the Psychoactive Plant Tabernanthe Iboga (Equatorial Africa)," *Integration* 5 (1995): 105–14.

27. Tobie Nathan, *L'Influence qui guérit* (Paris: Odile Jacob, 2009), 11. My translation.

Filmography

Après Mai (*Something in the Air*) (Olivier Assayas, 2012)
Ararat (Atom Egoyan, 2002)
Clouds of Sils Maria (Olivier Assayas, 2014)
Das Wolkenphänomen von Maloja (*Cloud Phenomena of Maloja*) (Arnold Fanck, 1924)
Der heilige Berg (*The Holy Mountain*) (Arnold Fanck, 1926)
Die bitteren Tränen der Petra von Kant (*The Bitter Tears of Petra von Kant*) (Rainer Werner Fassbinder, 1972)
Désordre (*Disorder*) (Olivier Assayas, 1986)
Fin août, début septembre (*Late August, Early September*) (Olivier Assayas, 1998)
Irma Vep (Olivier Assayas, 1996)
L'Eau froide (*Cold Water*) (Olivier Assayas, 1994)
La Désenchantée (*The Disenchanted*) (Benoît Jacquot, 1990)
La Fille de 15 ans (*The 15-Year-Old Girl*) (Jacques Doillon, 1989)
Les Quatre Cent Coups (*The 400 Blows*) (François Truffaut, 1959)
Les Vampires (Louis Feuillade, 1915–16)
Lygia Clark: Archive pour une œuvre-événement (Suely Rolnik, 2011)
Nuit et brouillard (*Night and Fog*) (Alain Resnais, 1956)
Paris s'éveille (*Paris Awakens*) (Olivier Assayas, 1991)
Personal Shopper (Olivier Assayas, 2016)
Rendez-Vous (André Téchiné, 1985)
Shoah (Claude Lanzmann, 1985)
Viaggio in Italia (*Voyage to Italy*) (Roberto Rossellini, 1954)

Bibliography

Agamben, Giorgio. *The Adventure.* Translated by Lorenzo Chiesa. Cambridge, MA: MIT Press, 2018.
American Psychiatric Association. *DSM-III: Diagnostic and Statistical Manual of Mental Disorders, Third Edition.* Washington, DC: American Psychiatric Association, 1980.
American Psychiatric Association. *DSM-5: Diagnostic and Statistical Manual of Mental Disorders, Fifth Edition.* Washington, DC: American Psychiatric Association, 2013.
Andrew, Dudley. *André Bazin.* New York: Oxford University Press, 1978.
Andrew, Dudley. *André Bazin, Revised Edition.* New York: Oxford University Press, 2013.
Andrew, Dudley. "The Ontology of a Fetish." *Film Quarterly* 61, no. 4 (Summer 2008): 62–66.
Andrew, Dudley. *What Cinema Is! Bazin's Quest and Its Charge.* West Sussex, UK: Wiley-Blackwell, 2010.
Angell, Marcia. "The Epidemic of Mental Illness: Why?" *The New York Review of Books.* June 23, 2011. https://www.nybooks.com/articles/2011/06/23/epidemic-mental-illness-why/.
Astruc, Alexandre. "The Birth of a New Avant-Garde: La Caméra-Stylo." In *Film Manifestos and Global Film Cultures: A Critical Anthology,* edited by Scott MacKenzie. Berkeley: University of California Press, 2014.
Aumont, Jacques, Alain Bergala, Michel Marie, and Marc Vernet. *Esthétique du film.* Paris: Fernand Nathan, 1983.
Barlow, David H., ed. "Special Section on the Dodo Bird Verdict." *Clinical Psychology: Science and Practice* 1, no. 9 (March 2002): 2–34.
Barsuglia, Joseph P., Martin Polanco, Robert Palmer, Benjamin J. Malcolm, Benjamin Kelmendi, and Tanya Calvey. "A Case Report SPECT Study and Theoretical Rationale for the Sequential Administration of Ibogaine and 5-MeO-DMT in the Treatment of Alcohol Use Disorder." *Progress in Brain Research* 242 (2018): 121–58.

Barthes, Roland. *The Pleasure of the Text*. Translated by Richard Miller. New York: Hill and Wang, 1975.
Baudry, Jean-Louis. "The Apparatus: Metapsychological Approaches to the Impression of Reality in Cinema." In *Film Theory and Criticism*, 7th ed., edited by Leo Braudy and Marshall Cohen, 171–88. New York: Oxford University Press, 2009.
Baudry, Jean-Louis. "Author and Analyzable Subject." In *Apparatus: Selected Writings*, edited by Theresa Hak Kyung, 67–83. New York: Tanam, 1980.
Baudry, Jean-Louis. "Ideological Effects of the Basic Cinematographic Apparatus." In *Narrative, Apparatus, Ideology: A Film Theory Reader*, edited by Philip Rosen, 286–97. New York: Columbia University Press, 1986.
Baumbach, Nico. "All That Heaven Allows: What Is, or Was, Cinephilia? (Part One)." *Film Comment*. March 12, 2012. https://www.filmcomment.com/blog/all-that-heaven-allows-what-is-or-was-cinephilia-part-one/.
Baumbach, Nico. *Cinema/Politics/Philosophy*. New York: Columbia University Press, 2019.
Bazin, André. "Cinema and Theology." In *André Bazin at Work: Major Essays and Reviews from the Forties and Fifties*, edited by Burt Cardullo, translated by Burt Cardullo and Alain Piette, 61–72. New York: Routledge, 1997.
Bazin, André. "De Sica: Metteur en Scène." In *André Bazin and Italian Neorealism*, edited by Bert Cardullo, 74–88. New York: Continuum, 2011.
Bazin, André. "Death Every Afternoon." In *Rites of Realism: Essays on Corporeal Cinema*, edited by Ivone Margulies, translated by Mark A. Cohen, 27–31. Durham, NC: Duke University Press, 2003.
Bazin, André. "In Defense of Rossellini." In *Bazin and Italian Neorealism*, edited by Burt Cardullo, 163–71. London: Continuum, 2011.
Bazin, André. "Ontology of the Photographic Image." In Bazin, *What Is Cinema? Volume 1*, translated by Hugh Gray, 9–16. Berkeley: University of California Press, 2005.
Bazin, André. "Ontology of the Photographic Image." In Bazin, *What Is Cinema? Volume 2*, translated by Timothy Barnard, 3–12. Montreal: Caboose, 2009.
Beller, Jonathan. *The Cinematic Mode of Production: Attention Economy and the Society of the Spectacle*. Hanover, NH: Dartmouth College Press, 2006.
Bellour, Raymond. *The Analysis of Film*. Edited by Constance Penley. Bloomington: Indiana University Press, 2000.
Belton, John. "If Film Is Dead, What Is Cinema?" *Screen* 55, no. 4 (2014): 460–70.
Bennion, M. R., G. Hardy, R. K. Moore, and Abigail Millings. "E-Therapies in England for Stress, Anxiety or Depression: What Is Being Used in the NHS? A Survey of Mental Health Services." *BMJ open* 7, no. 1 (2017): e014844.
Berardi, Franco "Bifo." "Freedom and Potency." *e-flux* 116 (March 2021): n.p. https://www.e-flux.com/journal/116/378694/freedom-and-potency/.
Berardi, Franco "Bifo." *The Soul at Work: From Alienation to Autonomy*. Translated by Francesca Cadel and Guiseppina Mecchia. Los Angeles: Semiotext(e), 2009.
Bickmore, Timothy W., Lisa Caruso, Kerri Clough-Gorr, and Tim Heeren. "'It's Just like You Talk to a Friend': Relational Agents for Older Adults." *Interacting with Computers* 17, no. 6 (2005): 711–35.

Bickmore, Timothy, Amanda Gruber, and Rosalind Picard. "Establishing the Computer-Patient Working Alliance in Automated Health Behavior Change Interventions." *Patient Education and Counseling* 59, no. 1 (2005): 21–30.

Brewin, C. R., J. D. Gregory, M. Lipton, and N. Burgess. "Intrusive Images in Psychological Disorders: Characteristics, Neural Mechanisms, and Treatment Implications." *Psychological Review* 117, no. 1 (2010): 210–32.

Brown, Nicholas J. L., Tim Lomas, and Francisco Jose Eiroa-Orosa, eds. *The Routledge International Handbook of Critical Positive Psychology*. London: Routledge, 2018.

Burch, Noël. *Theory of Film Practice*. Princeton, NJ: Princeton University Press, 2014.

Burkeman, Oliver. "Therapy Wars: The Revenge of Freud." *The Guardian*. January 7, 2016. https://www.theguardian.com/science/2016/jan/07/therapy-wars-revenge-of-freud-cognitive-behavioural-therapy.

Caldwell, Christopher. "Meet the Philosopher Who Is Trying to Explain the Pandemic." *New York Times*. August 21, 2020. https://www.nytimes.com/2020/08/21/opinion/sunday/giorgio-agamben-philosophy-coronavirus.html.

Cartwright, Lisa. *Screening the Body: Tracing Medicine's Visual Culture*. Minneapolis: University of Minnesota Press, 1995.

Casetti, Francesco. "Back to the Motherland: The Film Theatre in the Postmedia Age." *Screen* 52, no. 1 (Spring 2011): 1–12.

Casetti, Francesco. "Why Fears Matter: Cinephobia in Early Film Culture." *Screen* 59, no. 2 (Summer 2018): 145–57.

Chaudhuri, Shohini, and Howard Finn. "The Open Image: Poetic Realism and the New Iranian Cinema." *Screen* 44, no. 1 (2003): 38–57.

Combes, Muriel. *Gilbert Simondon and the Philosophy of the Transindividual*. Translated by Thomas Lamarre. Cambridge, MA: MIT Press, 2013.

Comolli, Jean-Louis. "Machines of the Visible." In *The Cinematic Apparatus*, edited by Stephen Heath and Teresa de Lauretis, 121–22. New York: St. Martin's Press, 1980.

Copjec, Joan. "Thriller: An Intrigue of Identification." *Ciné-Tracts: A Journal of Film and Cultural Studies* 3, no. 3 (Fall 1980): 33–38.

Cowie, Elizabeth. *Representing the Woman: Cinema and Psychoanalysis*. London: Macmillan, 1997.

Davis, A. K., et al. "Subjective Effectiveness of Ibogaine Treatment for Problematic Opioid Consumption: Short- and Long-Term Outcomes and Current Psychological Functioning." *Journal of Psychedelic Studies* 1 (2017): 1–9. https://doi.org/10.1556/2054.01.2017.009.

Dawkins, Roger. "Deleuze, Peirce, and the Cinematic Sign." *Semiotic Review of Books* 15, no. 2 (2005): 8–12.

De Castro, Eduardo Viveiros. "Intensive Filiation and Demonic Alliance." In *Deleuzian Intersections: Science, Technology, Anthropology*, edited by Casper Bruun Jensen and Hjetil Rödje. New York: Berghahn Books, 2010.

de Silva, Padmal. "Obsessional-Compulsive Imagery." *Behaviour Research and Therapy* 24, no. 3 (1986): 333–50.

DeLanda, Manuel. *Intensive Science and Virtual Philosophy*. London: Continuum, 2002.

Deleuze, Gilles. "The Brain Is the Screen: An Interview with Gilles Deleuze." In *The Brain Is the Screen: Deleuze and the Philosophy of Cinema*, edited by Gregory Flaxman, 365–73. Minneapolis: University of Minnesota Press, 2000.

Deleuze, Gilles. *Cinema 1: The Movement-Image*. Translated by Hugh Tomlinson and Barbara Habberjam. Minneapolis: University of Minnesota Press, 1986.

Deleuze, Gilles. *Cinema 2: The Time-Image*. Translated by Hugh Tomlinson and Robert Galeta. Minneapolis: University of Minnesota Press, 1989.

Deleuze, Gilles. *Difference and Repetition*. Translated by Paul Patton. New York: Columbia University Press, 1994.

Deleuze, Gilles. *Essays Critical and Clinical*. Translated by Daniel W. Smith and Michael A. Greco. London: Verso, 1998.

Deleuze, Gilles. "Mediators." In *Negotiations: 1972–1990*, translated by Martin Joughin, 121–34. New York: Columbia University Press, 1995.

Deleuze, Gilles, and Félix Guattari. *Anti-Oedipus: Capitalism and Schizophrenia, Vol. 1*. Minneapolis: University of Minnesota Press, 1986.

Deleuze, Gilles, and Félix Guattari. *A Thousand Plateaus: Capitalism and Schizophrenia, Vol. 2*. Translated by Brian Massumi. Minneapolis: University of Minnesota Press, 2009.

Deleuze, Gilles, and Félix Guattari. *What Is Philosophy?* New York: Columbia University Press, 1994.

Dermer, Shanon B., and Jennifer B. Hutchings. "Utilizing Movies in Family Therapy: Applications for Individuals, Couples, and Families." *American Journal of Family Therapy* 28 (2000): 164.

Derrida, Jacques. *Dissemination*. Chicago: University of Chicago Press, 1981.

Dimitrijević, Aleksandar. "What Is Trauma and How to Avoid and Heal It: Lecture I." Stillpoint Spaces Berlin. YouTube. April 3, 2017. https://www.youtube.com/watch?v=oqZ6nILqYd4&t=957s.

Doane, Mary Anne. "Film and the Masquerade: Theorising the Female Spectator." *Screen* 23, no. 3–4 (1982): 74–88.

Doane, Mary Ann. "Misrecognition and Identity." *Ciné-Tracts: A Journal of Film and Cultural Studies* 3, no. 3 (Fall 1980): 25–32.

Doane, Mary Ann. "Remembering Women: Psychical and Historical Constructions in Film Theory." In *Femmes Fatales: Feminism, Film Theory, and Psychoanalysis*, 76–98. New York: Routledge, 1991.

Dosse, François. *Gilles Deleuze & Félix Guattari: Intersecting Lives*. New York: Columbia University Press, 2010.

DP/30: The Oral History of Hollywood. "DP/30 @ TIFF: Clouds of Sils Maria, Olivier Assayas." YouTube. https://www.youtube.com/watch?v=qkZBosAanMI.

Duncan, Kevin David Beck, and Richard Granum. "Ordinary People: Using a Popular Film in Group Therapy." *Journal of Counselling and Development* 65 (September 1986): 50–51.

Eichelman, Burr. "Hypnotic Change in Combat Dreams of Two Veterans with Post-traumatic Stress Disorder." *American Journal of Psychiatry* 142, no. 1 (January 1985): 112–14.

Elsaesser, Thomas. "Cinephilia or the Uses of Disenchantment." In *Cinephilia: Movies, Love and Memory*, edited by Marijke de Valck and Malte Hagener, 27–44. Amsterdam: Amsterdam University Press, 2005.

Erickson, Milton H., and Ernest Lawrence Rossi. *Hypnotherapy, an Exploratory Casebook*. Irvington, 1979.

Evans, Jules. "David Clark on Improving Access for Psychological Therapy (IAPT)." Philosophy for Life. May 31, 2013. http://www.philosophyforlife.org/david-clark-on-improving-access-for-psychological-therapy-iapt/.

Fairfax, Daniel. "Glossary." In Jean-Louis Comolli, *Cinema Against Spectacle: Technique and Ideology Revisited*, translated and edited by Daniel Fairfax, 291–300. Amsterdam: Amsterdam University Press, 2015.

Ferenczi, Sándor. "Confusion of Tongues between Adults and the Child: The Language of Tenderness and of Passion." *Contemporary Psychoanalysis* 24, no. 2 (1988): 196–206.

Ferenczi, Sándor, and Otto Rank. *The Development of Psychoanalysis*. New York: Dover, 1956.

Fleming, Michael, and Ericka Bohnel. "Use of Feature Film as Part of Psychological Assessment." *Professional Psychology: Research and Practice* 40, no. 6 (2009): 641–47.

Florida, Richard. "The Lasting Normal for the Post-Pandemic City." Bloomberg CityLab. June 25, 2020. https://www.bloomberg.com/news/features/2020-06-25/the-new-normal-after-the-coronavirus-pandemic.

Flückiger C., A. C. Del Re, B. E. Wampold, and A. O. Horvath. "The Alliance in Adult Psychotherapy: A Meta-Analytic Synthesis." *Psychotherapy* 55, no. 4 (2018): 316–40.

Foucault, Michel. *Discipline & Punish: The Birth of the Prison*. Translated by Alan Sheridan. New York: Vintage Books, 1995.

Foucault, Michel. *Psychiatric Power: Lectures at the Collège de France 1973–1974*. Edited by Jacques Lagrange, François Ewald, Alessandro Fontana, and Arnold I. Davidson, translated by Graham Burchell. Basingstoke, UK: Palgrave Macmillan, 2006.

Freud, Sigmund. "Fetishism." In *The Standard Edition of the Complete Psychological Works of Sigmund Freud, Vol. XXI*, translated by James Strachey, 533–39. London: Hogarth, 1961.

Freud, Sigmund. "Fragment of an Analysis of a Case of Hysteria." In *The Standard Edition of the Complete Psychological Works of Sigmund Freud, Volume VII (1901–1905): A Case of Hysteria, Three Essays on Sexuality and Other Works*, translated by James Strachey, 1348–1456. London: Hogarth, 1966.

Freud, Sigmund. "Notes upon a Case of Obsessional Neurosis." In *The Standard Edition of the Complete Psychological Works of Sigmund Freud, Volume X: Little Hans and The Rat Man*, translated by James Strachey, 151–318. London: Hogarth, 1955.

Freud, Sigmund. *Totem and Taboo: Resemblances between the Psychic Lives of Savages and Neurotics*. London: George Routledge and Sons, 1919.

Friedberg, Anne. "A Denial of Difference: Theories of Cinematic Identification." In *Psychoanalysis and Cinema*, edited by Ann Kaplan, 36–45. New York: Routledge, 1990.

Gable, Shelly L., and Jonathan Haidt. "What (and Why) Is Positive Psychology?" *Review of General Psychology* 9, no. 2 (June 2005): 103-10.

Gaston, Louise, and Charles R. Marmar. "Manual of California Psychotherapy Alliance Scales (CALPAS)." Department of Psychiatry, McGill University, Montreal, Canada. http://www.traumatys.com/wp-content/uploads/2017/09/CALPAS-Manual.pdf.

Gelso, Charles J. "Special Issue: The Interplay of Techniques and the Therapeutic Relationship in Psychotherapy—Introduction to Special Issue." *Psychotherapy* 42, no. 4 (2005): 419-20.

Genosko, Gary. *Félix Guattari: A Critical Introduction*. London: Pluto, 2009.

Genosko, Gary. *Félix Guattari: An Aberrant Introduction*. London: Continuum, 2002.

Glick, Stanley D., Isabelle M. Maisonneuve, and Karen K. Szumlinski. "18-Methoxycoronaridine (18-MC) and Ibogaine: Comparison of Antiaddictive Efficacy, Toxicity, and Mechanisms of Action." *Annals of the New York Academy of Sciences* 914, no. 1 (2000): 369-86.

Gordon, Lewis R. *Existentia Africana: Understanding Africana Existential Thought*. New York: Routledge, 2013.

Guattari, Emmanuelle. *I, Little Asylum*. Cambridge, MA: MIT Press, 2014.

Guattari, Félix. *Chaosmosis: An Ethico-Aesthetic Paradigm*. Translated by Paul Bains and Julian Pefanis. Bloomington: Indiana University Press, 1995.

Guattari, Félix. "Cinema of Desire." In *Chaosophy: Texts and Interviews 1972-1977*, edited by Sylvère Lotringer, translated by David L. Sweet, Jarred Becker, and Taylor Adkins, 235-46. Los Angeles: Semiotext(e), 2009.

Guattari, Félix. "Machine and Structure." In *Psychoanalysis and Transversality: Texts and Interviews 1955-1971*, translated by Ames Hodges, 318-29. Los Angeles: Semiotext(e), 2015.

Guattari, Félix. *The Machinic Unconscious: Essays in Schizoanalysis*. Translated by Taylor Adkins. Los Angeles: Semiotext(e), 2011.

Guattari, Félix. "The Poor Person's Couch." In *Chaosophy: Texts and Interviews 1972-1977*, translated by David L. Sweet, Jarred Becker, and Taylor Adkins, edited by Sylvère Lotringer, 57-67. Los Angeles: Semiotext(e), 2009.

Guattari, Félix. "The Proliferation of Margins." In *Autonomia: Post-Political Politics*, edited by Sylvère Lotringer, translated by Richard Gardner and Sybil Walker, 108-11. Los Angeles: Semiotext(e), 2007.

Guattari, Félix. *Schizoanalytic Cartographies*. Translated by Andrew Goffey. New York: Bloomsbury, 2013.

Guattari, Félix. "The Transference." In *Psychoanalysis and Transversality: Texts and Interviews 1955-1971*, translated by Ames Hodges, 76-85. Los Angeles: Semiotext(e), 2015.

Guattari, Félix. "Transversality." In *Psychoanalysis and Transversality: Texts and Interviews 1955-1971*, translated by Ames Hodges, 102-20. Los Angeles: Semiotext(e), 2015.

Guattari, Félix. "The Vertigo of Immanence: Interview with John Johnston, June 1992." In *The Guattari Effect*, edited by Eric Alliez and Andrew Goffey, 25-39. London: Continuum, 2011.

Guattari, Félix, and Antonio Negri. *Communists Like Us: New Spaces of Liberty, New Lines of Alliance*. Translated by Michael Ryan. New York: Semiotext(e), 1990.

Guattari, Félix, and Antonio Negri. *New Lines of Alliance, New Spaces of Liberty*. Translated by Michael Ryan, Jared Becker, Arianna Bove, and Noe Le Blanc, edited by Stevphen Shukaitis. Brooklyn, NY: Autonomedia, 2010.

Guattari, Félix, and Suely Rolnik. *Molecular Revolution in Brazil*. Translated by Karel Clapshaw and Brian Holmes. Los Angeles: Semiotext(e), 2008.

Hagenaars, M. A., C. R. Brewin, A. Van Minnen, E. A. Holmes, and K. A. Hoogduin. "Intrusive Images and Intrusive Thoughts as Different Phenomena: Two Experimental Studies." *Memory (Hove, England)* 18, no. 1 (2010): 76–84.

Hagenaars, Muriel A., Agnes Van Minnen, Emily A. Holmes, Chris R. Brewin, and Kees A. L. Hoogduin. "The Effect of Hypnotically Induced Somatoform Dissociation on the Development of Intrusions after an Aversive Film." *Cognition & Emotion* 22, no. 5 (2008): 944–63.

Hardt, Michael. "Anti-Oedipus: Part 2." Reading Notes on Deleuze and Guattari Capitalism & Schizophrenia. http://people.duke.edu/~hardt/Deleuze&Guattari.html.

Hesley, John W., and Jan G. Hesley. *Rent Two Films and Let's Talk in the Morning: Using Popular Movies in Psychotherapy*. New York: John Wiley and Sons, 1998.

Heston, Melissa L., and Terry Kottman, "Movies as Metaphors: A Counseling Intervention." *Journal of Humanistic Education & Development* 23, no. 2 (December 1997): 92–99.

Hilton, Leon. "Mapping the Wander Lines: The Quiet Revelations of Fernand Deligny." *Los Angeles Review of Books*. July 2, 2015. https://lareviewofbooks.org/article/mapping-the-wander-lines-the-quiet-revelations-of-fernand-deligny/.

Holmes, Emily A., Arnoud Arntz, and Mervin R. Smucker. "Imagery Rescripting in Cognitive Behaviour Therapy: Images, Treatment Techniques and Outcomes." *Journal of Behavior Therapy and Experimental Psychiatry* 38, no. 4 (2007): 297–305.

Holmes, E. A., C. R. Brewin, and R. G. Hennessy. "Trauma Films, Information Processing, and Intrusive Memory Development." *Journal of Experimental Psychology: General* 133, no. 1 (2004): 3–22.

Holmes, E. A., N. Grey, and K. A. Young. "Intrusive Images and 'Hotspots' of Trauma Memories in Posttraumatic Stress Disorder: An Exploratory Investigation of Emotions and Cognitive Themes." *Journal of Behavior Therapy and Experimental Psychiatry* 36, no. 1 (2005): 3–17.

Horowitz, M. J. "Psychic Trauma. Return of Images after a Stress Film." *Archives of General Psychiatry* 20, no. 5 (1969): 552–59.

Horvath, Adam O., A. C. Del Re, Christoph Flückiger, and Dianne Symonds. "Alliance in Individual Psychotherapy." *Psychotherapy* 48, no. 1 (2011): 9–16.

Internet Encyclopedia of Philosophy. "Gilles Deleuze (1925–1995)." https://www.iep.utm.edu/deleuze/.

James, William. *Essays in Radical Empiricism*. Mineola, NY: Dover, 2003.

Janet, Pierre. *L'Amnésie et la dissociation des souvenirs par l'émotion*. Paris: F. Alcan, 1904.

Janet, Pierre. *L'État mental des hystériques: Les Stigmates mentaux*. Ancienne Librairie Germer Balliere et Cie, 1911.

Jodorowsky, Alejandro. *Psychomagic: The Transformative Power of Shamanic Psychotherapy*. Rochester, VT: Inner Traditions/Bear, 2010.

Jodorowsky, Alejandro, and Marianne Costa. *The Way of Tarot: The Spiritual Teacher in the Cards*. Translated by Jon E. Graham. Rochester, VT: Destiny Books, 2009.

Joiner, Lindsey. *The Big Book of Therapeutic Activity Ideas for Children and Teens: Inspiring Arts-Based Activities and Character Education Curricula*. London: Jessica Kingsley, 2012.

Kaslow, Florence W. "Foreword." In *The Cinematic Mirror for Psychology and Life Coaching*, edited by Mary Banks Gregerson, v–vi. Leavenworth, KS: Springer, 2009.

Keathley, Christian. *Cinephilia and History, or the Wind in the Trees*. Bloomington: Indiana University Press, 2005.

Kiluk, Brian D., Kelly Serafini, Tami Frankforter, Charla Nich, and Kathleen M. Carroll. "Only Connect: The Working Alliance in Computer-Based Cognitive Behavioral Therapy." *Behaviour Research and Therapy* 63 (2014): 139–46.

Kleinhans, Chuck. "Notes on Melodrama and Family under Capitalism." *Film Reader* 3 (1978): 40–47.

Konkoly-Thege, B., et al. "Relationship between Interpersonal Trauma Exposure and Addictive Behaviors: A Systematic Review." *BMC Psychiatry* 17, no. 1 (2017): 164. https://doi.org/10.1186/s12888-017-1323-1.

Kracauer, Siegfried. *Theory of Film: The Redemption of Physical Reality*. Princeton, NJ: Princeton University Press, 1997.

Kuiling, J. M. E., F. Klaassen, and M. A. Hagenaars. "The Role of Tonic Immobility and Control in the Development of Intrusive Memories after Experimental Trauma." *Memory* 27, no. 6 (2019): 772–79.

Kuntzel, Thierry. "The Film-Work." *Trivium-Estudos Interdisciplinares* 11, no. 2 (2019): 132–45.

Kuntzel, Thierry. "The Film-Work, 2." *Camera Obscura: Feminism, Culture, and Media Studies* 2, no. 2 (5) (1980): 6–70.

Lacan, Jacques. "The Function and Field of Speech and Language in Psychoanalysis." In *Écrits: A Selection*, translated by Alan Sheridan, 23–86. London: Routledge, 2015.

Lacan, Jacques. *Le Seminaire II: Le Moi dans la théorie de Freud et dans la technique de la psychanalyse 1954–1955*. Edited by Jacques-Alain Miller. Paris: Seuil, 1978.

Lacan, Jacques. *Le Séminaire, Livre XVII: L'Envers de la psychanalyse, 1969–70*. Edited by Jacques-Alain Miller. Paris: Seuil, 1991.

Lacan, Jacques. "On Freuds' 'Trieb' and the Psychoanalyst's Desire [1964]." In *Écrits: The First Complete Edition in English*, translated by Bruce Fink, 722–25. New York: W.W. Norton, 2006.

Lamarre, Thomas. *The Anime Ecology: A Genealogy of Television, Animation, and Game Media*. Minneapolis: University of Minnesota Press, 2018.

Lamarre, Thomas. *The Anime Machine: A Media Theory of Animation*. Minneapolis: University of Minnesota Press, 2009.

Lamarre, Thomas. "Diversity as Method." In David Lapoujade, *William James: Empiricism and Pragmatism*, translated by Thomas Lamarre, 77–118. Durham, NC: Duke University Press, 2020.

Lamb, C. Sue. "Hypnotically-Induced Deconditioning: Reconstruction of Memories in the Treatment of Phobias." *American Journal of Clinical Hypnosis* 28, no. 2 (1985): 56–62.

Lamb, C. Sue. "Negative Hypnotic Imagery/Fantasy: Application to Two Cases of 'Unfinished Business.'" *American Journal of Clinical Hypnosis* 24, no. 4 (1982): 266–71.

Lampropolous, Georgios K., Nikolaos Kazantzis, and Frank P. Deane. "Psychologists' Use of Motion Pictures in Clinical Practice." *Professional Psychology: Research and Practice* 35, no. 5 (2004): 535.

Langer, Susanne K. *Feeling and Form: A Theory of Art*. New York: Charles Scribner's Sons, 1953.

Laplanche, Jean, and Jean-Bertrand Pontalis. *The Language of Psychoanalysis*. Translated by Donald Nicholson-Smith. London: Karnac Books, 1973.

Lapoujade, David. *William James: Empiricism and Pragmatism*. Translated by Thomas Lamarre. Durham, NC: Duke University Press, 2020.

Layard, Richard, and David M. Clark. *Thrive: The Power of Evidence-Based Psychological Therapies*. London: Allen Lane, 2014.

Lazzarato, Maurizio. *Signs and Machines: Capitalism and the Production of Subjectivity*. Translated by Joshua David Jordan. Los Angeles: Semiotext(e), 2014.

Leader, Darian. "A Quick Fix for the Soul." *The Guardian*. September 9, 2008. https://www.theguardian.com/science/2008/sep/09/psychology.humanbehaviour.

Lellis, George. *Bertolt Brecht: Cahiers du Cinéma and Contemporary Film Theory*. Ann Arbor: UMI Research Press, 1982.

Lévi-Strauss, Claude. *The Elementary Structures of Kinship*. Translated by John Richard Von Sturmer and James Harle Bell, edited by Rodney Needham. Boston: Beacon, 1969.

Loree, Amy M., Kimberly A. Yonkers, Steven J. Ondersma, Kathryn Gilstad-Hayden, and Steve Martino. "Comparing Satisfaction, Alliance and Intervention Components in Electronically Delivered and In-Person Brief Interventions for Substance Use among Childbearing-Aged Women." *Journal of Substance Abuse Treatment* 99 (2019): 1–7.

Malchiodi, Cathy. "Foreword." In *Video and Filmmaking as Psychotherapy: Research and Practice*, edited by Joshua L. Cohen and J. Lauren Johnson, xiii–xvi. New York: Routledge, 2015.

Mandavia, A., et al. "Exposure to Childhood Abuse and Later Substance Use: Indirect Effects of Emotion Dysregulation and Exposure to Trauma." *Journal of Traumatic Stress* 29 (2016): 422–29. https://doi.org/10.1002/jts.22131.

Manning, Erin. *Always More Than One: Individuation's Dance*. Durham, NC: Duke University Press, 2013.

Manning, Erin. "Introduction." In *Nocturnal Fabulations: Ecology, Vitality and Opacity in the Cinema of Apichatpong Weerasethakul*, 7–17. London: Open Humanities, 2017.

Manning, Erin. *The Minor Gesture*. Durham, NC: Duke University Press, 2016.

Manning, Erin. *Relationscapes: Movement, Art, Philosophy*. Cambridge, MA: MIT Press, 2009.

Marcuse, Herbert. *Eros and Civilization*. Boston: Beacon, 1974.

Marcuse, Herbert. *One-Dimensional Man: Studies in the Ideology of Advanced Industrial Society*. London: Routledge, 2002.

Masson, J. Moussaieff. *Against Therapy: Emotional Tyranny and the Myth of Psychological Healing*. New York: Atheneum, 1988.

Massumi, Brian. "Fear (The Spectrum Said)." *Positions* 13, no. 1 (2005): 31–48.

Massumi, Brian. *99 Theses on the Revaluation of Value: A Postcapitalist Manifesto*. Minneapolis: University of Minnesota Press, 2018.

Massumi, Brian. *Ontopower: War, Powers, and the State of Perception*. Durham, NC: Duke University Press, 2015.

Massumi, Brian. *Parables for the Virtual: Movement, Affect, Sensation*. Durham, NC: Duke University Press, 2002.

Massumi, Brian. *Semblance and Event: Activist Philosophy and the Occurrent Arts*. Cambridge, MA: MIT Press, 2011.

Massumi, Brian. "Translator's Foreword: Pleasures of Philosophy." In *A Thousand Plateaus: Capitalism and Schizophrenia*, by Gilles Deleuze and Félix Guattari.

Metz, Christian. *Film Language: A Semiotics of the Cinema*. Chicago: University of Chicago Press, 1991.

Metz, Christian. "The Imaginary Signifier." *Screen* 16, no. 2 (1975): 14–76.

Metz, Christian. *Psychoanalysis and Cinema: The Imaginary Signifier*. Translated by Celia Britton, Annwyl Williams, Ben Brewster, and Alfred Guzzetti, edited by Stephen Heath and Colin MacCabe. London: Macmillan, 1982.

Miller, Arnold. "Brief Reconstructive Hypnotherapy for Anxiety Reactions: Three Case Reports." *American Journal of Clinical Hypnosis* 28, no. 3 (1986): 138–46.

Müller, John. "Lacan's Mirror Stage." *Psychoanalytic Inquiry* 5, no. 2 (1985): 233–52.

Mulvey, Laura. *Fetishism and Curiosity*. Bloomington and London: Indiana University Press and British Film Institute, 1996.

Mulvey, Laura. "Some Reflections on the Cinephilia Question." *Framework: The Journal of Cinema and Media* 50, no. 1-2 (Fall 2009): 190–93.

Mulvey, Laura. "Visual Pleasure and Narrative Cinema." In *Film Theory and Criticism, Seventh Edition*, edited by Leo Braudy and Marshall Cohen, 711–22. New York: Oxford University Press, 2009.

Mulvey, Laura, and Peter Wollen. "From Cinephilia to Film Studies." In *Inventing Film Studies*, edited by Lee Grieveson and Haidee Wasson, 217–34. Durham, NC: Duke University Press, 2008.

Nancy, Jean-Luc. "The Intruder." In *Extreme Bodies: The Use and Abuse of the Body in Art*, edited by Francesca Alfano Miglietti, 224–48. Milan: Skira, 2003.

Nathan, Tobie. *L'Influence qui guérit*. Paris: Odile Jacob, 2009.

Nathan, Tobie, and Isabelle Stengers. *Doctors and Healers*. Translated by Stephen Muecke. London: Polity, 2018.

Niemiec, Ryan M., and Danny Wedding. *Positive Psychology at the Movies: Using Films to Build Character Strengths and Well-Being*. 2nd ed. Boston: Hogrefe, 2014.

Norcross, John. "The Therapeutic Relationship, Individualized Treatment and Other Keys to Successful Psychotherapy." Kanopy.

Norcross, John C., and Michael J. Lambert, eds. *Psychotherapy Relationships That Work, Volume 1: Evidence-Based Therapist Contributions*. 3rd ed. Oxford: Oxford University Press, 2019.

Norcross, John C., and Bruce E. Wampold. "Compendium of Treatment Adaptations." *Psychotherapy in Australia* 19, no. 3 (2013): 34–37.
Nussbaum, Martha. *The Therapy of Desire: Theory and Practice in Hellenistic Ethics.* Princeton, NJ: Princeton University Press, 2009.
Pasolini, Pier Paolo. "The 'Cinema of Poetry.'" In *Heretical Empiricism*, translated by Ben Lawton and Louise K. Barnett, 167–86. Bloomington: Indiana University Press, 1988.
Patel, Trishna, et al. "Intrusive Images and Memories in Major Depression." *Behaviour Research and Therapy* 45, no. 11 (2007): 2573–80.
Pelbart, Peter Pál. "Modes of Exhaustion, Modes of Existence." *Inflexions* 10 (2017): 137–62. https://www.inflexions.org/exhaustion/PDFs/08_Pelbart.pdf.
Posner, Michael. "B.C. Doctor Agrees to Stop Using Amazonian Plant to Treat Addictions." *The Globe and Mail.* November 9, 2011. https://www.theglobeandmail.com/life/health-and-fitness/bc-doctor-agrees-to-stop-using-amazonian-plant-to-treat-addictions/article4250579/.
Rachman, Stanley. *The Treatment of Obsessions.* New York: Oxford University Press, 2003.
Rachman, Stanley. "Unwanted Intrusive Images in Obsessive Compulsive Disorders." *Journal of Behavior Therapy and Experimental Psychiatry* 38, no. 4 (2007): 402–10.
Rafanell i Orra, Josep. *En finir avec le capitalism thérapeutique: Soin, politique, communauté.* Paris: Éditions la Découverte, 2011.
Ratzinger, Joseph Cardinal. *Truth and Tolerance: Christian Belief and World Religions.* Translated by Henry Taylor. San Francisco: Ignatius, 2004.
Rodowick, D. N. "The Difficulty of Difference." *Wide Angle* 5, no. 1 (1982): 4–15.
Rodowick, D. N. *The Difficulty of Difference: Psychoanalysis, Sexual Difference and Film Theory.* London: Routledge, 1991.
Rogers, Carl R. *Client-Centered Therapy: Its Current Practice, Implications, and Theory.* Boston: Houghton Mifflin, 1965.
Rogers, Carl R., and Eugene T. Gendlin. *The Therapeutic Relationship and Its Impact: A Study of Psychotherapy with Schizophrenics.* Westport, CT: Greenwood, 1976.
Rolnik, Suely. "Molding a Contemporary Soul: The Empty-Full of Lygia Clark." In *The Experimental Exercise of Freedom: Lygia Clark, Gego, Mathias Goeritz, Hélio Oiticica and Mira Schendel*, edited by Rina Carvajal and Alma Ruiz, 55–108. Los Angeles: Museum of Contemporary Art, 1999.
Rose, Nikolas. "Brain, Self and Society." Andrew F. Holmes Dean of Medicine Distinction Lectures, McGill University, Montreal, Canada. October 27, 2016.
Rosen, Philip. *Change Mummified: Cinema, Historicity, Theory.* Minneapolis: University of Minnesota Press, 2001.
Rosen, Philip. "Preface." In Jean-Louis Comolli, *Cinema Against Spectacle: Technique and Ideology Revisited*, translated and edited by Daniel Fairfax, 7–16. Amsterdam: Amsterdam University Press, 2015.
Russell, Bertrand. *History of Western Philosophy.* London: George Allen and Unwin, 1961.
Samorini, Giorgio. "The Bwiti Religion and the Psychoactive Plant Tabernanthe Iboga (Equatorial Africa)." *Integration* 5 (1995): 105–14.

Schenberg, E., et al. "A Phenomenological Analysis of the Subjective Experience Elicited by Ibogaine in the Context of a Drug Dependence Treatment." *Journal of Psychedelic Studies* 1 (2017): 1–10. https://doi.org/10.1556/2054.01.2017.007.

Seligman, Martin. *Authentic Happiness: Using the New Positive Psychology to Realize Your Potential for Lasting Fulfillment.* New York: Free Press, 2002.

Seligman, Martin, and Mihaly Csikszentmihalyi. "Positive Psychology. An Introduction." *American Psychologist* 55, no. 1 (2000): 5.

Seligman, Martin, and Tamsin Shaw, "'Learned Helplessness' & Torture: An Exchange." *New York Review of Books.* April 21, 2016. http://www.nybooks.com/articles/2016/04/21/learned-helplessness-torture-an-exchange/.

Shaviro, Steven. *The Cinematic Body.* Minneapolis: University of Minnesota Press, 1994.

Shedler, Jonathan. "Bamboozled by Bad Science: The First Myth about Evidence-Based Therapy." *Psychology Today.* October 31, 2013. https://www.psychologytoday.com/us/blog/psychologically-minded/201310/bamboozled-bad-science.

Silverman, Kaja. *The Acoustic Mirror: The Female Voice in Psychoanalysis and Cinema.* Bloomington: Indiana University Press, 1988.

Silverman, Kaja. *The Subject of Semiotics.* New York: Oxford University Press, 1983.

Singer, Ben. "Film, Photography, and Fetish: The Analyses of Christian Metz." *Cinema Journal* 27, no. 4 (Summer 1988): 4–22.

Solomon, Gary. *The Motion Picture Prescription: Watch This Movie and Call Me in the Morning.* Santa Rosa, CA: Aslan, 1995.

Solomon, Gary. *Reel Therapy: How Movies Inspire You to Overcome Life's Problems.* New York: Lebhar-Friedman Books, 2001.

Speckens, Anne E. M., Ann Hackmann, Anke Ehlers, and Bea Cuthbert. "Imagery Special Issue: Intrusive Images and Memories of Earlier Adverse Events in Patients with Obsessive Compulsive Disorder." *Journal of Behavior Therapy and Experimental Psychiatry* 38, no. 4 (2007): 411–22.

Stam, Robert, Robert Burgoyne, and Sandy Flitterman-Lewis. *New Vocabularies in Film Semiotics: Structuralism, Poststructuralism and Beyond.* London: Routledge, 1992.

Stawarska, Beatta. "Defining Imagination: Sartre between Husserl and Janet." *Phenomenology and the Cognitive Sciences* 4 (2005): 133–53.

Stengers, Isabelle. *Thinking with Whitehead: A Free and Wild Creation of Concepts.* Translated by Michael Chase. Cambridge, MA: Harvard University Press, 2011.

Studlar, Gaylyn. "Masochism and the Perverse Pleasures of the Cinema." *Quarterly Review of Film & Video* 9, no. 4 (1984): 267–82.

Świderski, Stanislaw. "Les Récits bibliques dans l'adaptation africaine." *Journal of Religion in Africa* 10, no. 3 (1979): 174–233.

Świderski, Stanislaw. "Les Visions d'iboga." *Anthropos* 76, no. 3/4 (1981): 393–429.

Szymanski, Adam. *Cinemas of Therapeutic Activism: Depression and the Politics of Existence.* Amsterdam: Amsterdam University Press, 2020.

Szymanski, Adam. "*Uncle Boonmee Who Can Recall His Past Lives* and the Ecosophic Aesthetics of Peace." In *Nocturnal Fabulations: Ecology, Vitality and Opacity in the Cinema of Apichatpong Weerasethakul*, 48–78. London: Open Humanities, 2017.

The Third Wave. "The Ultimate Guide to Ibogaine." 2021. https://thethirdwave.co/psychedelics/ibogaine/.

TIFF Originals. "OLIVIER ASSAYAS | Master Class | Festival 2012." YouTube. October 4, 2012. https://www.youtube.com/watch?v=5ByOZP6Ph2o&t=1000s.

Truffaut, François. "A Certain Tendency of the French Cinema." In *Movies and Methods*, edited by Bill Nichols, 224–36. Berkeley: University of California Press, 2006.

"Understanding the Epidemic." Centers for Disease Control and Prevention. March 17, 2021. https://www.cdc.gov/drugoverdose/epidemic/index.html.

Van der Hart, Onno, Paul Brown, and Bessel A. van der Kolk. "Pierre Janet's Treatment of Post-Traumatic Stress." *Journal of Traumatic Stress* 2, no. 4 (1989): 379–95.

Van der Kolk, Bessel A. *The Body Keeps the Score: Brain, Mind, and Body in the Healing of Trauma*. New York: Penguin Books, 2015.

Van der Kolk, Bessel A., and Onno van der Hart. "The Intrusive Past: The Flexibility of Memory and the Engraving of Trauma." *American Imago* 48, no. 4 (1991): 425–54.

Walker, Janet. *Couching Resistance: Women, Film and Psychoanalytic Psychiatry*. Minneapolis: Minnesota University Press, 1993.

Walsh, Martin. *The Brechtian Aspect of Radical Cinema*. Edited by Keith M. Griffiths. London: BFI, 1981.

Wasson, Haidee. "Response to Dudley Andrew: Small Discipline, Big Pictures." *Synoptique*. May 2010. http://www.synoptique.ca/core/articles/wasson_haidee_dudley_andrew/.

Wasson, Haidee, and Charles Acland, eds. *Useful Cinema*. Durham, NC: Duke University Press, 2011.

Waxman, David. *Hypnosis (Psychology Revivals): A Guide for Patients and Practitioners*. Routledge, 2014.

Wedding, Danny, M. Boyd, and Ryan M. Niemiec. *Movies and Mental Illness: Using Films to Understand Psychopathology*. Cambridge, MA: Hogrefe and Huber, 2005.

Weil, Simone. *The Need for Roots: Prelude of a Declaration of Duties towards Mankind*. Translated by Arthur Willis. London: Routledge, 2002.

Whitney, E. Oliver. "Kristen Stewart Addresses the Irony of 'Clouds of Sils Maria.'" Huffington Post. October 9, 2014. https://www.huffingtonpost.ca/entry/kristen-stewart-clouds-of-sils-maria_n_5961102?ri18n=true.

Willemen, Paul. "Through the Glass Darkly: Cinephilia Reconsidered." In *Looks and Frictions: Essays in Cultural Studies and Film Theory*, 223–57. Bloomington: Indiana University Press, 1994.

Williams, Alan. *Republic of Images: A History of French Filmmaking*. Cambridge, MA: Harvard University Press, 1992.

Williams, Linda. "Discipline and Fun: Psycho and Postmodern Cinema." In *Reinventing Film Studies*, edited by Linda Williams and Christine Gledhill, 351–78. London: Arnold, 2000.

Winkelman, M. "Psychedelics as Medicines for Substance Abuse Rehabilitation: Evaluating Treatments with LSD, Peyote, Ibogaine and Ayahuasca." *Current Drug Abuse Reviews* 7 (2014): 101–16. https://doi.org/10.2174/1874473708666150107120011.

Wollen, Peter. "An Alphabet of Cinema." *New Left Review* 12 (November-December 2001): 115–33.

Wollen, Peter. "Godard and Counter-Cinema: *Vent d'Est*." *Afterimages* 4 (Autumn 1972): 7–16.

Wolz, Birgit. *E-Motion Picture Magic: A Movie Lover's Guide to Healing and Transformation*. Centennial, CO: Glenbridge, 2005.

Yazici, Esra, Fuat Ulus, Rabia Selvitop, Ahmet Bülent Yazici, and Nazan Aydin. "Use of Movies for Group Therapy of Psychiatric Inpatients: Theory and Practice." *International Journal of Group Psychotherapy* 64, no. 2 (2014): 254–71.

Younger, Prakash. "What Is Cinephilosophy? A Bazinian Paradigm, Part 1. A Philosophical Preamble, for the Love of Truth." *Offscreen* 13, no. 2 (February 2009): n.p. https://offscreen.com/view/what_is_cinephilosophy.

Younger, Prakash. "What Is Cinephilosophy? A Bazinian Paradigm, Part 2. André Bazin or, the Cinephilosophical Heritage of Film Studies." *Offscreen* 13, no. 2 (February 2009): n.p. https://offscreen.com/view/what_is_cinephilosophy_pt2.

Žižek, Slavoj. "Paul and the Truth Event." In *Paul's New Moment: Continental Philosophy and the Future of Christian Theology*, edited by John Millbank, Slavoj Žižek, and Creston Davis, 74–99. Grand Rapids, MI: Brazos, 2010.

Zur Institute. "Using the Power of Movies in the Therapeutic Process: Cinema Therapy." Zur Institute: Online Continuing Education for Mental Health Professionals. https://www.zurinstitute.com/cinematherapycourse.html.

Index

Page numbers in *italic* refer to figures.

absent presence, 89–90
Acland, Charles, 121n6
activism, therapeutic, 107
addiction, 25–26
adventure, 71–78, 79, 80
adventurousness, 77
aesthetics: Brechtian, 62; political, 17–18, 45, 66
affect theory, 19
Afflictions, 34
After May, 101
Agamben, Giorgio, 77–78
Alcoholics Anonymous, 25
alliance-making, 10
alterity, 47
American Psychological Association, 22
analysands, 14, 15, 45, 47, 119, 119–20n35
analysts, 3, 14, 66, 119–20n35, 125n5, 129n32; as ideal ego, 46; identification with, 46–47
Andrew, Dudley, 133–34n8, 133n6, 136n35
anxiety, 66, 79
apparatus theory, 40, 41–48, 90, 106, 126n12
Ararat, 83
art, 119n30; as monument, 97; politics and, 17; therapy and, 17, 104–5 (*see also* art therapy)
art cinema, 54
artificial intelligence (AI), 8

art therapy, 21–24, 121–22n14
Assayas, Oliver, 2, 79, 134n9, 136n33, 136n35; *After May*, 101; *Clouds of Sils Maria*, 59, 61, 62, 71–77, *73*, *74*, *76*, 80; *Paris Awakens*, 37–40, *38*, *39*, 56–58, *57*; *Personal Shopper*, 80, *81*, 84, 93–97, *95*, *96*; *A Post-May Adolescence: Letter to Alice Debord*, 101; *Rendez-Vous*, 72
Astruc, Alexandre, 1
auteurism, 2, 3
auteurs, 1–2
authoritarianism, 101
Autonomia Operaia movement, 101
autonomists, 101–2, 103–4
autonomy, 103–4
auto-poeisis, 103

Barthes, Roland, 39, 40, 124n2, 124–25n3
Baudry, Jean-Louis, 41–43, 44, 128n27
Baumbach, Nico, 46
Bazin, André, 1–2, 60, 63–64, 67, 68, 71, 76, 130n43, 133n6
becoming, 13–14
becoming-other, 13
behaviorism, 4
Bellour, Raymond, 40, 124–25n3
Berardi, Franco "Bifo," 17, 103, 104
Bergman, Ingrid, 69
Big Tech, 100

163

164 · INDEX

Binoche, Juliette, 59, 71, 72
biopolitical governmentality, 101
The Bitter Tears of Petra von Kant, 72
Black Francis, 56
Blair, Tony, 20, 117n15
Bohnel, Ericka, 28–29
borderline personality disorder (BPD), 25
Borromean knot, 44
Bouaziz, Sigrid, 96
Brazil, 104, 105
Brecht, Bertolt, 45, 101
Brechtian aesthetics, 62
Buñuel, Luis, 56
Bwiti religion, 108–10

Cahiers, 64, 65, 136n35
California Psychotherapy Alliance Scale, 7
Cameroon, 108
Canada, 108
capitalism, 101–2, 103–4, 107
Casetti, Francesco, 132n1
castration anxiety, 65
Castro, Eduardo Viveiros de, 12
cathexis, 85, 87, 139–40n20
Character Strengths and Virtues Handbook, 31, 31
Christian theology, 19
cine-love, 62. *See also* cinephilia
cinema(s), 5; alliance with the sick, 3–15, 79; as art producing revelatory cinephilic moments, 107; closure during coronavirus pandemic, 100, 107–8; as collective event, 55; commercial, 54 (*see also* Hollywood); curating existential health through therapeutic activism, 107; as dream, 45; as an experience or event, 77–78; as "a health," 2; indexicality as ontological basis of, 93; institutional use of in medical settings, 18, 21; instrumentalizations of, 17–35, 121n6; life-changing abilities of, 1; literature and, 1; as machine for transversality, 37–58, 79, 80, 107; "matters of expression" and, 53–54; medical literature on therapeutic use of, 35; narrative, 66; vs. photography, 135–36n27; political aesthetics and, 17–18; relationality and, 55–56; vs. still photography, 71; subjectifying powers of, 17; therapeutic value of, 2, 3–15, 17, 53, 58, 80, 89, 106–7, 110–11; as tool for assisting with talk therapy, 32–33
cinema spectatorship. *See* spectatorship
cinematherapy, 21, 24–26
cinematherapy writing, 26
cinematic image, 98
cinematographic apparatus: as apparatus of identification, 46. *See also* apparatus theory
cinephile-as-fetishist, 65, 66–67
cinephilia, 3, 35, 128n27, 133–34n8, 136–37n37, 137–38n3; adventure and, 59–78, 79, 80; *Cahiers*-style, 64–65; definition of, 70; as disease, 67; existential adventure and, 59–78, 79; fetishistic, 60, 62–67, 70; imaginary pleasures of, 45–46; as nonfetishistic, 134–35n16; revelatory, 60, 64–65, 67–70, 77, 107; spectatorial subjectivity and, 55–56; therapeutic value of, 47
cinephilic "attachment," 45
cinephilic disposition, 2–3
cinephilic moment(s), 67–70, 71, 77, 107
cinephilic spectatorship, 35
cinephobia, 132n1
Clark, David, 20, 117n15, 122n16
Clark, Lygia, 104–6
the clinic: logic of, 93; modelization as a "space of existence," 52–53
Clouds of Sils Maria, 59, 61, 62, 71–77, 73, 74, 76, 80
cognitive behavior therapy (CBT), 5, 7, 9, 20–21, 87–88, 97, 107
Cohen, Joshua, 23
commercial film, 54
Comolli, Jean-Louis, 126n12, 128n26
computerized therapy, 6–8
conformism, 125n5

Copjec, Joan, 44
coronavirus pandemic, 99, 101, 103, 107–8
Costa, Marianne, 143–44n17
counteractivity, 128n26
counter-cinema, 45
Cowie, Elizabeth, 129n32
creative arts therapies, 21–24
critical friendship, 32–34
critical theory, modern history of, 101
cultural studies, film studies and, 106

Dalí, Salvador, 56
Daney, Serge, 65–66, 67, 136n35
Da Silva, Luiz Inácio (Lula), 105
Das Wolkenphänomen von Maloja, or *Cloud Phenomena of Maloja*, 60–61, 62, 71, 75, 76
Deleuze, Gilles, 1–2, 3, 12, 13, 48–49, 97, 119n34, 125n5, 126n11, 139–40n20
Deligny, Ferdinand, 130n43
depression, 82, 99
depth psychology, 25, 26
Derrida, Jacques, 138n4
desire, 84; emancipatory politics of desire-in-the-making, 52; fetishistic structure of, 65–66; machinations of, 102; Oedipalized, 39; repression of, 101–2
de-subjectification, 54–55
determinism: technological, 43; unidirectional, 43, 52
Dewey, John, 19
diagnosis, power and, 34
dialectical behavioral therapy, 25
diegesis, 66
Dietrich, Marlene, 66
difference, 65; "denial of," 43; as lived mode of existence, 102
differentiation, act of, 102
digital technology, 6–7
discipline, 33–34, 118n29
dissent, 102
distanciation, Brechtian aesthetics of, 62
Doane, Mary Ann, 43, 127n16, 137–38n3
Dosse, François, 54

double consciousness, 46
dream interpretation, 9
DSM (Diagnostic and Statistical Manual of Mental Disorders), 4, 30, 33, 109

ego, in Lacanian thought, 44–45
Egoyan, Atom, 83
Eidinger, Lars, 59, 94
18-methoxycoronaridine (18-MC), 108–10
Elsaesser, Thomas, 136–37n37, 137–38n3
epimeleia heautou (care of the self), 18
epistemophilia, 45–46
Eros, 77, 100, 105
essentialism, 4
"evidence-based" therapies, 4, 19, 20–21, 107, 117n15
exchange, 10–11
existential adventure, 59–78, 79
existential co-creation, 97–98
existential health, 15, 98; definition of, 99; erosion of, 35; extinguished in the name of public health, 99–100; paradigm of, 4; vs. public health, 99–111
expressive therapies continuum (ETC), 23

Fairfax, Daniel, 126n12
familial imagos, 48–49, 51
Fanck, Arnold, 136n33; *Das Wolkenphänomen von Maloja*, or *Cloud Phenomena of Maloja*, 60–61, 62, 71, 75, 76
Fassbinder, Rainer Werner, *The Bitter Tears of Petra von Kant*, 72
Ferenczi, Sándor, 14, 15, 120n42, 131n52
fetishism, 2, 18, 60, 62–67, 79, 80, 134n15, 137–38n3
filming, 71
"film object," materiality of, 53
film philosophy, 9
film spectatorship. *See* spectatorship
film studies, 35, 64, 106, 133–34n8
film theory, 18, 21, 39, 41, 45, 132n1, 134n9, 137–38n3
film-work, semiotic labor of, 45

Fleming, Michael, 28–29
Foucault, Michel, 33
The 400 Blows, 49, 50, 130n43
France, 101, 107–8
Frankfurt school, 41
free association, 9, 84–85
freedom, 102, 103–4
French New Wave, 49
Freud, Anna, 15
Freud, Sigmund, 14, 44–45, 48–49, 80, 82, 84–88, 108, 129n33, 129n34, 134n15, 139n13, 140n23
Freudian School of Paris, 54
Friedberg, Anne, 43
Fromm, Erich, 41

Gabon, 108
the gaze, paternal, 58
Germany, 108
Godard, Jean-Luc, 101, 134n9
Godrèche, Judith, 37, *38*, *39*
Gray, Hugh, 64
Greece, ancient, 18
Guattari, Félix, 2–3, 12–13, 17–18, 48, 97, 101–3, 105, 107–8, 120n44, 125n5, 139–40n20, 142–43n4; at La Borde clinic, 2, 13, 52, 53, 102–3; Lacan and, 54; Metz and, 53–54; subjectivity and, 115–16n3; technology and, 130n45; transversality and, 52–53

Handel, George Frideric, 59, 75
healing arts, 41; Indigenous, 121–22n14; of seeing, 79
health: cinema as a, 3; existential, 3; illness and, 82; literature and, 3. *See also* existential health; public health
Hesley, Jan, 26
Hesley, Jon, 26
Hollywood, 27, 37, 63, 71
Holmes, Emily, 83–84
the humanities, 18, 19, 21

iboga, 108–10
identification, 2, 18, 127n16; with analyst, 46–47; apparatus of, 41–46; apparatus theory's schema of, 48; film theory and, 45; Freudian roots of, 44; imaginary, 45, 106; Lacan and, 44–45; with Oedipal imagos, 79; Oedipalism of, 52; primary, 41–42, 43, 106, 129n36; secondary, 41–42, 49, 106; technique of, 105–6; theory of, 80
identity, transcendental subject of, 44
illness, health and, 82
illusionism, 45, 46
imagery rescripting, 82, 92–93, 94, 97–98, 142n37
"imagery substitution" technique, 92
images: intrusive (*see* intrusive images)
the imaginary, 62
imagination, 92–93, 104
imago, as familialist image, 48
impression: "impression of reality," 42–43, 44, 45, 48, 126n12; language of, 126n11; metaphor of, 127n16
Improving Access to Psychological Therapies (IAPT) program, 20, 122n16
incest taboo, 10–11
indexicality, 67–68, 76, 89; indexical images, 64, 71, 78, 93, 97; photography and, 93; quantum of, 93; reality and, 63, 97
Indigenous healing techniques, 121–22n14
infant development, Freud's teleology of, 44
infantilism, 65
inpatient encounters, 21, 26–29
instrumentalizations, 17–35, 121n6
intrusive images, 97–98, 107, 140n23, 140n27; physical immobilization and, 90–91, 92; relational movement with, 92; seeing, 79–98; spectatorship and, 89–91
Iraq, U.S. invasion of, 34

Jacoby, Russell, 125n5
James, William, 19
Janet, Pierre, 90, 91, 92, 139n13, 141n35
Jodorowsky, Alejandro, 141n35, 143–44n17

Johnson, Lauren, 23
Jones, Kent, 2
Jung, Carl, 48–49
Jungian depth psychology, 25, 26

Kaslow, Florence W., 33
Keathley, Christian, 64, 68, 133n7, 136–37n37
King, Noel, 68, 69–70, 133n7
knowledge production, non-scientific modes of, 19
Kocaeli, Turkey, 27–28

La Borde clinic, 2, 13, 52, 53, 102–3
Lacan, Jacques, 41, 44–45, 46, 54, 128–29n30, 129n33, 129n36
Lamarre, Thomas, 130n45
Langmann, Thomas, 37, *38*, *39*
Lanzer, Ernst, 84–85
Lanzmann, Claude, 83
Laplanche, Jean, 43–44, 47–48
Lapoujade, David, 132n66
Layard, Richard, 20, 117n15, 122n16
lay therapeutic experimentation, 35
Lazzarato, Maurizio, 54–55, 119n31
Leader, Darian, 20–21
Léaud, Jean-Pierre, 39, 49, *50*
Lemelson, Robert, 34
Lévi-Strauss, Claude, 10–11, 12
libertarianism, 103
Lie, Anders Danielsen, 96
Lineham, Marsha, 25
literary authors, 1–2
literature, 5
Lukács, György, 101

Malchiodi, Cathy, 24
"Maloja snake" phenomenon, 59–60, 75, *76*, *77*
Manning, Erin, 17, 79
"manualized treatment," 5–6
Maoism, 101
Marcuse, Herbert, 4, 41, 100, 124n48
Masson, Jeffrey, 14–15
Massumi, Brian, 19, 121n11
Maté, Gabor, 121–22n14
May 1968 movement, 101

medical-industrial complex, 4, 35
medical power, hierarchies of, 52–53
medical practices, 17–35
Melville, Herman, 119n34
memory, 84, 90, 92
mental health, 3, 4, 17
mental illness, 3, 4, 13, 17
methadone, 109
Metz, Christian, 42–46, 53–54, 62, 65, 88–89, 106, 128n27, 142n41
Miller, Jacques-Alain, 54
mindfulness techniques, 25
MindMed, 108–10
mirror stage, 45, 51
modernism, 60, 62, 64, 65; discourse of, 42; political, 64
Moretz, Chloë Grace, 71
Müller, John, 46–47
Mulvey, Laura, 62–64, 66–67
Murnau, F. W., 39

Nancy, Jean-Luc, 82
narrative cinema, diegesis and, 66
narrative closure, 37
narrativity, 40
Nathan, Tobie, 18–19, 34, 55, 108, 124n47, 129n34
National Health Service (NHS), 117n15
naturopathy, 121–22n14
Negri, Antonio, 101, 115–16n3, 120n44, 142–43n4
neo-concrete movement, 104
neoliberalism, 8, 17
neorealism, 69, 135n20
neuroscience, 119n30, 126n11
neurosis: obsessional, 80, 84–86, 91–92; transference, 79
"new normal," 100
Niemiec, Ryan M., 30–32, *31*
Night and Fog, 83
Norcross, John, 5–6, 116n7, 117n10
the novel, 5
Nussbaum, Martha, 18

"observational learning," 31–32
obsessional neurosis, 80, 84–86, 91–92, 93–94

obsessive-compulsive disorder (OCD), 82, 87, 92, 141n35
Oedipal complex, 47, 67, 80, 85, 87
Oedipal identifications, 48; of identification, 52
Oedipal imagos, identification with, 79
Oedipal narrative, 39–40, 51–52, 124–25n3, 124n2
Oedipus complex, 39
Oedipus narrative, 139–40n20
ontology, 44
opioid crisis, 109
Oury, Jean, 102–3
outpatient psychotherapy, 21

pandemics, 99–100
parental imago, 41, 48–49, 56, 139–40n20. *See also* familial imagos
Paris Awakens, 37–40, *38*, *39*, 49, 51, 56–58, *57*
pathology, 34
patient sociality, cinema-initiated, 33–34
Pelbart, Peter Pál, 105
perception(s): failure of, 90; modes of, 80; multiplicity of, 96; pragmatics of, 82; transversal, 97
performativity, 52
Personal Shopper, 80, *81*, 84, 93–97, *95*, *96*
pharmaceutical industry, 93
pharmakon, 82, 89, 97, 107, 138n4
philosophers, 1–2
photography, 71, 93, 135–36n27
physical immobilization, 90–91, 92, 97, 140–41n31
Picasso, Pablo, 72
The Pixies, 56
Plato, *Phaedrus*, 138n4
Plato's cave, 43, 106, 140–41n31; allegory of, 47
pleasure principle, 37
pluralism, 80
political aesthetics, 17–18, 45, 66
political modernism, 62, 64, 65
politics: art and, 17; therapy and, 17
Pontalis, Jean-Bertrand, 43–44, 47–48
positionality, 97
positive psychology, 21, 29–32, *31*, 34

postmodern relativism, 64–65
post-traumatic stress disorder (PTSD), 82, 89–90, 92, 139n13, 141n35
power, diagnosis and, 34
pragmatism, 9
praxial crossroads, 71, 78
the "preindividual," 118n25
primordial lack, 65–66
professionalism, 10
progress, as instrument of domination, 4
psychedelics, research into, 108–10
psychiatry, 13; inpatient, 21, 26–29
psychoanalysis, 129n34, 140n23; conformism and, 125n5; Guattari's critique of, 107–8; as *pharmakon*, 107; repression and, 125n5; schizoanalytic, 13–14; as search for truth, 129n33; transference and, 47–48
psychoanalysts. *See* analyst
psychoanalytic theory, 4, 13, 21, 35, 39, 41, 45, 60, 64, 84–87, 106, 108. *See also* specific theorists
psychodynamic psychotherapies, 20
psychology, 9. *See also* specific schools
"psychomagic," 141n35
psychopharmacological treatment, 34
psychotherapy. *See* therapy
public health, 3, 4; cultural logic of, 100; vs. existential health, 99–111
pure experience, 132n66

Quincy Mental Health Center, Massachusetts Department of Mental Health, 28–29

Rachman, Stanley, 83, 87
radical empiricism, 19
Rafanell i Orra, Josep, 17
Rat Man, 82, 84–87, 88, 89, 90, 91–92, 93
Ratzinger, Joseph, 19
realism, 60, 64
reality: "impression of," 42–43, 44, 45, 48, 126n12; indexicality and, 76, 97; love of, 71. *See also* reality principle
reality principle, 35, 37
Reason, 4

"relational agents," 7–8
relationality, 55–56, 97–98, 118n25
Rendez-Vous, 72
repetition, 67; compulsive, 65–66, 84
repression, 35, 86, 101–2, 125n5
Resnais, Alain, 83
re-subjectification, 54–55
revelation, 77, 135n23
revelatory intellectual tradition, 60
Rodowick, D. N., 58, 139n14
Rogers, Carl, 116n7
Rolnik, Suely, 104–6
Rose, Nikolas, 32
Rosen, Phil, 126n12, 128n26
Rossellini, Roberto, 68–69

Salpêtrière Hospital, 90, 91
Sanders, Rupert, 72
Sartre, Jean-Paul, 102
schizoanalysis, 13–14, 56
scientism, 21
scopophilia, 137–38n3
Screen theory, 64
secondarization, logic of, 46
seeing: healing arts of, 79; through the eyes of another, 79, 92, 97–98
Seligman, Martin, 30–31, 34
semiotics, 48, 58; mixed, 53–55, 56, 67
Severn, Elizabeth, 14, 131n52
Shaviro, Steven, 106
Shedler, Jonathan, 20
Shoah, 83
Silverman, Kaja, 126n9, 134n11
Simondon, Gilbert, 118n25
singularity, 101–2; of subjectivity, 69–70
Slumdog Millionaire, 32
social dynamics, 37, 40
social media, 100
social transactions, 10–11
Socrates, 138n4
Solomon, Gary, 25–26, 29
Sontag, Susan, 134–35n16
spectacle, denunciation of, 62
spectatorial psyche, 126n11
spectatorial situation, transference and, 47–48
spectatorial sociality, 93, 97–98

spectatorial subjectivity, 2, 38–39, 41–46, 55–56, 65, 79
spectators, as visionaries, 93
spectatorship, 71; cinephilic, 35, 79, 82; fetishistic, 65–66, 67; film theory of, 2; intrusive images and, 89–91; pathologization of, 137–38n3; psychoanalytic theory and, 64; relationality and, 55–56; social contract of, 118n29; voyeurism and, 85–86
speculative pragmatism, 19, 121n11
"splitting up the doctor," praxis of, 52–53
Stalinism, 101
standardization, 52, 102
Stengers, Isabelle, 71
Sternberg, Josef von, 66
Stewart, Kristen, 59, 71, 72, 80, *81*
structural anthropology, 10–11
Studlar, Gaylyn, 137–38n3, 139n14
subjective petrification, 65–66, 84
subjectivity, 2–3, 101; collective, 2, 52; Guattari and, 115–16n3; Lacanian account of, 46–47; petrified, 65–66, 84; production of, 33, 38–39, 41, 43, 46–48, 52; recomposition of, 2–3, 8–9, 13–14, 18, 59, 67–69, 71, 78, 84, 102–3, 106–7, 115–16n3; singularity of, 69–70; spectatorial, 2, 38–39, 41–46, 55–56, 65, 79; standardization of, 102; transversal production of, 83; worker, 102, 107; worker subjectivity, 107
subjectivization, 35, 119n31
substitutionality, 7
suffering, 82
suture, 126n9
Switzerland, 108
the symbolic, 62
Szymanski, Adam, *Cinemas of Therapeutic Activism*, 99

Tabernanthe iboga (iboga), 108–10
tarot, 143–44n17
Téchiné, André, 72
technological determinism, 42–43
technology, 6–7, 42–43, 130n45

terminus, 132n67
theater, space of, 10
therapeutic activism, 13
therapeutic alliance, 5–6, 93, 116n7, 120n44; changing definition of, 6–7; between cinema and the sick, 9–15; "dodo bird effect" and, 117n13; machinic, 8–9, 14; traditional vs. computerized, 7–9
therapeutic insight, 68
therapist-client relationship, reappraisal of, 6–7
therapy, 92; art and, 17, 104–5; automation of, 6–7; countercultural approaches, 121–22n14; exchange in, 10; "manualization" of, 5–6; outpatient, 21, 24–26; person-centered approach to, 116n7; politics and, 17; scientific, 55; technologically disseminated, 6–7; "therapy wars," 20; two camps on change in psychotherapy, 116–17n9. *See also specific schools of therapy*
totalitarianism, 101
transference, 40–41, 52, 129n32, 129n34; as basis of therapeutic alliance, 47; fixicity, 52; imagos of, 46–52; non-familial, 48–49; parental imago and, 48–49; primary, 51; psychoanalysis and, 47–48; secondary, 51; spectatorial situation and, 47–48; types of, 48; without psychoanalysis, 47–48
transference neurosis, 79
transversality, 37–58, 59, 97, 111, 131n52; machine for, 52–58, 79
trauma, 83–84, 90–91, 139n13
"trauma films," 83–84, 90–91
Truffaut, François, 1, 49, 130n43
truth, love of, 71
twelve-step tradition, 25–26

Un Chien Andalou, 56
the unconscious, 58, 59, 108–9, 111, 139–40n20, 139n13

unidirectional determinism, 43
unidirectionality, 42–43, 48, 52
United Kingdom, 117n15
unpleasure, 66
"useful cinema," 121n6
U.S. military, 34

Van der Hart, Onno, 91, 139n13
Van der Kolk, Bessel, 91, 139n13
VHS tape technology, 24
Video and Filmmaking as Psychotherapy: Research and Practice, 23
VideoWork, 26
visionaries, 79, 93
visual pleasure, 118n29
Von Waldstätten, Nora, 93–94
Voyage to Italy, 68–70
voyeurism, 2, 18, 79–80, 84, 85–86, 88–90, 92–94, 97–98, 107, 137–38n3

WAI-Tech, 7, 9
Waldman, Diane, 125n5
Walker, Janet, 125n5
Wasson, Haidee, 121n6, 133–34n8
Watching Cinema Group Therapy program, 27–28
Wedding, Danny, 30–32, *31*
Weerasethakul, Apichatpong, 79
Weil, Simone, 70
Whitehead, Alfread North, 19
Willemen, Paul, 40, 68, 69–70, 133n7
Wollen, Peter, 63, 65
Wolz, Birgit, 25, 26
Woman-as-fetish, 66–67
woman-as-spectacle, 66
Worker's Party, 105
worker subjectivity, 102, 107
Working Alliance Inventory (WAI), 7
Wuhan, China, 99

Younger, Prakash, 70, 71, 134–35n16

Žižek, Slavoj, 135n23